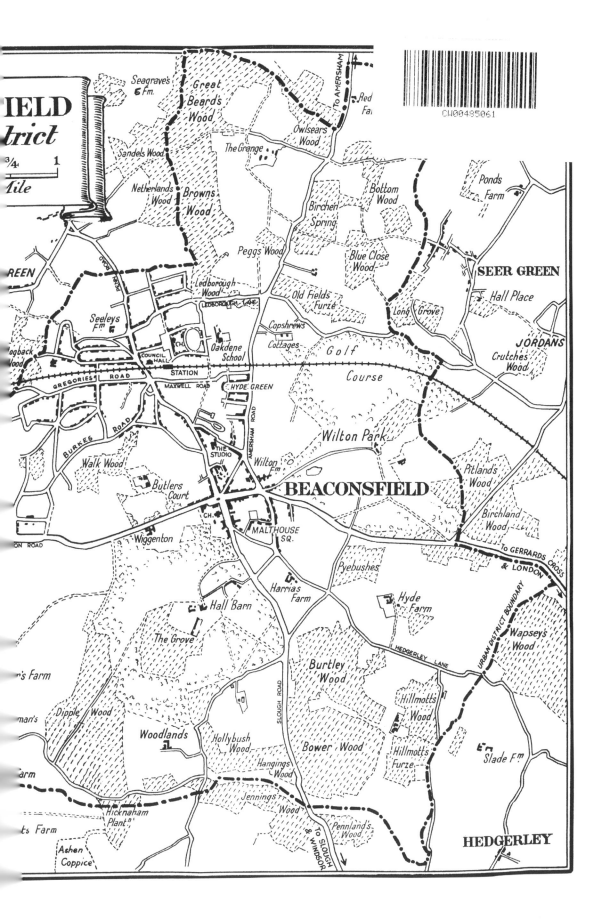

BEACONSFIELD

A History

Offices of Burgess, Holden & Watson, Burke's Parade, c.1920.

BEACONSFIELD

A History

Julian Hunt
and
David Thorpe

PHILLIMORE

2009

Published by
PHILLIMORE & CO. LTD
Chichester, West Sussex, England
www.phillimore.co.uk
www.thehistorypress.co.uk

© Julian Hunt and David Thorpe

ISBN 978-1-86077-497-3

Printed and bound in Malta

Contents

List of Illustrations

Frontispiece: Offices of Burgess, Holden & Watson, Burke's Parade, *c*.1920

LIST OF TABLES

Front Endpaper: Map of Beaconsfield Urban District, 1947
Back Endpaper: Beaconsfield street map, 1947

Acknowledgements

The majority of the photographs used in this book have come from the collection of Colin Seabright of Chesham Bois. These are numbered 5-7, 15, 17, 24, 32-4, 37-8, 40, 44, 51, 55, 59, 61-4, 66, 68-9, 71, 77-8, 81, 83-4, 86, 90, 93, 99-100, 105, 109, 111, 114, 124. Other illustrations are from the Beaconsfield and District Historical Society, nos. 2, 10, 23, 26, 29, 39, 47, 49-50, 79, 89, 91, 101, 108, 113; the Centre for Buckinghamshire Studies, frontispiece, 11-12, 16, 18, 20, 28, 36, 45, 52, 56, 58, 60, 67, 73, 75, 88, 95, 97, 103, 106-7, 112, 115, 119, 121-3, 125-7; the High Wycombe Library SWOP Project, 13, 46, 48, 76, 96; Buckinghamshire Archaeological Society, 98; A&Q Partnership, 53, 65, 70, 72, 87, 92, 94, 102, 104, 116-7; the National Monuments Record, Swindon, 8, 14, 19, 21-2, 25, 27, 35, 42-3, 57, 74, 85; the Frost Partnership, 120; the Earl of Clarendon, 4; Gary Bell, 82; and Alan Petford, 9.

Special thanks are due to Roger Bettridge and the staff of the Centre for Buckinghamshire Studies, Robin Darwall-Smith of Magdalen College Archives, Colin Harris of the Bodleian Library and the staffs of the National Archives and the British Library. Others who have provided help and encouragement include Marion Miller and John Brushe of South Bucks District Council, Chris Featherstone and Mike Dewey of the SWOP Project, John Stanbury and Russell Bayly of Beaconsfield and District Historical Society, Mike Power of A&Q Partnership, Alan, John and Nicola Frost of the Frost Partnership. Thanks are also due to Peter Hoare for copying several of the photographs and especially to Bill Hazlehurst of Halesowen who created the image used on the dust jacket.

Valuable assistance was provided by Dr Gary Bell of Hall Place, Mrs and Mrs F. Boys of Tahoe, the Sisters of Burnham Abbey, John Dodd of Chalfont St Giles, Alex Dunlop of the Old Town Garage, the Hon. Jenefer Farncombe of Hall Barn, Mrs R.A. Gale of Salters Ash, James Gurney of Reading, Michael Gurney of Framfield, Sussex, Mr Heal of Baylins Farm, Colin Macey of Martin Kleisser & Co., Mr and Mrs J. Martin of Upton Leigh, Mr and Mrs J. Minter, formerly of Netherlands, Mr and Mrs Nicholson of Overroads, Mr and Mrs T. Robinson of Fairlawn, Sue Ross of Pentacle Business School, Peter Safford, Liz Whetton of the Beaconsfield school and Fiona Wilson of Gregories.

Foreword

In April 2006, A&Q Partnership contributed several photographs and architectural drawings to an exhibition at Buckinghamshire County Museum celebrating the anniversary of the opening of the railway to Beaconsfield in 1906. Having recently moved offices to Bourne End, we have unearthed many more drawings of Beaconsfield houses, shops, schools and public buildings, prepared by our predecessors, Burgess, Holden & Watson. Many of these drawings are included in *Beaconsfield: A History*, the new book by Julian Hunt and David Thorpe, and will be on display at the exhibition at the Fitzwilliam Centre which is to coincide with the book's launch.

Amongst our archives, now deposited at the Centre for Buckinghamshire Studies in Aylesbury, is the certificate awarded to our founder, Julian Burgess, when he became a Fellow of the Royal Institute of British Architects. Burgess designed many of the early houses in Ledborough Lane and

Penn Road and with his partner, Legender Myers, laid out the Burke's Estate. He was responsible for the first Council Chamber in 1914 and superintended the building of Beaconsfield's early council houses. His young partner, Walter Holden, designed the firm's offices, which we are proud to see on the dust jacket of this new book. Holden also designed Top Meadow for G.K. Chesterton and Oakdene School for Miss Watts.

A&Q Partnership is delighted to have been involved in the production of this new book, which we hope will lead to a greater awareness of the importance of architecture in the understanding of our local history. At this time, many attractive Edwardian houses are being demolished to provide sites for new houses of sometimes less architectural clarity. We hoped that readers of this book will appreciate the rich architectural heritage handed down to us by the likes of Julian Burgess and preserve it appropriately.

Mike Power, A&Q Partnership, May 2009

Introduction

Beaconsfield and its Geographical Situation

Beaconsfield may be a rather small market town but it has always been a highly desirable place to live. It is situated 23 miles from London, on the main road to High Wycombe and Oxford. The market developed at the point where the Oxford road was crossed by an important local road running from Aylesbury to Windsor. The four roads around the market place were anciently called London End, Windsor End, Wycombe End and Holme or Aylesbury End. A fifth road, named Shepherds Lane, enters the market place from the north-east and provides not only a shortcut to Amersham, but also offers rear access to the large houses and business premises on the north side of London End. To the east of the junction between the Amersham and Oxford roads was the separate hamlet of Wilton Green. The farmhouses and cottages around the green were destroyed at the turn of the 18th and 19th centuries and taken into the grounds of Wilton Park. The old roads from Wilton Green to Chalfont St Giles and Chalfont St Peter were blocked off at this date, as were the roads leading to the green from London End and Pyebush Lane.

The parish of Beaconsfield covered an area of 4,873 acres. In 1934, however, parts of Burnham, Taplow and Wooburn were added, raising the area to 5,314 acres. The land rises from 241ft above sea level in the south to 378ft in the north. The soil is gravelly loam and the subsoil is chalk. Historically, about half the land was used for arable farming, about a quarter for pasture and another quarter for woodland. Much of the woodland was retained as a source of firewood to be transported to London by road or on the Thames. In more recent times woodland has been preserved so that visitors to large houses such as Hall Barn, Gregories and Wilton Park could enjoy the sport of shooting birds out of the air. Since the opening of the Great Central and Great Western Joint Railway in 1906, the land to the north of the Oxford road has been developed for high-quality housing and the new town has spilled over into the neighbouring parish of Penn. With the building of the M40 motorway in 1971, the south of the parish was cut off from the town. The original road to Windsor was blocked and the large house called Hall Barn is now approached via its own bridge over the motorway.

The Place Name

Beaconsfield was well known to travellers along the Oxford road, but the town assumed greater importance in 1876 when the newly ennobled Benjamin Disraeli chose to be called the Earl of

Beaconsfield. Disraeli, who had no property or direct connection with the town, insisted on pronouncing the name as *Beacons-field*. The locals had always called it *Beckons-field* and both pronunciations can still be heard in the town today.

This conflict sums up a basic problem in the origin of the name Beaconsfield. The Buckinghamshire volume in the English Place-name Society series was published in 1925. The editors were of the opinion that the first element was *beacon*, an Old English term used for land high enough to be the site of a signalling beacon. There is absolutely no evidence that during some ancient emergency, Beaconsfield was the site of such a beacon, either along the Oxford road or on some line from Windsor to the north.

Some of the earliest mentions of Beaconsfield are in conveyances of local farms copied into the Cartulary of Missenden Abbey. When Walter de Wyndlesores granted a virgate of land to Robert de Burnham in about 1200, the property was in *Bekenesfeld*. Similar spellings such as *Bekenesfelde* and *Beckenesfeld* occur in other early deeds, the common feature being the hard *beck* sound. Some students of English place-names have therefore suggested that the first element in Beaconsfield is *bece*, the Old English name for a beach tree. A good example of its use is in the parish name of Beachampton, in North Buckinghamshire. This origin suits the Beaconsfield landscape, where large tracts of deciduous woodland were deliberately preserved from the earliest times.

Beaconsfield is not mentioned in Domesday Book and at the time of the Conquest was part of the larger manor of Burnham. By the late medieval period, at least three large farms had become separate manors, their owners paying only a small chief rent to the lords of the manor of Burnham. These three estates, Hall Barn, Gregories and Wilton Park, continued to grow in importance right up until the 19th century, with their resident families vying for control of the economic, social, political and religious life of the community. The poet Edmund Waller in the 17th century and the statesman Edmund Burke in the 18th made the estates of Hall Barn and Gregories into household names. The Rectory of Beaconsfield was a valuable preferment and any resident rector also exercised considerable influence. After the English Civil War, a substantial part of the population, particularly the tradesmen and shopkeepers, followed the ejected minister of Beaconsfield and founded the Congregational Church.

Urban Growth

The commercial centre of Beaconsfield grew up around the crossing point of the Oxford and Windsor roads. By the 17th century there were at least six large inns serving the travellers on these roads and the town had become a meeting place for lawyers and merchants. The turnpiking of the Oxford road and developments in stagecoach design in the 18th century meant that travellers could easily reach Oxford in a day. Many of the coaching inns therefore closed, but their places were taken in the local economy by a multitude of boarding schools, for boys and girls, which sprang up in the 19th century. Beaconsfield was therefore well known amongst those who travelled to Oxford, did business in the south of Buckinghamshire, or who were educated in the town. The town acquired a Local Board of Health in 1850 and became an Urban District in 1894. Beaconsfield became something of an inland resort, with several large houses rented by genteel families, and many wealthy and cultured people visiting the great houses. The purchase of Hall Barn by Edward Lawson, proprietor of the *Daily Telegraph*, in 1881, ensured that Beaconsfield continued to be visited by the greatest in the land.

A High-Class Residential Suburb

When the railway reached Beaconsfield in 1906, the town already had a reputation as a healthy and stimulating place to live. Its natural and cultural advantages were exploited by the developers, who named the most select development the 'Burke's Estate'. The architectural quality of the houses and the spacious layout of the new roads attracted gentry, retired Indian and other colonial administrators, military officers, businessmen, lawyers, doctors, architects, journalists and leading figures from the arts. A civil or military decoration was almost a necessary condition of residence.

During the 20th century, the population rose from 1,500 to 10,679. From 1921, the town was home to a nationally known film studio which has more recently developed into the National Film and Television School. During the Second World War the town took on the mass production of aircraft engine parts and this huge factory, once employing 500 people, only closed down in the 1990s. Further employment was provided by a growing shopping centre in the New Town, which attracted all the multiple stores including Boots,

WH Smith, Woolworths, Waitrose and most recently Sainsbury's. In 1974, Beaconsfield Urban District joined the bulk of Eton Rural District in the new South Bucks District Council. There was a plan to move the new Council's offices from Slough to Beaconsfield, but in the event the councillors have rented offices in Denham.

Beaconsfield retains a very distinctive identity. Such is the desire to live in the town that some of the houses built near the railway station after 1906 have been demolished in order to build larger and more glamorous residences, or blocks of up-market flats. The Edwardian houses are beginning to be replaced by brash modern buildings of dubious architectural quality, more suited to Alderley Edge than Beaconsfield. Perhaps it is time to follow the example of nearby Gerrards Cross, where the Centenary Conservation Area now encompasses whole streets of Arts and Crafts houses, giving local people and their representatives more control over the development of the town.

One

Lords of the Manor

Buckinghamshire's Thames Valley parishes tend to be long and thin, running north from the river, well into the upland interior of the county. This arrangement was clearly deliberate, giving each parish a share of the rich meadowland beside the river, the arable land in the valley and the pasture and woodland on the higher ground. Most parishes had one or more sub-settlements on the higher land at the base of the Chilterns. Penn was thus a sub-settlement of Taplow. Sear Green was similarly a sub-settlement of Farnham Royal. Beaconsfield, as one of the sub-settlements of Burnham, probably dates from the time when the Burnham portion of this upland area was first ploughed.

Beaconsfield at the time of Domesday Book

The entry in Domesday Book for Burnham is as follows:

> Land of Walter Son of Otho
> In Burnham Hundred
> Walter himself owns Burnham. It is assessed at 18 hides. There is land for 15 ploughs. In the demesne are 3 hides, and on it are 3 ploughs; and 28 villeins with 7 bordars have 12 ploughs. There are 2 serfs, meadow sufficient for 3 plough (teams), woodland (to feed) 600 swine and supplying shares for the ploughs. In all it is worth 10 pounds; when received 6 pounds; Time of King Edward 10 pounds. This manor Elmar, a thegn of King Edward, held.

Before the conquest, Burnham had belonged to Elmar, a supporter of Edward the Confessor. By 1086, his manor had been given to Walter, son of Otho, who also held the valuable 10-hide manor of Eton.

Burnham itself was valued at 18 hides, a high taxation compared with the average Buckinghamshire assessment of 10 hides. If we accept the popular idea that a hide equated to 120 acres of arable land, then the figures suggest that there were more than 2,000 acres under cultivation in Burnham. The demesne or home farm accounted for three hides, or one-sixth of the total, with the remainder cultivated by 35 tenant farmers. It seems that these farmers worked co-operatively, for they had to share 12 ploughs. A good proportion of the arable land would have been in the open fields of Burnham, which survived well into the 19th century. Here, farmers owned or rented strips in a number of common arable fields and sewed and harvested the crops according to a system of rotation. It is likely, however, that part of Burnham's cultivated land was at Beaconsfield, for, as we have seen, the 'field' element in the place name implies open field agriculture.

According to Domesday Book, there was also sufficient woodland in Burnham to pasture 600 pigs. This may have been the area now known as Burnham Beeches, but the figure probably includes further woodland to the north around Beaconsfield. The landscape around the town is still one of large enclosures cut out of older woodland. The Domesday entry suggests that some of the wood was used for making plough shares. It is unlikely that ploughs at this date were actually made of wood. It is more plausible that the wood was turned into charcoal for making iron plough shares.

Beaconsfield Hertfordshire

To the north-west of Beaconsfield was a huge area of common grazing known as Wycombe Heath. The farmers of Wycombe, Hughenden, Great and Little Missenden, Amersham, Penn and perhaps Beaconsfield as well all had access to the heath. They were free to pasture their sheep and cattle there and to take wood for building and for their hearths. As pressure on land increased, settlements like Penn Street, Woodrow and Winchmore Hill grew up on the edge of the Heath. At the eastern end of Wycombe Heath was the hamlet of Stock, later to be known as Coleshill. Stock must have been on part of the Heath anciently claimed by farmers from one of the Hertfordshire parishes, for, until the boundary changes of 1844, Coleshill formed a detached part of the county of Hertford.

The parish boundary between the Burnham hamlet of Beaconsfield and the Amersham hamlet of Coleshill ran east to west between Luckings and Stockings Farms to the north and Whites (now The Grange) and Oldfields farms to the south. This boundary was anciently marked with a series of crosses, strongly suggesting that there had been some doubt or dispute as to its exact course. The situation was further complicated by the fact that the county boundary ran further to

the south along Ledborough Lane, placing the Beaconsfield farms of Whites and Oldfields in Hertfordshire. The owners of these farms may have paid their tithes to the rector of Beaconsfield and their poor rates to the Beaconsfield overseers, but their hearth and land taxes were collected by the Hertfordshire authorities. Freeholders there even had a vote in the elections for Knights of the Shire of Hertfordshire.

The legal origin of this strange double boundary is partly explained by reference to early charters to do with the Hertfordshire parish of Tring. The Domesday Book entry for Tring includes a two-hide 'berewick', or distant farmstead, where eight farmers had two ploughs. Tring was given by King Stephen and his wife Matilda as an endowment for their new Abbey at Faversham in Kent. When their son confirmed this grant in 1154, Tring is conveyed along with a distant sub-settlement called 'Stoches'.[1] Stephen's successor, Henry II, also confirmed the gift of Tring to Faversham, but he retained Stock, granting it to the Mandevilles, the then lords of the manor of Amersham.[2] Right up until the 19th century, the owners of Whites Farm in Beaconsfield were obliged to pay a chief rent of 10s. to the Drake family, as lords of the manor of Amersham. Coleshill remained in Hertfordshire until 1844 when an Act of Parliament caused various detached parts of English counties to be absorbed into the surrounding counties.

Gift of Land to Missenden Abbey

Following the Norman Conquest, Burnham and the hamlet of Beaconsfield remained in the ownership of Walter, son of Otho, and his descendants. This family held extensive lands on both the Buckinghamshire and Berkshire sides of the Thames, along with the important office of Castellan of Windsor Castle. Because of this association, Walter son of Otho's family eventually assumed the surname of Windsor.

The Cartulary of Missenden Abbey contains a series of deeds by which Walter de Windsor and his nephew Ralph de Hodeng transfer several farms in Beaconsfield to a local man, probably a relative, named Robert de Burnham. These conveyances all date from about the year 1200 and are some of the earliest surviving documents relating to Beaconsfield. The conveyances to Robert de Burnham, copied into the Missenden Cartulary, can be summarised as follows:

1 virgate of land in Beaconsfield held by Robert de Grave
1 virgate of land in Beaconsfield held by Lambert de Holeweia
¼ virgate of land held by Edward Geri
1 virgate of land in Beaconsfield held by Helric the forester
1 virgate of land in Beaconsfield held by Osbert de Odefeld
½ virgate held by Agnes widow of William son of Estrild
1 virgate of land held by Sired son of Alwin
All land held by Alwin son of Derwin
100 acres of heathland
½ hide of land held by Alfred the priest
Alstanescroft in Beaconsfield which Geoffrey son of Sired held
52 acres of land in Alkehulle

These conveyances suggest that large farmsteads such as Holloways and Oldfields farms were already in existence by 1200. The conveyances not only grant the farms to Robert de Burnham, but also the tenants and their issue. This is the classic form of villeinage tenure, where the tenant is technically the property of the lord and cannot marry or leave the manor without the lord's permission. It is tempting to imagine a typical English village with each of the tenants farming strips in a series of common arable fields. Old maps of Beaconsfield show no evidence of this system, however; nor is there any evidence of the ridge and furrow which characterises the North Buckinghamshire landscape. Instead, the ancient farms are scattered around the parish and linked by a complex network of old roads. The only

unenclosed areas were common grazing land, such as Latchmore, on the eastern boundary of the parish.

There are two further deeds in the Cartulary of Missenden Abbey whereby Robert de Burnham gave all this land to the Abbey.[3] In the second conveyance, he makes it clear that, as a major donor, he expects to be buried in the Abbey church. As the owners of Wiltons (later Wilton Park) paid a chief rent to Missenden Abbey, we may assume that the bulk of the land accumulated by Robert de Burnham was in the north-east part of the parish around that house.[4]

Huntercombe Manor

With the death of Walter de Windsor in 1202, the Windsor family holdings in Burnham and Beaconsfield were divided between Walter's sisters, Gunnora de Hodeng and Christiana, wife of Duncan de Lascelles. Gunnora's son Ralph de Hodeng received that part of the manor of Burnham centred on the manor house called Huntercombe (now a private hospital), along with a part of the manor of Beaconsfield. Ralph de Hodeng also inherited the advowson, or right to appoint the priest at Beaconsfield. The descendants of the Hodengs assumed the surname de Huntercombe and continued in possession of their half of Beaconsfield until the 16th century. The accounts of Robert Hunte, agent for the Butler family in Beaconsfield, show that a chief rent of 24s. a year was paid to the lord of the manor of Huntercombe in 1420.[5]

The Foundation of Burnham Abbey

At the division of Walter de Windsor's land, Duncan and Christiana de Lascelles received the other half of Burnham, the advowson of Burnham church and the remaining part of Beaconsfield. Duncan and Christiana's son,

1   *Huntercombe Manor, Burnham, 1965.*

It is clear from 15th-century rentals of Burnham Abbey that the freeholders of Beaconsfield paid their chief rents to the same steward, whether they were tenants of Huntercombe or of the Abbey. The Abbey rental of 1430 shows that the tenants if Beaconsfield paid a total to £5 7s. 9½d. The largest chief rent of 40s. was paid by William Hunte 'for divers lands and tenements lately belonging to Hugh Berwyk'. This payment relates to the manor of Halle, later to be known as Hall Barn, The next largest chief rent was 30s. paid by Thomas Ballard for 'merlonde', later to be known as Gregories.[6] In a rental of 1462, both the big estates on the west side of Beaconsfield are in single ownership. The manor of Halle is referred to as 'William Hunte, now Boteler, for divers lands and tenements late Hugh Berwyk'. Gregories is listed as 'Robert Ballard now Boteler for the farm of Merlonde'.[7] It is clear from

Thomas de Lascelles, sold this property to Richard, Earl of Cornwall, some time prior to 1255. In 1266, the Earl of Cornwall gave his part of Burnham and Beaconsfield to the newly founded Burnham Abbey. Successive Abbesses of Burnham were therefore lords of part of the manor of Beaconsfield for the next 250 years. We should not overestimate the importance of the Huntercombe family or of the Abbess of Burnham. These lords of the manor derived a small income from their manor courts, but as most of their Beaconsfield tenants were freeholders, the tributes or chief rents they paid to their respective lords only amounted to a few pounds.

contemporary sales and leases that Berewyk, Hunte and Boteler were successive owners of Hall Barn and that the Butlers had added Gregories to their growing empire.

The Dissolution of the Monasteries

In 1522, the Abbess of Burnham's estate in Beaconsfield was valued at £5 per year. This compares with £10 from her lands in Burnham itself, £10 from Burnham Rectory, £10 from Dorney Rectory and £10 from the manor of Holmer in Little Missenden. The Beaconsfield income was made up of market tolls, fines from the manor courts and chief rents due from freehold property. In Henry VIII's *Valor Ecclesiasticus* of 1535, the income from the Abbey's possessions in Beaconsfield is unfortunately included amongst the figures for the manor of Burnham. There was £11 2d. from lands which the Abbey farmed itself and £18 4s. 6d. from lands rented out to tenants. The lawyer holding the post of bailiff at Beaconsfield was Robert Waller, whose salary was 20s. per year.[8]

Burnham Abbey was surrendered to the Crown in September 1539. Most of its property was retained by the Crown, and the site of the Abbey was leased out. The Abbey's interest in the manor of Beaconsfield, however, was sold in 1545 to Robert Brown, a London goldsmith.[9] He sold it in 1549 to Sir John Williams of Thame, who had been a Visitor to the Monasteries under Henry VIII and

held the lucrative posts of Master of the Jewels and Treasurer of Augmentations. Williams had himself bought several former monastic properties and had recently purchased the Butler estates in Beaconsfield.[10] Williams obtained a grant to hold a Wednesday market at Beaconsfield in 1551. Despite his involvement in the Dissolution of the Monasteries, Sir John Williams promoted the cause of Queen Mary against the claim of Lady Jane Grey. This change of course was highly successful, for in 1554 he was created Lord Williams of Thame and made Chamberlain to King Philip. Lord Williams almost fell from grace in 1556 when an audit of his accounts as Master of the Jewels found that he owed the Crown £25,000. A contemporary remarked that Williams was 'fayent to brake up his howse and to lyve at Beconfeld because of the Queen's lack of generosity'.[11] Lord

2   *Burnham Abbey, c.1920.*

Williams died in 1559, when his property passed to his daughters, Isabell wife of Richard Wenman and Margaret, wife of Henry Norreys.[12] Henry and Margaret Norreys sold their share of the manor of Beaconsfield to Richard and Isabell Wenman in 1561.

Richard Wenman was descended from an Oxfordshire clothier, but his father, Thomas Wenman, had married Ursula Giffard, heir to the manor of Twyford near Buckingham. Richard Wenman had also made a shrewd marriage to Isabell Williams. His father in law, John Williams, was a very wealthy man and no doubt smoothed the way for Wenman to become MP for Northampton in 1547. When Richard Wenman died in 1572 he was buried at Twyford, where there is a large monument to him erected by his widow Isabell. The Beaconsfield estates passed to Richard and Isabell's son, Thomas Wenman, who was MP for Buckingham in 1571. Thomas Wenman died young in 1577, leaving his property to his son Richard Wenman, then only five years old. Isabell Wenman had married Richard Huddleston, and when she died in 1587 an inquisition post mortem found that her grandson, Richard Wenman, was entitled to the manors of Beconsfield, Hawle alias Hall Barne, Penn alias Pennlands, Gregories, Hyde and Wiltons, as well as land in Boveney, Farnham Royal, Chalfont St Peter, Chalfont St Giles, Hitcham, Coleshill, Little Marlow,

Chepping Wycombe, Wooburn, Amersham, and Penn.[13] As Lord Williams and his descendants were all absentee landlords, living at Thame or Twyford, their manor of Beaconsfield was leased out. The tenant in 1579 was a local lawyer, Richard Tredway, who lived at Gregories.

During the reign of James I, Richard Wenman of Thame Park and his wife Agnes began to break up their Beaconsfield estate. By 1604 they had sold Dawbeneys Ground (later Davenies Farm) to Richard Tredway. In 1607 they sold Hyde Farm to Elizabeth, widow of Thomas Waller of the Brick Place (later Little Hall Barn). In 1608, Richard and Agnes sold Hall Barn and the manor of Beaconsfield to Ralph Smith and his wife Martha,[14] and in 1611 they sold Wiltons to Richard Baldwin. They also sold several houses and land to Thomas Waller and his wife Dorothy for, when he died in 1627, Thomas Waller owned Gregories and five other messuages 'late the perquisites of Richard Wenman'. Some of the Wenmans' property was later to form the basis of another great estate in Beaconsfield. Hyde Farm was sold by Elizabeth, widow of Thomas Waller, to her cousin Robert Waller. Robert Waller's widow, Anne Waller, and her son Edmund Waller the poet, made further purchases and eventually bought Hall Barn and the manor of Beaconsfield from Ralph Smith in 1624.[15]

Two

Great Houses

Beaconsfield has no large house called the Manor House. This is perhaps because its farmers originally paid their rents at the manor courts of Huntercombe and Burnham Abbey, who shared the manorial rights. Several Beaconsfield farmsteads did, however, develop into agricultural estates where the owners took on some of the rights and responsibilities of a lord of the manor. No matter how exalted these landlords became, they nevertheless continued to pay modest chief rents to the Huntercombe family or to the Abbess of Burnham.

The proprietors of these local estates often had commercial, legal and political interests far beyond the boundaries of Beaconsfield. It was very useful for a medieval man of affairs to have a house one day's ride from London, either as a retreat from the capital or as a stopping off point on regular journeys to the West Midlands or Wales. Their owners may have purchased several farms in order to build up an estate in the town and the building of a modern, comfortable house in the centre of their domain may have been the final stage in a long process. Although estates like Hall Barn, Gregories, Hyde and Wiltons were partially recreational, they each had a number of agricultural tenants and so came to be regarded as sub-manors within Beaconsfield.

The Manor of Halle or Hall Barn

In the 1330s, the manor of Halle belonged to the Loveday family, lords of the manor of Hedsor.[1] John Loveday of Hedsor leased the manor of Halle to a local man named Richard Gregory. The term of the lease was for the life of Richard Gregory, who was to pay £2 10s. per year rent for the first seven years and the substantial sum of £20 per year thereafter.[2] In 1358, John Loveday sold the manor of Halle in Beaconsfield to Sir Hugh de Berewyk, a wealthy lawyer who acted for several abbeys and priories, including those at Bisham and Medmenham. Hugh already owned land in Beaconsfield, for in 1349 he gave a messuage and land at Fleet Marston to Medmenham Abbey, but his manor of Hyde in Beaconsfield was specifically excluded from the transaction. The purchase price of the manor of Halle in 1358 was 200 marks of silver, a very large sum for the period.[3] Hugh gradually extended his land holdings in Beaconsfield. A 1372 court roll, preserved amongst the Egerton Rolls in the British Library, is endorsed 'Court of Hugh Berwik, Penlond, Hallbarne'.[4] A similar roll of 1385, amongst the Hall Barn papers, is endorsed 'Hugh de Berewyk & Equida his wife, Lord and

Lady of the Manor of Whelton'.[5] It lists Hugh's tenants at Halle, Wiltons and Pennlands.

The Butler Family

Hugh de Berewyk died in 1403, leaving his property to his son, Thomas.[6] He died in about 1415, when his sister and heir, Margaret de Berewyk, married Ralph Butler of Badminton, Gloucestershire. Ralph Butler did not reside in Beaconsfield, but any one of the large houses on his new Beaconsfield estate would have been useful to a man who travelled regularly between Gloucester and London. His rents at Beaconsfield were collected by an agent called Robert Hunte, whose account for 1420 shows a chief rent of 40s. paid to Burnham Abbey.[7] A court roll of 1425, giving the tenants of the manors of Pennlands, Halle, Wiltons and Hyde, is endorsed with the names of 'Ralph Botelar & Margaret his wife, lord and lady of the said manors'.[8]

The manors of Halle, Wiltons and Pennlands were inherited by Ralph and Margaret's son, Sir John Butler, who was born in 1400 and lived at Badminton. He was MP for Gloucestershire in 1439 and 1445 and Sheriff in 1441, 1446 and 1473. Sir John Butler was also MP for Buckinghamshire in 1467, and Sheriff in 1465 and again in 1472. Sir John Butler died on 15 June 1477. At an inquisition post mortem held at High Wycombe, it was established that he held the manors of Hall and Gregories from Burnham Abbey, at rents of 40s. and 30s. per year respectively. Wiltons was held of Missenden Abbey by the rent of 8s. 4d. and Pennlands was held of Oliver Manningham at the rent of 16s. 4d. Sir John Butler also held lands in Gloucestershire, Somerset, Wiltshire and Oxfordshire. His heir was John, aged 29, the son of his deceased son William Butler.[9]

According to the 1522 Certificate of Musters, John Butler had land in Beaconsfield to the value of £28 per year, whilst an Aves Butler, probably his mother, had land valued at £18. This compares with the Abbess of Burnham's interest in the town, valued at only £5 per year.[10] When John Butler died in 1525, his property passed to his grandson, also named John Butler. According to the inquisition post mortem, Butler's Beaconsfield properties included the manors of 'Whyltons, Hallelonds, Penlond and Grovelond, a messuage with 100 acres of land and 10 acres of wood called Gregory's, another messuage with ... acres of land and 30 acres of wood called The Hide, and 60 acres of land and three acres of wood called Ledborowes'. The inquisition post mortem also lists the overlords to whom John Butler paid his various chief rents. The manor of Halle was held by John Butler from George Rotherham as of his manor of Cold Norton. Rotherham was a descendant of the Hodengs and owned part of Eton. Hyde Manor was held of Edmund Brudenell. Pennlands was held of Richard Sacheverel as lord of the manor of Stoke Poges.[11] Whilst there is no evidence that the Butlers regarded Beaconsfield as a principal residence, a Mrs Avis Butler was buried at Beaconsfield in 1543.[12] The Butlers finally disposed of their Beaconsfield properties in 1545, when John Butler and his wife Silvester conveyed the manor of Halle to Sir John Williams of Thame.[13]

Hall Place

Although the descent of the manor of Halle is well documented, there is no mention in any of the early deeds of a great house there, nor is there any early reference to a John of the Hall or to any other individual who might have been the tenant. When Robert Waller made his will in 1545 he left his son Francis a lease of 'Hawe Farm' in Beaconsfield. Francis Waller died at Amersham in 1549, leaving the lease of Hall Farm to his brother Thomas Waller, but neither lived there. Amongst the Hall Barn papers, however, is a 1625 deed conveying a large house near the churchyard of Beaconsfield which has obviously fallen on hard times. The vendors, John Wolward of Beaconsfield, labourer, and his wife Alice, are obscure, but the purchasers are none other than Anne Waller of Beaconsfield, widow, and Edmund Waller the poet, her son and heir apparent. The property, which changes hands for the modest sum of £30, is:

> All those two messuages and two gardens which were heretofore a barn a kitchen a cellar and a solar situate lying and being in Beaconsfield aforesaid in said County of Bucks in a street there called Wycombe End adjoining to the churchyard there on the east side and to the inheritance of James King on the north side thereof which said two messuages and gardens are now in the possession of him the said John Wolward and Alice his wife and one of them was lately in the possession of one William Molyngton of Beaconsfield aforesaid.[14]

The bounds given locate the property near to the present house called Hall Place. The 18th-century deeds to Hall Place, now held at Magdalen College, in fact call the house 'The Place', which would be a very pretentious description if the house had not been the centre of a large estate, perhaps of the manor of Hall. The earliest deed, dated 1736, is a conveyance of the house from John Briars of Beaconsfield, carpenter, to John Crook of Pall Mall, perfumer, for £550. It describes The Place as:

> All that capital messuage or mansion house with the appurtenances now or heretofore commonly called or known by the name of The Place situate and being in Beaconsfield aforesaid in the said County of Bucks.
>
> And also all the housing called the College or otherwise howsoever the same is called and also all other the houses edifices buildings barns stables yards orchards gardens courts backsides pews in the church seats passages profits commodities hereditaments and appurtenances whatsoever to the same now or heretofore belonging or appertaining or therewith used occupied or enjoyed.

> Together with the three cottages or tenements and other the houses and buildings erected on part of the said ground.
>
> And the little plot of ground adjoining to the gate standing between the yard and the meadow.
>
> All which premises now are or late were in the tenure or occupation of Anne Gibbs widow Mrs Bellenden Mr Edmund Pilkington Isaac King Richard Inkershold and John Dorrell or their respective undertenants.
>
> And also so much of the lane or passage leading from the street of Beaconsfield to the before granted and released premises as did or doth belong to the said John Briars or which he hath or ever had right to grant.
>
> All which premises are situate lying and being in Beaconsfield aforesaid and do adjoin the street or highway of Beaconsfield aforesaid on the north, to the Churchyard there and the Parsonage yard on the east, to the meadow heretofore of Edmund Waller Esq and after in the occupation of Robert Bates butcher on the south, and to the meadow formerly of the said Edmund Waller and late of Dorothy Reading widow on the west as the same now is or heretofore had been severed and used …

The Place was evidently in multi-occupation in 1736, but still warranted a very thorough and almost reverential description by the lawyer.

The reference to 'the housing called the College' probably refers to a school room. The 1736 conveyance of Hall Place refers to a previous occupant, Samuel Clarke, the Presbyterian minister at Beaconsfield, possibly a relative of the noted preacher Samuel Clarke, who enjoyed the patronage of Lord Wharton at nearby Wooburn. Summers' history of the Congregational Churches of South Buckinghamshire suggests that Clarke ran a school at Beaconsfield, which may in fact have been a theological college for Presbyterian ministers.

John Crook probably bought Hall Place as a weekend retreat from the pressures of business in London, with a view to retiring there in due course. It was probably an old-fashioned, timber-framed

3 *Hall Place, rebuilt by John Crook, c.1750.*

building, for soon after purchasing the property he had it thoroughly rebuilt in red brick with elegant sash windows. When he made his will in 1764, John Crook made bequests to the daughters of 'John Briars deceased, who built my dwelling house and justly dealt by me therein'.

Hall Barn

When the manor of Hall was bought by Anne Waller and her son Edmund Waller, in 1624, there was evidently no suitable house for the new owners to occupy. Instead, Edmund Waller took a lease of the Brick Place (now Little Hall Barn) in Windsor End. It was not for another 50 years that he built the new mansion called Hall Barn.

The Waller family originally came from Groombridge in Kent, but by 1457 a Richard Waller of Kent had married the daughter of Edmund Brudenell, owner of the manor of Raans in Amersham.[15] When Brudenell died in 1469, Richard Waller inherited the Brudenell estate at Wormsley in Stokenchurch, and it may be this good fortune which brought the family to the Beaconsfield district. In 1472, a John Waller was witness, along with Sir John Butler and Robert Bulstrode, to a conveyance by William Bulstrode of land in Windsor End.[16] Probably the same John Waller made his will in 1498, leaving property in Beaconsfield to his wife Joan, his son Robert and his brother William. He was sufficiently wealthy to be buried within the church of Beaconsfield and he left 3s. 4d. towards the repair of the church bells. His wife Joan died in 1521, desiring to be buried in the high chancel and leaving 20s. towards the cost of building the steeple. She left £6 'for a priest to sing for my soul and my husbands one whole year'. Joan Waller's son, John, also died in

1521. He desired to be buried in the high chancel and left the same sum, 20s., towards building the steeple. He left property to his wife Elizabeth, his sons William, Robert and Thomas, and his brother Robert.

Robert Waller was a lawyer, acting not only for the Bulstrodes, but also for the Abbess of Burnham. In 1535 he is shown as receiving a salary of 20s. per year as the Abbey's bailiff in Beaconsfield.[17] He held the lease of 'Hawe Farm', presumably Hall Barn, and the lease of Wiltons, but chose to live in London End. When he wrote out his own will in 1545, he desired to be buried in the church and left 20s. towards the cost of finishing the steeple 'to be paid when the workmen work on it'. He also made modest bequests to the churches of Wooburn, Iver, Chalfont St Giles, Chalfont St Peter, Fulmer, Hedgereley and Farnham Royal, reflecting his wider commercial network in South Buckinghamshire. He divided his portfolio of property between his wife, Elizabeth, and his seven sons. The eldest, Anthony, was given a tenement in London End, plus the lease of Wiltons; John received a tenement called Taylor's in Beaconsfield, along with three closes in Beaconsfield, Hertfordshire; William received property in High Wycombe; Francis was to receive the mansion house in Beaconsfield where Robert Waller lived after the death of his wife Elizabeth and also the lease of 'Hawe Farm in Beaconsfield'; Ralph was given the tenement 'sometime called the *George* but now the *Bull*' in the occupation of Nicholas Cooke; Thomas was given a tenement in Beaconsfield late in the occupation of Michael Tomson; and Edmund was given a tenement in Beaconsfield in the tenure of Nicholas West.

Despite the attention to detail in Robert Waller's will, it was found necessary to hold an inquisition post mortem. This listed all the property mentioned, but also referred to the 'messuage with appurtenances in Beaconsfield opposite the *Saracens Head* there in which the same Robert inhabited'. Robert Waller's widow,

Elizabeth, married Thomas Ball, who moved into the Waller family home. Thomas Ball died in 1559, making bequests to his own and to his wife's family. Elizabeth Ball died in 1570, leaving 20s. to the poor of Beaconsfield and 3s. 4d. towards 'new casting of the bell in Beaconsfield'.

Robert Waller's son Francis held a lease of the manor of Coleshill and lived at the manor house there called Stock Place. He made his will in 1548 leaving 40s. each to the poor of Amersham and Beaconsfield. He left his lands, including 'my mansion house in Beaconsfield' and 'my lands and tenements that I bought of my brother Ralph Waller', to his wife Anne for her natural life. He left 'the lease of Hall Farm' to his brother Thomas Waller. Francis Waller was buried at Amersham in 1549. An inquisition post mortem was held, listing all his property. This included 'one messuage with appurtenances situate in Beaconsfield aforesaid opposite the *Saracens Head* there where Thomas Ball lately inhabited'. The only substantial houses opposite the *Saracens Head* where Waller's mother and step-father could have lived were the building which became the *Swan Inn* in about 1600 and the house which was named the *Kings Head* in about 1650.

Robert Waller's youngest son, Edmund, lived in London where he was a citizen and draper.[18] He nevertheless added to his property in Beaconsfield and renewed his brother Francis's lease of the manor of Coleshill. Edmund Waller's eldest son, Robert, born in 1560, was sent to Kings College, Cambridge in 1578. Edmund and his son Robert were both shrewd businessmen. A 1607 rental of Thomas Brudenell, who owned the freehold of the manor of Coleshill, shows that his tenants Edmund and Robert Waller paid only £12 7s. rent for the manor of Coleshill, yet they had 'felled all the woods at their pleasure which were very good and great'.[19] Edmund Waller made his will in 1603, making bequests to the poor of Amersham and Beaconsfield but desiring to be buried in Amersham church, 'near my wife, my eldest brother Francis and my daughter Ursula'.

Edmund Waller's son, Robert, made perhaps the most advantageous marriage of any of his family by securing the hand of Anne, daughter of Griffith Hampden, one of the wealthiest and most powerful men in Buckinghamshire. Robert and Anne were married in 1600. An elaborate marriage settlement was drawn up, to which the Wallers contributed the manor of Knottinge in Bedfordshire, whilst the Hampdens provided £800.[20] The couple initially lived at Stock Place, Coleshill, where their eldest son, Edmund, was born in 1606. They later moved to the Waller family home in Beaconsfield. Robert Waller made his will in 1615, desiring to be buried in the churchyard among the poor, 'deeper than usual'. His children were 'to be brought up according to my degree, in virtue, learning and good manners. My wife is to obtain the wardship of my children, whether it fall to the King or to some other lord, raising on my lands money sufficient for the purpose.' These lands, listed in an inquisition post mortem of 1617, included the manor of Knottinge in Bedfordshire, the manors of Tiddington and Kidlington in Oxfordshire and a manor in Dinton, near Aylesbury. Robert Waller's property in Beaconsfield included the 'messuage in which the said Robert Waller inhabited', Holloways Farm in the tenure of George Lovett, the 'inn called the *Bull* with divers lands situate in the parish of Beaconsfield in the Counties of Bucks and Herts in the tenure of George Grymsdale', and a number of smaller properties and plots of land, all held of Sir Marmaduke Dayrell as lord of the manor of Huntercombe.

Edmund Waller
(1606-87)

Edmund Waller was born on 3 March 1606, at Coleshill. After his father's death in 1617, he and

4 *Edmund Waller the poet (1606-87).*

his mother moved to a house in Chalfont St Giles called the Stone. Edmund Waller went up to King's College, Cambridge, in 1621. In 1624, he and his mother purchased the manor of Beaconsfield and the freehold of Hall Barn from Ralph Smith and his wife Martha. This transaction was registered in the Court of Chancery but the actual deed has been lost.[21] The Lawson family attempted to trace it in the 1980s, even commissioning a search of 250 Beaconsfield deeds in the Wakefield Collection, then in the Library of Congress, but now in the Centre for Bucks Studies in Aylesbury.[22]

Edmund Waller and his mother Anne appear to have lived at the Brick House in Windsor End (later known as Little Hall Barn). This was leased to Edmund Waller for 21 years in 1627 by his cousin, the Rev. Walter Waller of Chalk in Wiltshire.[23] In 1624, Edmund Waller, under the guidance of his cousin, John Hampden, embarked on his Parliamentary career as MP for Ilchester in Somerset. In the Parliament of 1626 he was given one of the seats belonging to the Borough of Chepping Wycombe. In 1628 he was offered a seat at Amersham, one of the three new Parliamentary boroughs established by Hampden in 1624. Despite his association with Hampden, whose opposition to Charles I was ever more vociferous, Waller became a popular figure at court and his poetry was much admired in literary circles.

In 1631, Edmund Waller made a very advantageous marriage to Anne, daughter of John Bancks, a London mercer. She came with a dowry of £8,000. The couple had one son and one daughter before Anne died in childbirth in 1634. It is not clear exactly where the family lived at this stage. Hall Barn itself was not built until the 1670s, so it is likely that the Wallers were still living at Little Hall Barn. When an inspection of parish churches was made in 1637, it was reported that the pews in Beaconsfield church belonging to 'Mr Waller of the Town' and 'Mr Waller of Gregories' were too high.[24]

When Charles I was forced to call the Short Parliament in April 1640, Waller was again returned for Amersham, but by November of that year he had secured a seat in the Borough of St Ives, in Cornwall. When Charles I fled from London in 1642 and the English Civil War began, Edmund Waller remained in London, where he advocated a compromise with the King. In 1643 he was party to a secret plan for the King to march on London where moderates like Waller would raise the population in his support. When the conspiracy, later known as 'Waller's Plot', was discovered, Waller was arrested for treason and did not scruple to implicate his friends and even his brother-in-law, Nathaniel Tomkins, in order to save his own life. Having bribed selected MPs, he was allowed to address the House of Commons, where he begged for his life with all the eloquence he could muster under such pressure. It appears that whilst a prisoner in the Tower, he secretly married Mary Bressy, a member of a family which was trying to secure his release. She was 15 years younger than Waller and was to bear him four sons and seven daughters. By

mortgaging or selling all his property and raising loans from family and friends, he was able to pay a huge fine of £10,000 and was allowed to go into exile in November 1644.

Edmund Waller returned to England in 1652 and wrote the famous 'Panegyrick to my Lord Protector' in 1855. This was not only a brilliant poem in praise of Cromwell but also an argument for the legitimacy of the Protectorate. When Charles II was restored to the throne in 1660, Waller penned the equally ingratiating lines 'To the King upon His Majesty's Happy Return'. It is remarkable that Edmund Waller had retained sufficient of the family fortune to build himself a fine new house at Beaconsfield. Hall Barn was built sometime during the 1660s or 1670s, but there is no record of the precise date, the architect or the builder. The house was very modern, three storeys high, five bays wide, with a hipped roof and a lantern between the tall chimneys on the roof.

In the Restoration Parliament, Edmund Waller sat as MP for Hastings. He was appointed to numerous committees and the House of Commons enjoyed his regular and witty contributions on the issues of the day. He generally argued for toleration in religious affairs, but he was not an MP in 1679, when many Parliamentarians were trying to exclude the Catholic Duke of York from succeeding Charles II. He evidently had Quaker friends, for Thomas Ellwood, who held the Quakers' monthly meeting at his home at Ongar Hill in Coleshill, lent him money to buy the manor of Coleshill in 1683.[25] This was evidently a sentimental purchase, for he allowed the vendor, Henry Child, also a Quaker, to remain as tenant on the condition that Waller could use a specific parlour and bedroom and have access to the stable and coach house.[26]

Now in his eighties, Edmund Waller served as MP for the Cornish Borough of Saltash in James II's Parliament of 1685. He died at his London house in 1687 and is buried at Beaconsfield. His elaborate tomb, surmounted by

5   *Hall Barn, built by Edmund Waller, c.1670.*

an obelisk, was erected in Beaconsfield churchyard by the children of his second marriage, some time after 1700.

Edmund Waller
(1652-1700)

Edmund Waller the poet was succeeded in 1687 by his eldest surviving son, also Edmund, born in 1652. He was not a strong man and was prone to melancholy. He was returned as MP for Amersham in 1689, 1690, and again in 1695. He joined the Society of Friends in 1698 and died at Bath in 1700. He was buried in the Quaker burial ground there. By his will of 30 August 1699 he gave the large sum of £100 each to the overseers of Beaconsfield and Amersham to purchase lands, whose rents were to be distributed to the poor of each parish forever.

Stephen Waller
(1654-1706)

Edmund Waller was succeeded in 1700 by his brother, Stephen. Stephen Waller married Judith, daughter of Thomas Vernon of Haddon, Berkshire, in 1693. The couple had two sons, Edmund, born in 1699, and Harry, born in 1701. Stephen Waller died in 1706, leaving his two sons to be brought up by their mother. In 1713, Judith Waller married John Aislabie, MP for Ripon, who came to live at Hall Barn. Aislabie was Chancellor of the Exchequer from 1714-18 and secretly increased his fortune dealing in South Sea stock. When the South Sea bubble burst, Aislabie was forced to resign and was expelled from the House of Commons in 1721. He kept much of his fortune and was able to make his house at Studley Royal, near Ripon, something of a showcase. Judith Aislabie bought the 'Brick House' in Windsor End from the executors of Caroline Carne. She renamed the house Little Hall Barn and it has remained as a dower house for the Hall Barn family until modern times. Judith Aislabie died in 1740, leaving the house to her husband, John Aislabie, who died in 1742.

Edmund Waller
(1699-1771)

When Stephen Waller died in 1706 his son and heir Edmund was only seven years old. Even before he became of age, the young Edmund Waller was acting on behalf of his step-father, John Aislabie, dealing in large quantities of South Sea stock. He married Aislabie's daughter, Mary, who gave him four sons and two daughters. He used his South

6 *Little Hall Barn, the property of Judith Aislabie, 1740.*

Sea fortune to extend Hall Barn, building a south wing which almost doubled the size of the house. The new rooms looked south over the garden, which was laid out to the designs of the celebrated architect Colen Campbell. Lord Percival, visiting Hall Barn in August 1724, wrote:

> Friday morning left Beaconsfield; we went half a mile out of our way to see Hall Barn, Mr. Waller's house a London box, if I may so call a house of seven windows every way. He was gone a hunting, so we did not go into the house, which promised nothing extraordinary, but we spent a full hour and half in viewing the gardens, which you will think are fine, when I tell you they put us in mind of those at Versailles. He has 80 acres in garden and wood ... All this fine improvement is made by himself or Aislabie, his father-in-law, who had this house and the lands about it, in right of his wife's jointure, but gave it up in the South Sea year to his son-in-law. There is a great deal more still to be done, which will cost a prodigious sum, but this gentleman by marriage, South Sea and his paternal estate [is able] to do what he pleases.[27]

7 *Hall Barn gardens, created for Edmund Waller, c.1720.*

Edmund Waller also used his wealth to promote his Parliamentary career. He was elected MP for Marlow in 1721, despite a petition from an opponent claiming Waller had employed excessive bribery.[28] He retained the seat in 1727 and 1734. Edmund Waller was also cultivating Chepping Wycombe, where the two MPs were chosen by 50 members of the Corporation. His brother Harry captured one of these seats in 1726 and retained it in 1727 and 1734. Both Edmund and Harry Waller were elected for Wycombe in 1741, without opposition. In 1747, Harry Waller gave way to his nephew Edmund, so two Edmund Wallers represented the town. From 1754, the two seats were shared amicably between the Wallers of Hall Barn and the Earls of Shelburne, owners of the property now known as Wycombe Abbey. Edmund Waller's son, John, took one seat that year, and his younger son, Robert, held it from 1761 to 1784. No outsider presumed to contest the Wycombe seats throughout this period.

It was Edmund Waller who purchased the manor of Farmington in Gloucestershire. Here he built Farmington Lodge, a classical pile which was later to become the Wallers' principal residence. When Edmund Waller died in 1771, he was succeeded by his son Edmund.

Edmund Waller
(1725-88)

Edmund Waller was born in 1725. He married Martha, daughter of Rowland Phillips of Orlandon, Pembrokeshire. He was chosen as MP for Chepping Wycombe in 1747. That same year he obtained the Mastership of St Katherine's Hospital, a lucrative sinecure, which he held for life. Having become an alcoholic, he was forced to give up the Wycombe seat to his elder brother John in 1754, but held the seat again from 1757-61 after his brother's death. His father prudently put the Hall Barn Estate in trust, so that when Edmund Waller inherited in 1771, he was unable

to touch the capital. He died in 1788 and was succeeded by his son Edmund Waller.

Edmund Waller
(1757-1810)

Edmund Waller, who inherited Hall Barn in 1788, was already well established at Farmington Lodge in Gloucestershire. He let Hall Barn to Alexander Blair Esq. whose mother died at Beaconsfield in 1794. Later tenants included Thomas Sutton Wood Esq., whose son was buried at Beaconsfield in 1801, and Hugh Maxwell. In 1809 he leased Little Hall Barn to the celebrated writer William Hickey, who lived at Beaconsfield for seven years.[29] In 1805, Edmund Waller exchanged 125 acres of land south of Wiltons Green for 54 acres of land more convenient to the Hall Barn Estate belonging to James Du Pre of Wilton Park. Following this exchange, the Hall Barn Estate owned most of the land to the south of the Oxford road, leaving the Du Pres of Wilton Park controlling most of the land north of the road. Edmund Waller died in 1810, leaving £5,000 for the benefit of the poor of Beaconsfield and Farmington in Gloucestershire. He was succeeded by his brother, the Rev. Harry Waller.

Harry Waller
(1760-1824)

Harry Waller, who inherited Hall Barn and Farmington Lodge in 1810, had been the rector of Farmington since 1788. He continued to let Hall Barn. He died in 1824, leaving the two properties to his son, Harry Edmund Waller.

Harry Edmund Waller
(1804-69)

By 1831, Harry Edmund Waller had clearly decided to sell Hall Barn and a thorough survey was made of the whole estate. The mansion, gardens and parkland extending to 136 acres was let to Sir John Robinson at a rent of £500 a year. Hall Barn was advertised for sale in the same year. 'The mansion is calculated for a family of the first distinction and in contiguity to Windsor and London renders the property eminently desirable for a nobleman or gentleman holding any high official appointment.'[30] In 1833 the estate was sold for £84,000 to Sir Gore Ouseley.

Sir Gore Ouseley
(1769-1844)

Sir Gore Ouseley was an able diplomat who had promoted British interests in India, Persia and Russia during the Napoleonic Wars.[31] He was created a baronet in 1808. He was also an expert in oriental languages and President of the Society for Publication of Oriental Texts. Sir Gore Ouseley had the wealth not only to purchase Hall Barn at the price of £84,000,[32] but also to rebuild the south wing, where the ceilings were twice the height of those in the original house. He died at Hall Barn on 18 November 1844 and was succeeded by his son, Sir Fredrick Arthur Gore Ouseley, the church musician. Sir Fredrick sold Hall Barn in 1847 to John Hargreaves.[33]

John Hargreaves
(1797-1873)

John Hargreaves was a calico printer and colliery owner, living at Broad Oak, Accrington. Hargreaves was a keen collector of art and a juror at the 1851 Exhibition. Although his principal home was in Lancashire he would have found Hall Barn a useful base for his visits to London. Hargreaves employed his head gardener, George Smith, as his steward, who rebuilt several farmhouses on the estate, including Woodlands, Holloways and Harrias Farms. John Hargreaves died in 1873, leaving an estate valued at £400,000, but much of this was in Lancashire. He left £500 to the

Beaconsfield church Day School, then nearing completion. His collection of more than 450 works of art, 'formed with great taste over 40 years', raised £42,000 at auction.[34] Hargreaves' executors sold the Hall Barn Estate to Allan Morrison in 1874.[35]

Allan Morrison
(1842-80)

Allan Morrison was a director of the Fore Street Warehouse Company Ltd. This concern was founded by his father, James Morrison, whose motto was, 'small profits and quick returns'. Allan Morrison had inherited a fortune of between £3-4m and was a major figure in the City of London. He was on the committees preparing the British contribution to the Paris Exhibition in 1867, and the British Regatta in Paris in that year, rubbing shoulders with the Prince of Wales and the Duke of Edinburgh. Allan Morrison bought Hall Barn by private contract in 1874. He enjoyed it for only six years, dying at Hall Barn on 7 April 1880, at the early age of thirty-eight. He was succeeded by his brother, Charles Morrison. Hall Barn, along with Little Hall Barn and 13 farms, was put up for sale in June 1880 but was still unsold a year later.

Edward Levy-Lawson
1st Baron Burnham
(1833-1916)

The Hall Barn Estate was purchased in 1881 by Edward Levy-Lawson. Born Edward Levy in 1833, he became the editor of the *Daily Telegraph* soon after its purchase by his father, Joseph Moses Levy, in 1855. He married, in 1862, Harriette Georgiana, only daughter of Benjamin Nottingham Webster, the actor-manager. He changed his name from Levy to Lawson in 1875 and transferred his support from Gladstone's Liberals to Disraeli's

Tories in 1879. Lawson was made a baronet in 1892 and created Lord Burnham in 1903. He used Hall Barn for entertaining in a way that was appropriate to his position as the proprietor of a major newspaper. He was to dominate the social and economic life of Beaconsfield in the same way that the Wallers had done in the 17th and 18th centuries.

When Lawson's heir, Harry, came of age in 1883, the 'great party' necessitated the construction of a new ballroom wing on the east side of Hall Barn. The most celebrated gatherings at the house were the annual shooting parties attended by the Prince of Wales and then King George V.

The major change in the relationship between Hall Barn and the town was the way in which Lord Burnham bought up property. By 1910 he owned all the cottages on the west side of Aylesbury End, with two exceptions, up to no. 25, plus no. 39 and the block numbered 49-69. On the east side he owned the workshops used by the chair manufacturing company and no. 28, a house and yard rented by the carrier, Horace Roberts. This property had stabling for six horses. He also owned all the properties on the north side of London End, with one exception, up to no. seventeen. Further to the east he continued to own Bull Farm and the associated cottages. On the south side of London End he owned no. 18 (the Old Post House) and 13 of the properties from no. 24 (Wendover House) to no. 60, next to the *Old Swan Inn*.

It was in Windsor End where his dominion was greatest; of the 68 properties he owned all but 10, most of which were public houses and associated cottages. He owned the largest house of all, Little Hall Barn, valued at £5,032, and the substantial Hall Cottage, bought in 1906 and valued at £2,012. He also owned the freehold of two newly built houses in Hedgerley Lane, the White House, valued at £2,150, and Redcroft, £1,500, both held on 99-year leases from 1904. In Wycombe End, he owned the two cottages next to the Reading Room

and the three next to the *Cross Keys Inn*. On the north side of the road he owned 14 cottages and Factory Yard. Finally, he owned the block within the market place comprising Uriah Day's shop and the fire engine house.

It is not clear why Lawson made such extensive purchases in the town. At a meeting in 1897 with Lawson's daughter, Mrs Halse, arranged to discuss the decoration of the chancel, the rector 'pressed on her the disgraceful state of many of the houses in the town belonging to Sir Edward Lawson. This is a matter which urgently requires attention. How can we expect the people to lead clean and wholesome lives when their houses are in a state of dirt, neglect and shocking over-crowding'.[36]

Sir Edward Lawson was a founder member the Urban District Council (hereafter U.D.C). In July 1897 he was complaining at the Council meeting about the state of the village green near the church. In the same year he donated a bathing pool in New Pond Meadow to mark the Queen's Diamond Jubilee. It was arranged 'completely in all details of cleanliness and safety and provided with dressing places'. It is possible that it was only with his elevation to the peerage in 1903 and retirement from the *Daily Telegraph* that he devoted his full energies to running the estate. Surviving ledgers show that he required everything to be accounted for in detail. The 1910 valuation shows that in the 1900s he spent considerable sums to improve some of the larger cottages, but is silent on most of the smaller ones. He spent £500 on Hall Barn Cottage and £1,000 on Chester House, Windsor End, but only £50 on the cottages in Factory Yard, which must have been some of those in the worst condition in the town. For many years Lord Burnham's agents were John and Robert Rolfe of Wiggentton House. In about 1910, however, Richard Spencer Britten became the agent, living at Holloways Farm. Britten consulted the Country Gentleman's Association on extensions to the farmhouse in 1914. The estate usually employed the architects Burgess & Myers to design new houses or to restore old property in the town. They greatly enlarged Harrias Farm in 1913 to accommodate Lord Burnham's daughter, Dorothy, and her husband, the Hon. John Coke. Lord Burnham died in January 1916, aged 82, and was succeeded by his son, Harry Lawson Webster Levy Lawson.

Harry Lawson Webster Levy Lawson Viscount Burnham (1862-1933)

Harry Lawson Webster Levy Lawson was Liberal MP for West St Pancras, 1885-92, and for Cirencester, 1893-5. He represented Mile End as a Unionist in 1905-6 and again in 1910-16. He succeeded his father as 2nd Lord Burnham in 1916 and was made Viscount Burnham in 1919. He was managing proprietor of the *Daily Telegraph* from 1903-28. Life at Hall Barn in the inter-war years is covered in the delightful memoir written by his daughter, Lucia Lawson.[37] During this period, the agent was Walter Joseph Craft, who established the Hall Barn Estate Office in the former lock up in Aylesbury End. When the 2nd Lord Burnham died in 1933, the Viscountcy became extinct, but

the Barony passed to his brother, William Arnold Webster Levy Lawson.

William Arnold Webster Levy Lawson 3rd Baron Burnham (1864-1943)

William Arnold Webster Levy Lawson was born in 1864. In 1887, he married Sybil Mary, daughter of Lt-Gen. Sir Frederick Marshall. He served in the South African War and in the First World War. He succeeded his brother as 3rd Lord Burnham in 1933. He died in 1943 and was succeeded by his son, Edward Frederick Lawson.

Edward Frederick Lawson 4th Baron Burnham (1890-1963)

Edward Frederick Lawson was born in 1890. In 1920 he married Mary Enid, daughter of Hugh Scott Robson. He served with the Royal Bucks Hussars in the First World War and fought at Dunkirk in the Second World War. From 1943-5 he was Director of Public Relations at the War Office. He succeeded his father as 4th Lord Burnham in 1943. He was general

8 *Hall Barn Estate Office, 1948.*

manager of the *Daily Telegraph* 1927-39, and from 1945-61. He published *Peterborough Court, the Story of the Daily Telegraph*, in 1955. He died in 1963 and was succeeded by his son William Edward Harry Lawson.

William Edward Harry Lawson
5th Baron Burnham
(1920-93)

William Edward Harry Lawson was born in 1920. In 1942 he married Mary, daughter of George Gerald Petherick of the Mill House, St Cross, Winchester. He served in the Scots Guards in the Second World War. He succeeded his father as 5th Lord Burnham in 1963. It was he who remodelled Hall Barn between 1969 and 1972, demolishing the east wing and restoring the house to the size and shape of that built by Edmund Waller in the 17th century. The work was carried out under the supervision of the architects Bird & Tyler Associates of Chenies. Lord Burnham died in 1993 and was succeeded by his brother, Hugh John Frederick Lawson. The Hon. Jenefer Anne Lawson, daughter of the 5th Baron Lawson, married Andrew David Farncombe in 1985 and now lives at Hall Barn.

Hugh John Frederick Lawson
6th Baron Burnham
(1931-2005)

Hugh John Frederick Lawson was born in 1931. In 1955 he married Margaret, daughter of Alan Hunter of Perth. He worked for the *Daily Telegraph* from 1955-86 and was assistant managing director from 1984-6. He succeeded his brother as 6th Lord Burnham in 1993. He was Deputy Chief Whip for the Conservatives in the House of Lords and became an elected member in 1999. He lived at Woodlands Farm until his death in 2005. He was succeeded as Baron Lawson by his son, Harry Frederick Alan Lawson, who was born in 1968 and also lives at Woodlands Farm.

Wilton Park

Wilton Park, formerly Wiltons, emerged as a manor in the medieval period when Walter de Windsor and Ralph de Hodeng, as lords of the manor of Burnham, conveyed several farms in Beaconsfield to Robert de Burnham, almost certainly a close relative.[38] Robert de Burnham appears to have created a deer park at Beaconsfield, for parts of a great ditch survive, enclosing 100 acres of land around the big house. In about 1200, Robert de Burnham granted the chief rents of his Beaconsfield property to Missenden Abbey and expressed a desire to be buried in the Abbey.[39] In 1291 Missenden Abbey was receiving a rent of 8s. per annum from its land in Beaconsfield.[40]

Wiltons seems to have acquired its name from a later owner called Thomas de Whelton, who witnessed several deeds in Beaconsfield between the years 1325 and 1344. He received permission from the Bishop of Lincoln to have a private chapel at his house in Beaconsfield. His property is mentioned in a 1344 lease of 'a croft called Lymesmere, opposite the gate of Thomas de Whelton, between two roads, one to Chalfont St Peter and the other to Chalfont St Giles, next to the common called Willeshul'.[41] Thomas de Whelton's son, Richard de Whelton, mortgaged the estate and eventually sold it to Hugh de Berewyk.[42] Hugh may have resided at Wiltons, for in 1387 he gave a three-life lease of a cottage in Beaconsfield to Richard Grum, his wife Emma and their son William, the rent of 13s. 4d. to be paid 'at his court at Wheltons'. Richard agreed to serve Hugh de Berewyk as his groom for £1 6s. 8d. per year, plus clothes at Christmas and horses to ride in his service.[43] Hugh de Berewyk also held the manor of Hall Barn, then called Hallond. A 1385 court roll, preserved with the Hall Barn deeds, lists tenants of the manors of Pennlands, Wiltons and Hallond and is endorsed with the names of 'Hugh de Berewyk and Equida his wife, lord and lady of the Manor of Whelton'.[44]

In 1415, Ralph Butler of Great Badminton in Gloucestershire married Margaret de Berewyk and thus became the owner of Wiltons. His affairs at Beaconsfield were conducted by Robert Hunte, whose account for 1420 shows a chief rent of 8s. 4d. paid to Missenden Abbey.[45] In 1477, his son John Butler died holding Wiltons from the Abbot of Missenden at a rent of 8s. 4d. per annum.[46] None of the Butlers lived at Wiltons and the property appears to have been leased to a branch of the Bulstrode family of nearby Temple Bulstrode.

The Bulstrode Family

The Bulstrodes who settled in Beaconsfield in the 15th century were probably a junior branch of the Bulstrodes of Temple Bulstrode in Hedgerley. Richard Bulstrode of Upton was MP for Wallingford in 1450 and MP for Buckinghamshire in 1472. He was a collector of customs duties at Bristol and Dover. The family estate was situated in a detached portion of Upton, now part of Gerrards Cross, where the big house is still called Bulstrode Park. There is an impressive array of monumental brasses to the Bulstrodes in Upton church, but several members of the family chose to be buried at Beaconsfield.

It is apparent from successive family wills that the Bulstrodes had built up a substantial portfolio of property in Beaconsfield. Robert Bulstrode was a witness to several Beaconsfield conveyances from 1461. In 1470, William Bulstrode of Upton conveyed property in Beaconsfield to his son Robert and his wife Margaret.[47] Another son, William Bulstrode, citizen and draper of London, left instructions in his will of 1478 that he was to be buried in the chancel of Beaconsfield church, where his executors were 'to make a tomb over my sepulture'. There is a large table tomb of this period in the chancel of Beaconsfield church.

William Bulstrode of Beaconsfield, son and heir of Robert Bulstrode, was MP for Wallingford

in 1491, and collector of customs in the Port of London. He was one of the Gentleman Ushers of the Chamber, serving Henry VII's Queen Elizabeth, and Henry VIII's Queen Katherine. He made his will in 1520, leaving property both in London and in Beaconsfield. He instructed his wife Maud to pay £20 of his goods towards building 'the aisle of Trinity in the Church of Beaconsfield'. He also mentions his deceased brother Walter, and his sister, Anne Broke. He desired to be buried in St Anne's Aisle, between his mother and father and his son Reynold. There is a large table tomb in the arcade of the south chancel of the church, which is probably that of William Bulstrode. The base has panels containing shields, those on the south side being carved with the arms of Bulstrode.

William Bulstrode may well have employed Robert Waller to conduct his business in Beaconsfield. He left Robert Waller a rent of 10s. a year to be taken out of his lands in Beaconsfield called Blackcroft. Blackcroft was a piece of land situated near the junction of the Oxford road and Lakes Lane. Robert Waller was later to be an executor of William Bulstrode's widow. In 1522, William Bulstrode Esq. had land in

9 *Coat of arms of the Bulstrode family on a tomb between the chancel and south aisle of Beaconsfield church.*

Beaconsfield to the value of £20 per year. Soon after her husband's death in 1527, Maud Bulstrode conveyed her 'capital messuage in Beaconsfield wherein William Bulstrode did live' to Charles Bulkeley and other trustees.[48]

Walter Bulstrode, who died in 1529, also desired to be buried in Beaconsfield church. He left '10 marks every year to be taken from my lands for 80 years for a chantry for my wife and myself in Beaconsfield'. This sum was to pay a priest who would say mass daily for their souls at one of the altars in Beaconsfield church. Maud Bulstrode, who made her will in 1531, specified that she was to be buried 'in the Trinity aisle of Beaconsfield church, near my husband'. She requested that the curate, John Foster, 'sing for me in Beaconsfield Church for one year' and left him £6 13s. 4d. for his trouble. She confirmed the bequest of the land called Blackcroft to Robert Waller and left 'my gown furred with mink and my little coffer' to Elizabeth Waller. The Wallers seem to have acquired most of the Bulstrode land, for it formed the bulk of Robert Waller's property when he died in 1545.[49]

In 1545, John Butler sold his Beaconsfield estates, including the freehold of Wiltons, to John, later Lord Williams of Thame. The sitting tenant was Robert Waller who left the lease of Wiltons to his son Anthony in his will of 1545. Lord Williams' daughter Isabell married Richard Wenman, and their grandson, Richard Wenman, still owned the property in 1611, when Wiltons was sold to Richard Baldwin of Beaconsfield yeoman. The 1611 conveyance comprised:

> Messuage and demesne called Whiltons in Beaconsfield with the Mead, Ponde Close, Ponde Close Meade, Hazell Field, Pease Croft, the Heath, Wyde Field, Wyde Field Heath, Spring, Rendall Field, Three Legged Crosses, Great West Field, Little West Field, Barn Field, Pooke Field, Reddinge Field, Reddinge Field Spring, Little Chiswicke Great Chiswicke, Ferny Fields, Byrchin Spring, Byrchin Spring Pightell and Horse Leasowes.[50]

The Baldwins came to Beaconsfield some time in the mid-16th century. Thomas, son of John Baldwin, was baptised in the parish church in 1575. When William Baldwin died in 1610 his estate at Beaconsfield was the subject of an inquisition post mortem.[51] The family had property in Chesham and also owned the brewery in Amersham.[52] Richard Baldwin died in 1661, leaving Wiltons to his son-in-law Edward Baldwin and his wife Elizabeth. Edward Baldwin was a lawyer. He was appointed Recorder of High Wycombe in 1683 and represented Wycombe in Parliament from 1685-90. His son, Henry Baldwin, went up to Oxford in 1679 aged 16, but died a year later. His younger son Richard, who matriculated at Oxford in 1686 aged 17, thus became the heir to Wiltons. In 1690, Richard Baldwin, now a barrister at the Inner Temple, married Anne Monteth, who came with a dowry of £3,000. An elaborate marriage settlement was drawn up where Wiltons was described as:

> Wiltons capital messuage with land impaled and stocked with conies, Pond Close, The Grove, Pond Close Mead, the Pightle adjoining to Pond Close, Wallnutt Tree Close, Rye Close, Shawes Mead, Limers Mead, Thrums Pightle, Thrumswood, Piersons Spring, Well Redling Wood, Sheppards Spring, Hores, Barne Field Hedgegrove, Widfeild Heath Spring, The Bottome Woodlands, Hasle Field Hedgroves, Birchen Spring, Pitlands Coppice, Groves Field (totalling 162 acres) in Beaconsfield, Chalfont St. Giles, and Chalfont St. Peter.

> Messuage adjoining the capital messuage, Willis Hill Farm at Wiltons Green in Beaconsfield; Orchard Garden and Rush Plott, Great Mead, Well Field, Little Mead, Leachmore Grounds, Little Wide Field, Heath Wide Field, Rendall Field, Hores Redding Field, Great and Little Chiswicks, Chalford Chiswicks, Barne Field, Peasecroft, Hasle Field, Well Redding, Hither, Middle and Further Pitlands, Durants Heath (totalling 180 acres) in Beaconsfield, Chalfont St. Giles and Chalfont St. Peter.[53]

The families were wise to put such a valuable estate as Wiltons in trust. Edward Baldwin died in 1691. His son Richard Baldwin died in 1698, obviously in debt. His widow, Anne Baldwin, obtained a private Act of Parliament in 1700 to enable her to sell the messuage called Wiltons and other lands in Buckinghamshire left in her husband's will.

Martin Cawfield Basil

The purchaser of Wiltons in 1700 was Martin Cawfield Basil Esq. of Lincoln's Inn, Middlesex. He paid £2,799 to clear the existing mortgage on Wiltons, plus £706 to Richard Baldwin's widow Anne. £400 went to Stephen Baldwin, £400 to Thomas Baldwin, £583 to Maria Baldwin, £520 to Sarah Baldwin and £91 to Elizabeth Mitton, all of these being brothers and sisters of Richard Baldwin.[54] One of the perquisites of Wiltons was the right to bury members of the family in the south chancel aisle of Beaconsfield church. At the visitation of 1706, the rector stated that there were burying places in the two wings of the chancel, one belonging to Mr Waller of Gregories and the other to Mr Baldwin's family, late of Wiltons.[55]

Martin Basil was High Sheriff of Buckinghamshire in 1724. He died in 1735 and was succeeded by his son William Basil. In 1738, William Basil made a significant addition to the estate by buying the *Saracens Head* from Thomas Rutt. He in turn was succeeded by his sons Martin and Edmund Basil, Edmund being chosen as High Sheriff of Buckinghamshire in 1770. In 1777, Edmund Basil of White Barns, Hertfordshire, sold Wiltons to Josias Du Pre for £37,000. It was described as:

> All that capital messuage commonly called Wiltons … With all barns stables dovehouses buildings orchards gardens yards and appurts … containing together by estimation 2 acres situate standing and being in the parish of Beaconsfield in the said County of Bucks heretofore in the tenure or occupation of Ann Baldwin her assignee or assigns and afterwards of Martin Caulfield Basil his assignee or assigns.[56]

The conveyance also included the *Saracens Head* in Beaconsfield, then in the tenure of Joseph Jagger.

Josias Du Pre

Josias Du Pre had made his fortune as Governor of Madras and soon began the rebuilding of Wiltons. He died at Beaconsfield in 1780, aged 54, but his widow, Rebecca, a sister of the 1st Earl Caledon, continued building the house to be called Wilton Park. The writer of *Beauties of England* enthused, 'The house was built from the designs of Mr Jupp, late surveyor to the East India Co., by the late Governor Du Pre, but finished by his widow about twenty years since. The rooms are embellished with a few good pictures; some of which were purchased from the late Mr Purching's celebrated collection.'[57] Rebecca Du Pre died in 1800.

James Du Pre

James Du Pre, son of Josias and Rebecca, was born in 1778. In 1801 he married Madelina, daughter of Sir William Maxwell of Monreith, Wigtownshire. In 1805, James Du Pre received permission from the Quarter Sessions to close

10 *Wilton Park, built by Josias Du Pre, c.1780.*

the road from Beaconsfield to Wilton Green, which came inconveniently close to his house. He then built a new road to Chalfont St Giles and Chalfont St Peter, skirting Wilton Park. This road became known as Pot Kiln Lane, as it cut through the property of William Wellings of Beaconsfield, brickmaker and potter.[58] Also in 1805, James Du Pre exchanged 54 acres of his land in Beaconsfield for a farmstead and 125 acres of land south of Wilton Green, belonging to Edmund Waller of Hall Barn.[59] In 1807 he purchased a farmhouse and malting at Wiltons Green, formerly belonging to James Boddy.[60] Both these farmhouses were demolished and the land was added to Wilton Park.

James Du Pre was elected MP for Aylesbury in 1802 but was mired in the infamous bribery case which followed. He bought the Quarrendon Estate, just to the north of Aylesbury, in order to secure his position in the town. He was High Sheriff of Buckinghamshire in 1825. James Du Pre had three sons, including Caledon George Du Pre, after whom Caledon Road is named. Another son, William Maxwell Du Pre, married Catherine, daughter of Sir Thomas Baring, and became Vicar of Wooburn. His daughter, Catherine Anne, married Pascoe St Leger Grenfell, heir to a copper and banking fortune. His four unmarried daughters played a significant local role in maintaining the girls' school, which later became part of Beaconsfield's National School. The Du Pres contributed a significant amount to the £1,500 needed for the building of the new Congregational Church in Aylesbury End in 1875. James Du Pre died in 1870, aged 92, and was buried at Beaconsfield. His address in the burial record is 40 Portland Place. His heir was his son, Caledon George Du Pre, born in 1803.

Caledon George Du Pre

Caledon George Du Pre was MP for Buckinghamshire from 1839-74 and, although never holding ministerial office, he seems to have been a trusted backbencher who took his duties in the House of Commons seriously. As the sixth-largest landowner in the county in 1872, it might have been thought that he would have relied heavily on the votes of his tenants and neighbours. However, he drew votes from all four of the county's divisions almost equally in 1852 and even obtained 27 more votes than his Conservative running mate, Benjamin Disraeli.

Caledon George Du Pre did not live permanently at Wilton Park. In 1882, the reversion of the Wilton Park Estate was advertised, but was not sold:

> Wilton Park Estates, comprising the Beaconsfield, Wooburn, Quarrendon, Chippenham Court, Chalfont St Peter's estates with the fine old mansions and parks of Wilton-hall and Wooburn-house, several country houses, and many well-cultivated farms with substantial buildings, the mills and brickfield the whole extending over an area of 6000 acres and with an estimated rent roll of £14,000. The reversion is contingent on the present tenant for life who is now aged 79 years and whose wife is deceased, dying without male issue and is subject to certain annuities and charges. There will be included also the benefit of two policies of assurance.[61]

George Caledon Du Pre died in 1886, aged eighty-three. The executors of his will were his nephews, Arthur Riversdale Grenfell and Henry Edward Thornton. He left £356,000 in personal estate and gave legacies to his gamekeeper, shepherd, coachman and other servants. His oil paintings, books, fixed mirrors and pictures were left to the tenant-in-tail of the mansion house of Wilton Park. As his sons had predeceased him without male issue, Wilton Park passed to his great nephew, William Baring Du Pre, grandson of his brother, the Rev. Maxwell Du Pre, one-time rector of Wooburn. William Baring Du Pre was only 11 when he inherited Wilton Park. His parents lived modestly in Hampshire, so he may not have visited Beaconsfield very often. Wilton

Park was therefore leased to his wealthy cousin, Pascoe Du Pre Grenfell. The scale of society associated with his use of the house can be seen in the 1891 census return. Staying at Wilton Park with Pascoe Du Pre Grenfell were no less than 17 family members and friends. Amongst the visitors, three of whom brought their own servants, were four business associates: a copper merchant, an insurance agent, a brewer and a stockbroker. They were looked after by 23 servants, and there were a further 24 employees living in the lodges, stables, laundry and gardener's cottage.

William Baring Du Pre

Pascoe Du Pre Grenfell had vacated the house by 1896 when the heir, William Baring Du Pre, came of age. The young man had begun a military career but had decided to live at Wilton Park with his mother and two sisters, along with two brothers who were still at Eton. The way the people of Beaconsfield celebrated this event suggests that they pinned a great deal of hope on the patronage that a resident squire might provide:

> Mr. Du Pre arrived from London at the Wooburn Green station at a quarter past two, and accompanied by his mother, he was at once driven to Beaconsfield. Upon entering the town the carriage was met by a number of sons of tenants on the Wilton Park estates, who took the horses out, and, substituting ropes for the traces, pulled the vehicle to a point nearly opposite the *Saracens Head Hotel*. Here the carriage was surrounded by a numerous gathering of the inhabitants, who heartily cheered Mr. Du Pre. The bells of the Parish Church were also ringing at the time, while cannon were fired in Wilton Park in honour of the event. Subsequently a series of rural sports were indulged in the grounds and at night there was a display of fireworks, a huge bonfire being also lighted. The attendance of the parishioners of Beaconsfield was very numerous, and all were highly delighted with the festivities.[62]

In the event, William Baring Du Pre did not stay long at Wilton Park. From 1897 to about 1903

he let the house to Henry White, the Secretary of the American Embassy and acting Ambassador. White entertained many prominent figures there, including on one occasion Lord Kitchener, the Duke and Duchess of Devonshire, the Earl of Rosebery, Mr Balfour, Lord and Lady Curzon, Lord Stavordale, Countess Grosvenor, Lord and Lady Elcho, Mr and Mrs Grenfell of Taplow Court and Mr George Wyndham MP. The Empress Frederick (The Princess Royal) joined the party on the Sunday afternoon.[63] Another tenant was Sir John Aird, who died at Wilton Park in 1911. Aird had been MP for Paddington, 1887-1906, and was a famous engineer, having earlier in life been responsible for moving the Crystal Palace from Hyde Park to Sydenham and later for the construction of reservoirs on the Nile.

Meanwhile, William Baring Du Pre travelled extensively and served in the Boer War. He was an all-round sportsman and laid out a nine-hole golf course near to Wilton Park in 1902. He was

11   *William Baring Du Pre, 1905.*

world champion at croquet and his putting style reflected this as he stood facing the hole and swung the club between his legs. The course was later extended to 18 holes and a new clubhouse, designed by Stanley Hamp, was opened in July 1914. When the new Great Western and Great Central line cut through Wilton Park, a halt was provided to serve the golf course.

William Baring Du Pre was only too anxious to cash in on the development brought by the railway. He gave his name to Baring Road where building plots were sold from 1905 and, in 1907, he sold 293 acres of Gregories Farm for development for £58,690. He was living at Taplow House when his daughter was born in 1910, and his only son died there in 1912. Another daughter was born at 4 Upper Berkeley Street in 1912. He was High Sheriff of Buckinghamshire in 1911, and was MP for the Wycombe Division from 1914-23. By December 1915, Taplow House had been converted into a maternity home for officers' wives and, although William had resumed his military duties, serving in the Middle East, his family had moved back to Wilton Park. The family remained there until 1939 although they travelled a good deal. When Mrs Du Pre's maid advertised for a position in 1937 she described herself as an experienced traveller.[64] In 1939, Wilton Park was requisitioned by the army and William Baring Du Pre moved to Tetworth, near Ascot, where he died in 1946. Wilton Park was used as a reception and interrogation centre for high-ranking German officers. After the war, it became the Army College of Military Education. The old house was demolished in 1967 and replaced by a rather ugly high-rise block.

Gregories

Gregories was another sub-manor of Beaconsfield, taking its name from the Gregory family, who flourished here from the 13th to the 15th centuries. A Ralph Gregory witnessed a deed of 1250 and a conveyance from about 1260 transferred a messuage and land between the road from Wycombe to London and the land of Ralph Gregory.[65] A similar deed from about 1290 refers to property between the land of Ralph Gregory and the road from Penn to Windsor.[66] In 1316, Agnes, widow of John, son of Ralph Gregory, claimed dower in a messuage in Beaconsfield.[67] Richard Gregory and his wife Edith survived the Black Death and were involved in many subsequent land transactions. Their son, Richard, also lived through the Black Death and witnessed innumerable sales and leases of Beaconsfield land up to the 1390s. Lawrence Gregory, citizen of London, probably his brother, also acquired considerable property in Beaconsfield. Alice, widow of Richard, son of Richard Gregory, still had a life interest in Gregories in 1402, when she came to an agreement with the heir, Gregory Ballard (probably her nephew), that she could continue to take firewood and pasture her animals on the land.[68]

In the 1430 rental of Burnham Abbey, a Thomas Ballard paid 15s. per half year for 'the farm of Merlonde', an alternative name for Gregories.[69] Ballard soon sold out to John Butler, owner of Hall manor, for in a similar rental of 1462 there is a 30s. chief rent due from 'Robert Ballard now Boteler for the farm of Merlonde, Fuller Fylde and Stonyfeld'. In the inquisition post mortem of Sir John Butler in 1477, the 'manor called Gregorys' is held of the Abbess and convent of Burnham at a rent of 30s.

Gregories was part of the estate at Beaconsfield sold in 1545 by John Butler to Lord Williams of Thame.[70] In 1556, Lord Williams leased the house to his servant, George Hanford. It was described as 'all that capital messuage or tenement called Gregories otherwise called Butler's Court or Place'.[71] The Hanfords clearly intended to build up a significant estate at Beaconsfield, for in 1566, Thomas Hanford bought the advowson of Beaconsfield church from Ralph Scudamore. When the rector Thomas Goodrich died in 1576, the Hanfords appointed a relative, Nicholas Taverner, to the vacancy. Although the Hanfords soon after sold their land in Beaconsfield, the family retained the right to appoint the rector until 1673.

George Hanford died in 1580, leaving 40s. a year to the poor of Beaconsfield. His widow, Cecily, married Edward Dun Lee. This may explain why the rector, Nicholas Taverner, resigned in 1589, to be replaced by Simon Lee. In 1584, Edward Dun Lee sold the lease of Gregories to the Beaconsfield lawyer Richard Tredway for £580. When it emerged that Lee had fallen behind on his rent, and that Lord Williams's successor, Richard Wenman, could reclaim the property, Tredway started an action in the Court of Chancery to recover his costs.[72] This court case must have been successful, for Richard Tredway continued to live at Gregories. He acquired further land in Buckinghamshire, including the Rectory of Stoke Poges, which was purchased in 1589 for his son, Sir Walter Tredway. Sir Walter died in 1604, owing his father a large sum of money. Sir Walter's young son, Edward Tredway, became the ward of Henry Saville, Provost of Eton. Richard Tredway died in the same year, leaving his affairs in the hands of his executors, one of whom was his son in law and partner in his law firm, Richard Gosnold. When Richard Tredway's widow Ellen removed household goods and jewellery from Gregories, Gosnold took her to court, claiming that the goods were required to pay Tredway's debts and the legacies given in his will.[73] Ellen Tredway died in 1608 and was buried near to her husband in the church of Beaconsfield.

Gregories should have passed to Richard Tredway's grandson, Edward Tredway. Instead, it became the home of Richard Tredway's other executor, Thomas Waller, Prothonotary of the Court of Common Pleas. Thomas Waller had married Dorothy, daughter of William Gerrard of Harrow on the Hill. Their youngest son, Thomas Waller (1605-82) became Clerk of the Assize for

Buckinghamshire. It seems that Thomas Waller himself took over the lease of Gregories, and later bought the freehold from the Wenman family.

Thomas Waller the elder died at Beaconsfield in 1627. His is the first of a series of elaborate family gravestones set into the floor of the north aisle of Beaconsfield church. It shows a man and woman kneeling beneath the coat of arms of Waller, being three walnut leaves in a bend. The Latin inscription roughly translated means:

> Here lies the body of Thomas Waller Esq., Prothonotary of the Bench, and Dorothy his wife. She departed this life in the year 1626, he in the year 1627.

An inquisition post mortem was held to establish the inheritance. Thomas Waller held 'one messuage called Gregories alias Botelers Corte alias Botelers Place with the appurtenances in Beaconsfield' and also … gardens, two granaries, 12 acres of land, 10 acres of meadow, 80 acres of pasture and 100 acres of wood in Beaconsfield in the County of Bucks, late in the occupation of Felix Gerrard and William Gerrard also formerly the property of Richard Wenman. Thomas Waller also owned the *Crown Inn*, Beaconsfield.[74] His heir was his son, Edmund Waller, born about 1593.

Edmund Waller of Gregories is not to be confused with his younger cousin, the poet Edmund Waller (1606-87), who built the mansion called Hall Barn. In 1627, when making a lease of Glory Mills in Wooburn to Richard King, he styles himself Edmund Waller of Gregories alias Botelers Court.[75] Edmund Waller, son of Thomas, went up to Christ Church, Oxford, in 1608, aged fifteen. In 1616 he married Mary, daughter and heir of Anthony Smith of St Pauls Cray in Kent. Thomas Waller refers to their marriage settlement in his will of 1621, noting that he had paid off Mary's wardship and £1,200 worth of his son's debts. Edmund Waller had at least four children by his first wife, including a son, Thomas, born about 1622. Helen Gabriel, 'servant to Mr Waller of Gregories', was buried at Beaconsfield in 1631. In 1632, Mary Waller was one of seven gentlewomen given specific licence by the rector to eat meat during Lent.[76] At an inspection of the parish church in 1637, however, it was reported that the pew belonging to 'Mr Waller of Gregories' was too high.[77] In his will, dated 6 March 1652, Edmund Waller left 20s. to Richard Gould, his coachman. Richard Skinner, 'servant of Edmund Waller of Gregories', was buried in 1662. Edmund Waller of Gregories married secondly Lucy, daughter of Sir Richard Grobham Howe.

Edmund Waller of Gregories died in 1667. His gravestone in the church reads:

> Edmund Waller of Gregories in the parish of Beaconsfield and County of Bucks died 21 Sept 1667 and lieth here underneath interred; who was the son and heir of Thomas Waller and Dorothy his wife which Dorothy was the daughter of William Gerard of Harrow upon the Hill in the County of Middlesex Esq.

When his widow Lucy died in 1686, there was a similar attention to detail:

> Here lieth the body of Lucy Waller wife of Edmund Waller of Gregories Esq second daughter of Sir Richard Grobham Howe Kt & Bart who departed this life 28 Dec 1686.

The pedigree of the heir, Thomas Waller of Gregories, who died in 1682, was similarly recorded:

> Thomas Waller of Gregories in the parish of Beaconsfield and County of Bucks Esq. died the 30 day of May 1682 and lieth buried under this stone; who was the son and heir of Edmund Waller Esq.

The heir of Thomas Waller was his son Edmund Waller of Gregories, who was chosen as High Sheriff of Buckinghamshire in 1689. His wife, Theophila, was buried at Beaconsfield in 1708. The Wallers evidently had a London house

for when Edmund Waller died in 1713, his address was given as St James, Westminster. Perhaps he had already given possession of Gregories to his son and heir, John Waller.

In about 1712, John Waller employed an architect called Thomas Milner to design a new house at Gregories. It was typical of small country houses of the period, being two storeys high over a basement and seven bays wide. The architect's drawing, published in 1717, shows that the central three bays projected slightly and were topped by a shallow pediment, beneath which was an elaborate carving in stone of a naval scene. Either side of the house was a curved colonnade leading to domestic quarters on the west and stables on the east. The drawing shows a massive statue of a horse and groom in a niche in the stable wall.[78] The old house, situated some distance to the north, was retained as a home farm.

John Waller was the last of the Wallers to live at Gregories. In his will of 1722, John Waller left Gregories to his ailing son, Henry Waller, on whose death it was to pass to his nephew, Francis Fuller, whom he hoped would take the surname of Waller. Francis Fuller was the son of Waller's deceased sister Mary, who had married Edward Bostock Fuller of Tandridge, in Surrey. Francis Fuller did not change his name to Waller, but inherited Gregories nonetheless. So as to secure the transfer of the estate, John Waller's widow Frances agreed in 1731 to sell to Francis Fuller her own entitlement to a third of her late husband's estates for £12,955.[79]

Francis Fuller was a career soldier. He was appointed a Lieutenant and Captain in the 1st Foot Guards in 1711 and rose to be Colonel of the 29th Foot (later the Worcestershire Regiment) in 1739. Fuller sold a substantial part of the Gregories Estate to Edmund Basil of Wiltons, in 1739.[80] Francis Fuller was made a Major General in 1743. When he died in 1748,[81] Gregories passed to his eldest son, Edward, who was also a military man. It was Major General Edward Fuller who sold Gregories to William Lloyd in 1757. The

12   *The architect's drawing of Gregories which appeared in Colen Campbell's* Vitruvius Britannicus *in 1717.*

Fullers still owned the *Crown Inn*, however, and the family appears to have removed there when it ceased to trade in about 1759.[82] Edward Fuller died in 1762. His mother, Christiana, died in 1765 and his brother, John, died in 1777. They were all buried at Beaconsfield. John's widow, Anne, still owned the former *Crown Inn* in 1783.[83]

William Lloyd

William Lloyd may have been related to the Fullers as both he and Christiana Fuller made bequests to members of the Gwyn family in their wills. Lloyd was a wealthy socialite and collector. In 1754, he married Elizabeth Collins, who came with a dowry of £6,000.[84] He purchased Gregories from Edward Fuller in 1757 for £12,964.[85] Lloyd lived at Gregories for only 10 years, but several of his children were baptised at Beaconsfield and his wife died there in 1761.

By 1767, William Lloyd was heavily in debt and was negotiating with the politician, Edmund Burke, for the sale of Gregories for £20,000. Lloyd died in June 1768 before the purchase was complete. He left his property to trustees to be sold for the benefit of his eldest son, John

William Lloyd, who was under 21, and his second son, William Lloyd. In his will, made in 1764, he made specific bequests of 'marble busts standing in my hall at Gregories' and another bust on top of a bookcase in his study there. William Lloyd's second son, William, born at Beaconsfield in 1760, evidently inherited his father's taste for art and antiquities. He went up to Wadham College, Oxford, in 1776 and was Keeper of the Ashmolean Museum 1796-1815.

Edmund Burke

Edmund Burke had agreed to buy Gregories, including William Lloyd's notable art collection, for £20,000. Burke was slow to pay the purchase money to Lloyd's trustees. Earl Verney, who not only gave Burke a Parliamentary seat at Wendover, also had to lend him £6,000 to buy the house. When Verney himself was in deep financial trouble in 1783, he sued Edmund Burke for repayment, but Burke refused to acknowledge the debt.[86] Burke renamed Gregories as Butler's Court, seeming to prefer the name of one medieval owner rather than another. Burke took pleasure in managing the home farm, which was situated some way north of

13 *Gregories, when occupied by Edmund Burke. Note the absence of the colonnades and pavilions shown on the elevation of 1717.*

14 *Gregories, home of James Louis Garvin, editor of the* Observer, *1908-42.*

the mansion. He conducted worthy experiments in cultivation and husbandry and was visited by the agriculturalist Arthur Young. Amongst his philanthropic activities was the founding of a school at Penn, at the house of his friend General William Haviland, for the children of those who fled to England during the French Revolution.

Edmund Burke died at Butler's Court in 1797 and was buried at Beaconsfield. His wife, Jane, lived on at Butler's Court. Although short of money, and at one stage advertising the house for sale, she maintained a team of ageing servants, several of whom were later buried at the parish church. These included her coachman, Charles Franks, in 1805, her footman, Francis Adams, in 1808, her gardener, John Heard, in 1809, her bailiff, Joshua Wade and her butler, William Webster, in 1810, and her servant, Sarah Webster, who survived her, in 1818. Butler's Court was sold shortly before Mrs Burke's death in 1812. Burke's library and the art collection he bought from William Lloyd were taken to London for auction. This was fortunate, as the house was burnt to the ground in 1813, never to be restored.

The new owner of Gregories was James Du Pre of Wilton Park, whose tenant at the home farm now cultivated the former parkland as well. When William Baring Du Pre sold Gregories Farm for development in 1907, the farmhouse had already been gentrified and was in the occupation of the local solicitor, A.E.W. Charsley. In 1921, the remaining parts of Gregories Farm were bought by James Louis Garvin, editor of the *Observer* from 1908-42.[87] He worked from home and converted several buildings to house his huge library. After Garvin's death in 1948, Gregories was split into four dwellings: the main house retained the name Gregories; the east wing, which Garvin had used as his study, was split off as Shepherds Corner; the building to the west, which had housed part of his library, was sold as the Old Coach House; and the former stables, which had housed the remainder of Garvin's library, became a house named Piebalds.[88]

Butler's Court

The large Victorian house known as Butler's Court was built in 1891 by Arthur Riversdale Grenfell. The Grenfell family came from Cornwall where they had extensive mining interests. Pascoe Grenfell (1761-1838) became a partner with Thomas Williams in the copper-finishing works at Temple Mills, near Marlow, and lived at Taplow Court. He was MP for Marlow from 1802-20. His son, Pascoe St Leger Grenfell, married Catherine Anne, daughter of James Du Pre of Wilton Park, in 1824. Their eldest son, Pascoe Du Pre Grenfell, lived for a time at Wilton Park. It was their third son, Arthur Riversdale Grenfell, who built Butler's Court in 1891 on land belonging to Gregories Farm. The architect was Arthur Vernon of High Wycombe.

When Arthur Riversdale Grenfell died unmarried in November 1895, Butler's Court passed to his brother, Francis Wallace Grenfell (1841-1925), a career soldier, who had fought in the Zulu Wars. He was created Lord Grenfell in 1902 and became a Field Marshal in 1908. He put the house on the market in May 1896 when it was described as:

> A very attractive freehold residential property, known as Butler's Court, Beaconsfield. The house is approached by a carriage drive through the park and contains entrance and staircase halls, three reception rooms, 13 bed and dressing rooms, bathroom and capital offices. Electric light is installed. Stabling for three horses, coach-house, tastefully laid-out pleasure grounds in all about 60 acres.

Butler's Court did not find a buyer and remained a home of Field Marshal Grenfell for many years. Grenfell was a noted Egyptologist and two tablets with Egyptian and Coptic hieroglyphics are set into the walls of the house. The best pieces of his collection were acquired by the British Museum at a sale in 1917. Butler's Court was eventually sold to Francis Reckitt, joint chairman of the Hull firm, who died there in 1917, aged 90,

15 *Butler's Court, built by Arthur Riversdale Grenfell, 1891.*

leaving more than £1m. The next owner was Capt. Shirley Sutton Timmis, a retired soap manufacturer and J.P. for Lancashire. Timmis was Vice Chairman of the U.D.C. in 1924 and High Sheriff of Buckinghamshire in 1938-9 and 1940-1. The Butler's Court gardens were opened for charity to the public in the late 1930s. Like the Du Pres, the Timmis family spent a considerable time abroad. It was during such an absence in 1934 that the house was seriously damaged by fire, but it was rebuilt to its original plan. During the Second World War, Butler's Court was a convalescent home for Free French forces. London County Council bought the site in 1948, intending to open a special school there. This plan was not proceeded with and the L.C.C. sold it in 1952 to George Pitcher of Seeley's Farm. The house became the research centre for the papermakers Wiggins Teape in 1956.[89] In the 1960s, the builders George Wimpey bought half of the 40 acres of land still owned by the trustees of Shirley Sutton Timmis. By 1966 they were advertising large four-bedroomed houses at £8,150 freehold on their Butler's Court estate. Butler's

Court itself has recently been sold by Wiggins Teape for redevelopment, but the current plans are for the house to continue as offices.

16 *Field Marshal Francis Wallace Grenfell (1841-1925).*

Three

Farms and Farmers

Away from its urban centre, Beaconsfield has a landscape of scattered farmsteads amongst preserved woodland. There is no evidence that the farmers had strips in common arable fields like those of nearby Burnham. Nor were there any extensive areas of common pasture, besides Latchmore, a small common with a pond near Wilton Green, which was enclosed in the 18th century. The farms on the west side of Beaconsfield may have been able to graze their animals on Holtspur Heath in Wooburn parish. Some of Beaconsfield's farms take their names from topographical features like Woodlands Farm, but most are named after particularly important owners or tenants.

Davenies Farm

Davenies Farm probably takes its name from John Dabney or Dawbeney, an innkeeper who died in 1510, leaving his house near the *Crown Inn* and extensive property and leasehold land in Beaconsfield. The freehold of some of this land was acquired from the lord of the manor by the Beaconsfield attorney Richard Tredway. He put it in trust for his son, Sir Walter Tredway, and refers to 'Dawbeneys' in his will of 1604:

> And whereas I did likewise purchase to Sir Walter Tredway knight deceased my late son and to the said Thomas Goddard and to their heirs in trust for me and my heirs of Sir Richard Wenman Knight certain arable land pasture and wood ground in Beaconsfield aforesaid called Dawbeneys ground with two meadow plots thereto belonging or reputed parcel thereof all which premises are now in the said Thomas Goddard by title of survivor.

By 1678, Davenies Farm was owned by the Waller family of Gregories and rented by Richard Clarke of Beaconsfield, a maltster.[1] When Clarke died in 1715, he divided his farming stock into two, one half going to his widow and the other to his son, Zachary, who continued to run the farm.

Davenies passed with the rest of the Gregories Estate to James Du Pre of Wilton Park in 1812. From 1841-91, Davenies was tenanted by the Hearne family. Thomas Hearne was born in Penn and in 1824 was a founder member of the Methodist Church in Beaconsfield.[2] He was an early chairman of Beaconsfield Local Board of Health. His son, Walter Hearne, took over the tenancy of Davenies Farm in about 1871. The last farmer at Davenies was John Thomson, formerly of Wilton Park Farm. With the coming of the railway in 1906, much of the land was laid out in building plots by the Wilton Park Estate and the farmhouse and neighbouring barn was then converted into a large country house by the

17   *Davenies Farm, converted into a country house by the architect Stanley Hamp, c.1909.*

well-known London architect, Stanley Hamp, who came to live at Davenies.[3] In 1940, Davenies became a school run by the Rev. R.E. Newton.

Gregories Farm

When John Waller built the new house called Gregories in the early 18th century, he chose a site some way to the south of the original house. The old house became the home farm and was purchased in about 1812, along with the rest of the Gregories Estate, by James Du Pre of Wilton Park. The 19th-century farmers at Gregories included Richard Piggott, Henry Briggs and Jesse Betts. In 1871, John Foster was the tenant of Gregories, farming 499 acres with the help of eight men and three boys. The last farmer at Gregories was William Gee and, by 1901, Gregories was the home of the solicitor A.E.W. Charsley. When the farmland was cut in two by the new railway line, the owner, William Baring Du Pre, laid out building plots north of the station. In 1907, he sold the remaining land south of the station to

James and William Gurney who developed the Burke's Estate. Charsley then bought the freehold of Gregories farmhouse and developed several houses in the vicinity. In 1921, Gregories became the home of the journalist J.L. Garvin.

Harrias Farm

Harrias was a small farm on Hedgerley Lane, about half a mile south-east of the old town. In the 17th century it was sold by the attorney, George Gosnold, to Michael Rutt, innkeeper, along with the house in London End, later called the *Kings Head*. In 1664, Rutt sold the land called Harrias, with a cottage erected on it, to Edward Lee of Westminster, probably as a country retreat. Edward Lee died in 1686, aged 86, and was buried at Beaconsfield. His son, John Lee, who also lived at Harrias, erected a memorial to him in the church.[4] John Lee sold Harrias Farm in 1717 to Charles Dickinson of London. His widow, Elizabeth Dickinson, was buried at Beaconsfield in 1756, having left the farm to her nephew, Freeman Taylor. The 1763 map of the Hall Barn Estate shows Harrias Farm as a house and land belonging to Mr Freeman Taylor. When Taylor died in London in 1766, the farm was sold to William Anthony, who also held nearby Hyde Farm. By 1820, the farm had been added to the Hall Barn Estate and was let to William Batting. An 1831 survey of the Hall Barn Estate described Batting as:

> A very industrious man, who does ample justice both to himself and his landlord in the management he pursues, and by selling milk to the inhabitants of Beaconsfield, and employing the leisure time of himself and horses to hire continues to put a decent livelihood for himself and family, suitable for his education.[5]

Batting was probably the last genuine farmer at Harrias. In about 1860, the farmhouse was replaced by a larger house, built some distance to the south. This was occupied by a gentleman farmer, Henry Reginald Sykes. There is a stained glass window to his memory at the east end of the south aisle of Beaconsfield church. Sir Edward

Lawson established a model dairy at Harrias Farm with a herd of Jersey cows. In 1884, Harrias Farm became the first home of Harry Webster Lawson, later 2nd Lord Burnham. From 1903-11, Harrias was rented by a Mrs Cunard. The house was further enlarged in 1913 to the designs of Burgess & Myers. The new accommodation comprised a drawing room, dining room, smoking room, servants' hall, nursery, five bedrooms, a night nursery and eight servants' bedrooms.[6] The new occupant was the Hon. John Spencer Coke, son of the Earl of Leicester, who in 1907 had married Dorothy Olive, daughter of the 1st Viscount Burnham. In 1937, Dorothy Olive Coke sold Harrias House to Sir John Reith, Director General of the BBC. When Reith sold Harrias House in 1955, it became a home for '25 elderly people of slender means'.[7]

Hillmots Farm

Hillmots and Gods Farms were situated in the east of the parish, just south of Hedgereley Lane.

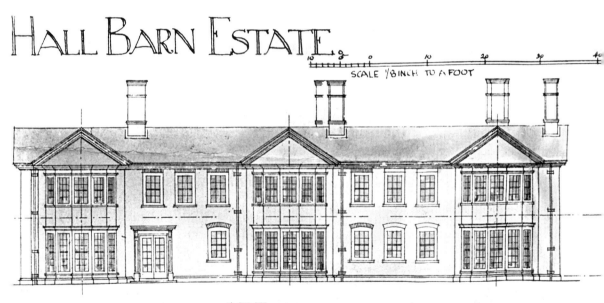

18 *Additions and alterations to Harrias Farm, 1913.*

19 *Hillmots Farm, 1948.*

For many years they formed part of the Duke of Portland's Bulstrode Estate, but they were purchased in about 1805 by Edmund Waller as a useful addition to the Hall Barn Estate. The two farms comprised 114 acres and were let to Isaac Mills, proprietor of the *White Hart Inn*.[8] Esther Mills of Hillmots Farm was buried at Beaconsfield on 11 May 1828 aged twenty-eight. Isaac Mills was still the tenant in 1831 and died in 1839.

Holloways Farm

Holloways Farm was situated about a mile south-west of the old town just before Burnham Road dips into a distinct hollow. The farm probably took its name from Lambert de Holeweia who was living at Beaconsfield as early as 1200.[9] The last of the family to live there was John Holway, who died before 1414, when his widow conveyed his land to trustees.[10] Their daughter, Joan Holway, sold Holloways Farm to William Gardner of Beaconsfield, a draper, in 1430.[11] In 1553 William Gardner sold the farm, then described as a 'capital messuage', to Thomas Ball of Beaconsfield, yeoman, for the high price of £814 3s. 4d. Thomas Ball married Elizabeth, widow of Robert Waller, and the farm descended to her

grandson Robert Waller, father of the poet. In his inquisition post mortem of 1616, the farm is described as:

> One messuage or farm called Holloways Farm in Beaconsfield and Burnham in said County of Bucks in the tenure of George Lovett ... held of Sir Marmaduke Dorrell as of his manor of Huntercombe in the County of Bucks.[12]

When Holloways Farm was listed in a Waller family settlement of 1660, the tenant was Henry Holt.[13] By 1692, Holloways was in the tenure of the Anthony family who also farmed Woodlands.

SOUTH ELEVATION

20 *Elevation of Holloways Farm, 1902.*

When John Anthony the elder made his will in 1720, he made the following bequests regarding his two Beaconsfield farms:

> I give to my wife Mary all goods, bed, bedding and furniture in and belonging to the chamber over the parlour in the messuage wherein I dwell, and also my silver tankard. I give to my wife all the stock in husbandry, corn, grain, hay, wagon, cart etc on or about the farm and lands called Holloways in my own occupation.

> I give to my son John all the stock etc belonging to the farm called Woodlands in my occupation in Beaconsfield. If the value of the two farms is not equal, they shall be divided equally between my wife and son John.

During the 18th century, some of the cultivated land belonging to Holloways Farm was taken to extend the gardens of Hall Barn. In 1743, Edmund Waller of Hall Barn let the remainder to Thomas Battin of Holloways, Beaconsfield, a husbandman, for 21 years at a rent of £92 a year.[14] The increase in farm rents over a century is apparent from a 21-year lease of Holloways Farm, made in 1830 by Harry Edmund Waller to Thomas Brown of Dorchester, gentleman, at a yearly rent of £210. The farm was measured at 147 acres and the New Park at 98 acres, both in the occupation of John Hare.[15] Later tenants of the farm included Henry Bamford, Andrew Graham, and George Gibson.

Some time after 1847, the farmhouse was replaced by a new house sited north-west of the farm buildings and nearer to the Burnham road. Its modern Victorian style suggests that it was built for a better class of farming tenant. It had two tall gables facing south, with bay windows to the principal living rooms. In 1914 the tenant, Captain Robert Spencer Britten, was in correspondence with the Architecture Department of the Country Gentleman's Association, regarding further improvements to Holloway House. The drawing room and the bedroom above were to be extended south into the garden, and the new accommodation included a drawing room, dining room, smoking room, study, three bedrooms, nursery, night nursery and one servant's bedroom. The sash windows were to be replaced with casements in the Arts and Crafts style.[16] The house was later occupied by the High Court Judge Sir Frank Douglas MacKinnon. Holloway House was demolished in 1960 and replaced by the present Fairview House.

Hyde Farm

Hyde Farm is situated about a mile south-east of the old town and is approached via Pyebush Lane. The house has 16th- or 17th-century timber framing on its east side and there is a substantial chimney of 17th-century brick, now reduced in height, on the east gable of the north wing.

The Hyde, or Hyde Farm, was one of the early freehold farms purchased by Hugh de Berewyk when he built up his Beaconsfield estate in the 14th century. It is listed in the rentals of his successor, Ralph Butler, as a separate manor,[17] but it was in fact occupied by a tenant farmer. Hyde Farm passed with the rest of the Butler estate in 1545 to Lord Williams of Thame and from him to his son-in-law, Richard Wenman. In 1563, Wenman leased Hyde Farm to George Langton for 31 years at a rent of £12 16s. 8d.[18] Two years later, the lease was assigned by Joan, widow of George Langton, to Edmund Waller of Coleshill.[19]

By 1607, Richard Wenman of Thame was disposing of his Beaconsfield estate. In that year he sold Hyde Farm to Elizabeth, widow of Thomas Waller of Beaconsfield.[20] She sold it to her cousin, Robert Waller, in 1614.[21] When Robert Waller died in 1616, the farm passed to his wife, Anne, and their son, Edmund Waller the poet. Anne and Edmund Waller purchased the remaining manorial rights to all the former Wenman property, including the manor of Hyde, in 1624.[22] In 1656, Edmund Waller leased Hyde Farm to John Witney of Stoke Mandeville for 21 years at a rent of £50 a year.[23]

21 *Hyde Farm, 1912.*

By 1692, the lease of Hyde Farm was held by the Anthony family, who continued to farm there for more than 100 years. In 1763, William Anthony of the Hyde, Beaconsfield, a yeoman, took out a new 19-year lease on the farm at the high rent of £106 a year.[24] In 1780, William Anthony of Hyde Farm, near Beaconsfield, a farmer, insured his household goods in his dwelling house there for £80. His farming stock in a nearby barn and rick-yard amounted to £150. In 1798 he had 16 horses, the largest number employed on any of the Beaconsfield farms. Some of these may however have been employed in the coaching trade.

Hyde Farm was maintained as a working farm long after other farmhouses on the Hall Barn Estate had been let out as gentlemen's residences. Hyde Farm now belongs to the Portman Burtley Estate and the farm buildings are leased to a variety of tradesmen.

Oldfields Farm

Oldfields Farm is situated about one and a half miles north-east of the town, on the east side of the Amersham road. Although in the parish of

Beaconsfield, it was within a detached part of Hertfordshire until 1844. The farm may take its name from one Osbert de Odefeld, who held a lease of a virgate of land in Beaconsfield in about 1200.[25] Nicholas Cooke, who held the *Bull Inn* in Beaconsfield, mentions Oldfields Farm in his will of 1562:

> Roger Cooke shall freely dwell at Old Fields during the term of my lease ... I will that my wife shall bestow among the poor in Beaconsfield five loads of wood and faggots during my lease of Old Fields which I bequeath to her ...

The property later became part of the Gregories Estate and was occupied by several generations of the Grimsdale family. Oldfields Farm was part of the estate sold in 1739 by Francis Fuller to Edmund Basil of Wilton Park.[26] It passed to the Du Pre family with the rest of Wilton Park in 1777. The tenant was Elisha Grimsdale of Oldfields Farm, who insured his property in Chalfont St Giles with the Sun Insurance Company in 1786.[27] Subsequent tenants of the Du Pres at Oldfields Farm included William Rainer, James Hatch, George Rance, Thomas Wilson, William Taylor, John Henry Robarts and W. Baylis.

Overs Farm

Overs Farm is situated about a mile west of the old town and included land in Beaconsfield and Wooburn parishes. The farm takes its name from a 16th-century tenant, John Over of Beaconsfield, a husbandman, who left a will in 1543. Richard Over of Beaconsfield, a yeoman, also left a will in 1594. It appears that the former Wattleton Farm, which once stood on the north side of the Oxford road and was later absorbed into the grounds of Butler's Court, was part of Overs. Both farms are mentioned in the 1621 will of Richard Gosnold of Beaconsfield, gentleman, in which he leaves to his son Richard Gosnold:

> My farm called Overs Farm with all the land thereunto belonging lying and being in the parish of Beaconsfield in the said County of Bucks (except Waddendon) with the house there upon lately erected and built.

In 1622, Richard Gosnold leased Overs Farm to Samuel Atkinson,[28] but soon after the farm appears to have been occupied by one of the Aldridge family from nearby Woodlands. Richard Aldridge of Overs Farm left a will in 1634. The farm was later occupied by Richard Dell and William Nash. Robert Charsley, writing in 1787, described it as a messuage and lands called Overs

22   *Overs Farm, 1948.*

Farm, in Beaconsfield and Wooburn, Bucks, were purchased of Thomas Ligo and wife on 27 May 1721. Edmund Waller of Hall Barn leased Overs and Lilly Fee Farms in 1781 for 14 years to Jacob Howard at an annual rent of £140.[29] The Howard family continued at Overs Farm until the late 19th century.

Seeleys Farm

Seeleys Farm was part of the Gregories Estate and was situated in the north of the parish, just to the west of the road to Penn. It probably takes its name from the Cely family who were living in Beaconsfield in the 16th century. William Cely and his wife Joan are mentioned in the will of William Bulstrode in 1520. A William Cely married Edith Robbyns at Hedgerley in 1549, and a William Cely died in 1606 leaving an heiress, Edith Cely, then aged two. In the early 18th century, Seeleys Farm was leased by Francis Carter, a Beaconsfield maltster, who also owned land at Westhorp in Little Marlow. In his will of 1721, Francis Carter of Beaconsfield, gentleman, left to his son Francis 'the lease I have of the messuage farm and lands from John Waller Esq now in my own possession situate lying and being in the parish of Beaconsfield'.[30] When Francis Carter died in 1723, his friends made a detailed inventory of his farming stock.[31] These included:

Item all the Corn in the ground ploughing and seed valued at	68	15	0
Item in Carts Wagons Ploughs Harrows and Roles valued at	24	2	6
Item all the Sheep Racks and Hurdles valued at	99	10	0
Item a Pump Cistern and pipes	3	0	0
Item for Roots	7	4	0
Item Cows and Hogs in the Yard valued at	15	12	0
Item in the Stable Horses and harness all valued at	57	6	0
Item in the Granary all the Corn valued at	38	16	0

23 *Seeleys Farm, c.1910.*

Item in the Rickyard all the Wheat Ricks Stands and Hay and Tares valued at	199	0	0
Item all the implements of Husbandry and about the House and Barns	3	1	0

The landlord mentioned in the will of Francis Carter was John Waller of Gregories, who died in 1726. He was the last of the Waller family to own the estate before it was broken up. Seeleys Farm was sold to Ashetton Curzon of Penn, who leased it to David Anthony.[32] Seeleys Farm remained in the ownership of Earl Howe until the farmland was divided into building plots in the early 20th century. The farmhouse remains, surrounded by modern housing. It has a timber frame behind a brick façade, and has fireplaces in the east and west wings, dated 1572 and 1693 respectively.

Wattleton Farm

Wattleton Farm stood on the north side of the Oxford road, opposite the present Wiggenton Farm. Wattleton is mentioned in the 1621 will of the attorney Richard Gosnold, who left it to his wife, Elizabeth, with the remainder to his son George Gosnold. The farm was later owned by another attorney, Thomas Smith, who married Mary Gosnold in 1670. Thomas Smith died at Wattleton in 1707, leaving the house and extensive property in Beaconsfield to be sold for the benefit of his second wife, Anne.

Wattleton was purchased by Benjamin Young Esq., but was sold on to Edmund Waller of Hall Barn in 1749. In 1765 it was leased to David Anthony for 21 years at £139 per year.[33] Several members of the Anthony family occupied Beaconsfield farms during the 18th century, including Holloways, Hyde, Woodlands and Seeleys. On a map of Beaconsfield prepared in 1790, Wattleton is marked as Anthony's Farm. Wattleton was next leased and subsequently purchased by John Rolfe, a local land agent whose father, James Rolfe, had been agent for Edmund Burke at Butler's Court.

In a survey of the Hall Barn Estate made prior to its sale in 1832, the tenant of Wattleton Farm is singled out for praise:

Wattleton Farm … is in the highest state of cultivation. The land on this farm may be considered naturally as poor as any about Beaconsfield, but very much improved and very much better than immediately adjoining by a judicious and liberal mode of cultivation, alike beneficial to himself and his landlord, and he is a most desirable tenant, and one deserving every encouragement.[34]

Wattleton was occupied by three generations of the Rolfe family and was last farmed by William James Rolfe, one-time chairman of Beaconsfield's Local Board of Health. In 1891 the farmhouse was demolished and replaced by the gatehouse to the newly built Butler's Court.

Whites Farm

Whites Farm, now known as The Grange, was a large estate situated to the west of the Amersham road in the Hertfordshire part of Beaconsfield. It was probably so-called after a farmer called 'White', but the earliest record of it is in 1443, when the manor called Whites, in Hertfordshire, was sold by Thomas Ballard and Philippe his wife to John Boteler.[35] Ballard was the one-time owner of Gregories, and Boteler had married the daughter of Hugh de Berewyk, heiress to the manors of Hall Barn and Wiltons. There is a brass in the centre aisle of Beaconsfield church to John Warren, who died at Whites Farm in 1609.

> Here resteth the body of John Warren of Whites Farm who lived in marriage with Elizabeth his wife 23 years and by her had issue 4 sons and 2 daughters. He died being aged 60 years, the 16th December 1609.

The brass also shows small figures of his children Richard, Henry, William, John, Phyllis and Elizabeth.[36]

Whites Farm must have been a very large house, for the occupant in 1662, Dorothy Brown, paid tax on six chimneys.[37] Dorothy Brown was buried at Beaconsfield on 9 November 1665; John

Brown paid the church rates on Whites Farm in 1678 and Zachary Brown of Beaconsfield, yeoman, left a will in 1732.

Whites Farm was next owned by James Gallopine, a citizen and cooper of London, who used it as a country retreat. Gallopine was evidently a non-conformist, for, in his will of 1763, he left £100 to the minister and elders of the Dissenting Congregation at Beaconsfield. Whites Farm passed to Gallopine's son Daniel, a sugar broker in Tower Street, London, and then to Daniel's sister Mary, the wife of Joseph Stevenson, a London grocer. Stevenson had a tea warehouse in Love Lane, London, and used Whites Farm as his country home. He, too, supported the Congregational Church in Beaconsfield and, in 1790, his daughter Elizabeth married the minister, John Geary. The couple's first child, baptised at the Old Meeting House, Beaconsfield, on 28 December 1791, was named John Stevenson Geary. When Joseph Stevenson made his will in 1799 he left his son Joseph Stevenson:

> All books, furniture, prints, wine, liquors, coals and stores of housekeeping in my houses at Botolph Lane, London, and at Whites in the parish of Beaconsfield. Also all stock of corn, grain, hay, straw, utensils and implements of husbandry and live and dead stock about my farm and lands called Whites.

He also left £100 to the 'Congregation of Protestant Dissentors of Beaconsfield in the County of Bucks whereof my son-in-law John Geary is now pastor'. Stevenson was a supporter of the campaign to abolish slavery and left each of his children two £50 shares in the Sierra Leone Company. This organisation, founded in 1791, established the settlement of Freetown as a safe haven for freed slaves from Jamaica and the southern American colonies.

Joseph Stevenson died in 1808 and Whites Farm duly passed to his son, Joseph. By 1828, however, Whites Farm had become the home of John Stevenson Geary. He sold the farm in 1840 to William Dawkins, a gentleman farmer and founder member of Beaconsfield Board of Health. The farm was described as:

> All that capital messuage and farm with the appurtenances commonly called or known by the name of Whites Farm situate and being within the parishes of Beaconsfield and Agmondisham alias Amersham or one of them in the Counties of Bucks and Hertford … containing in the whole by estimation 111 acres … heretofore in the tenure possession or occupation of Robert Bradley afterwards of Henry Brown … Hine and Thomas Parker respectively and now or late of Daniel Gallopine.[38]

By 1877, Whites Farm had changed its name to 'The Grange' and was owned by George Henry Wood. In 1881, Wood was living there with his brother, a solicitor, and three servants. In 1891, Charles Sage was in residence with only two servants. He was the grandson of a cotton company director and the son of a clergyman. In 1901 the house was occupied by James Gurney, who, with his brother William, developed the Burke's Estate in Beaconsfield. By 1910 the house was owned by a Mrs Chaplin, but the occupant was a Mrs Williams. The house had 145 acres attached and was valued at £5,500, placing it next in importance to Hall Barn, Wilton Park and Butler's Court. The Grange was advertised for sale in the The Times, 18 August 1919:

> Preliminary notice is given of the sale of a very choice estate on the fringe of the Chilterns, known as The Grange, Beaconsfield, extending to about 430 acres. The house is of moderate size, with a smaller residence near it, and there are two sets of farm buildings with a large area of woodland.

The Grange was bought by John Henry Guy, a leading figure in the confectionary business. When Guy died in 1955, The Grange was bought by John Bernard Whitefield, a director of Jameson's

Chocolates. He died in 1974. In the 1980s, The Grange was the home of Chelsea Football Club's flamboyant owner, Ken Bates.

Wiggenton Farm

Wiggenton Farm is a red-brick, three-storey house of the mid-18th century, standing on the south side of the Oxford road as it leaves Beaconsfield. Like Wattleton Farm on the opposite side of the road, Wiggenton belonged to the Beaconsfield attornies Richard Gosnold and his son George Gosnold. In 1678, Wiggenton was leased for 40 years to the Beaconsfield attorney Thomas Smith, who had married George Gosnold's daughter, Mary, in 1670.[39]

Thomas Smith died in 1707 and Wiggenton Farm passed to William Low, who leased it to the Beaconsfield butcher and grazier, Robert Bates. William Low and his wife Mary sold Wiggenton Farm in 1747 to John Crook of Hall Place.[40] In 1804, Robert Crook leased the farm to Thomas Green of Beaconsfield, a shopkeeper.[41] When Robert Crook died in 1812, Wiggenton Farm passed to his daughter, Nelly Clay. It is described in some detail in an 1812 family settlement:

> All that capital messuage or tenement formerly in the tenure or occupation of Thomas Smith his undertenants or assigns commonly called or known by the name or names of Widgenden otherwise Widgendon otherwise Wigindon … all that courtyard and one other yard with the appurtenances adjoining to the said last mentioned messuage or tenement one of which was formerly paled in from the other but now are both joined together and near or adjoining to the said last mentioned messuage … wash house and brewhouse … barn and granary with the hogstye and hen houses adjoining … stable with granary over it … little garden … orchard heretofore planted with trees and containing 1 ½ acres … garden with the appurtenances as the same were formerly planted with fruit trees and used for a kitchen garden … little orchard or garden with appurtenances lying between Widgenden pond and the said highway.[42]

Nelly Clay, then living in Leamington, sold Wiggenton Farm to Harry Edmund Waller, owner of Hall Barn, in 1828.[43] One of the last to farm Wiggenton was James Honour, who in 1881 was described as a farmer of 147 acres and a hurdle and birch broom manufacturer. He was also a member of the Local Board. Wiggenton Farm became a private residence in about 1900, occupied by Esther Heath and Sarah Fry, teachers at the Church of England School. From 1918 it was the home of the High Court Judge, Sir Frank MacKinnon.

Wilton Park Farm

On the 1763 map of the Hall Barn Estate, no house is shown on the north-east corner of the Amersham and London roads, but the land is marked as belonging to Mr Davis.[44] Matthew Davis, innkeeper and maltster, occupied the *Kings Head*, London End, from 1745-75. He sold the *Kings Head* and other property to Edmund Basil of Wiltons in 1776. His brother, James Davis, was innkeeper at the *Saracens Head*, which also belonged to Edmund Basil. In 1777, Basil sold Wiltons to Josias Du Pre and it may be at this time that Wilton Park Farm was built on the former Davis property as a home farm.

The newly built farmhouse was occupied by Joseph Jagger, who had been innkeeper at the *Saracens Head* from 1769-87, but had settled down to farming by 1792. He had 10 horses, three wagons and four carts in 1798. It seems likely that Jagger was steward to the Wilton Park Estate, for Joseph Hare, his successor at Wilton Park Farm, held that position from 1810-69. Joseph Hare initially cultivated the land attached to Wilton Park Farm, but from 1851 there was a separate tenant for the farm. Joseph Hare died in 1869 aged 83, but his son, Joseph, succeeded him as steward on the estate, and continued to live at Wilton Park Farm. By 1877, however, John Perryman had taken over as steward, and Joseph Hare had moved to Windsor End. Wilton

24 *Wiggenton Farm, c.1905.*

Park Farm was then occupied by Henry King, who was farming 375 acres and employing five labourers in 1881. The farm was later held by John Thomson, who also rented Davenies Farm from the Du Pres. He was a member of the Local Board of Health.

25 *Wilton Park Farm, 1948.*

Woodlands Farm

Woodlands Farm was a brick-built, multi-gabled house, probably of the 17th century. It was situated in the south-west of the parish, just to the north of Burnham Road. Some historians have suggested that Woodlands was the original manor house of Beaconsfield, but it was in fact the home of the prolific Aldridge family, who were witnesses to innumerable local deeds in the 14th and 15th centuries. Robert Aldridge, who died in 1612, had sufficient wealth to warrant an inquisition post mortem. Henry Aldridge of Woodlands, gentleman, left a will in 1618 and Robert Aldridge paid tax on six hearths in 1662.

Perhaps the last of the Aldridge family to farm here was John Aldridge of Woodland, a yeoman, who was buried at Beaconsfield in April 1712. John Anthony, whose will of 1720 has been mentioned in connection with Holloways Farm, appears to have taken over the farm. He was succeeded by William Carter, a maltster. From notes on the Hall Barn deeds made in 1787, it seems that the freehold of the farm was purchased by the Wallers from John Aldridge on 26 June 1762.[45] The Wallers took much of the land north of the farmhouse into Hall Barn Park some time after 1763.[46] Their tenant in 1851 was Philip Woodman, who farmed 150 acres. In about 1860, a new house and modern farm buildings were built west of the old house, which then became labourers' cottages. In 1881, the tenant, Thomas Harrison, was farming 1,000 acres with a workforce of 20 men. When Sir Edward Lawson took over the Hall Barn Estate there was clearly a change in policy. The arable land was consolidated into fewer farms and the better farmhouses were let to upper middle-class families. By 1891, Woodlands Farm was rented by John Fox, a retired civil servant. In 1901, the house was occupied by William Penfold, a dental surgeon. More recently it has been the home of Lord Burnham himself.

Beaconsfield Farms in the 19th Century

A full survey of the Hall Barn Estate was made in 1831, prior to its sale by the Waller Family. The estate as a whole extended to 2,500 acres and brought in an annual rental of £2,800. The

26 *Woodlands Cottages, c.1900.*

27   *Woodlands Farm, 1948.*

agent was keen not to give a false impression of its value if it were put on the market:

> The land is generally on a poor pebbly soil, with the exception of some few instances, and some lands and premises immediately adjoining the town of Beaconsfield, which enhances the value of the whole, and leaves it yielding about a pound an acre after deducting the rentals of the Mansion, upon average. The tenants, with some few exceptions may be considered men without small capitals, barely sufficient to carry on their businesses – but an industrious hard working class of frugal habits and trifling affluence, and thus it is that many of them go on and they do, but in the event of bad harvests they have little to depend upon for *kind* beyond the growing of crops – and are therefore with an honest and honourable spirit and intention to pay, unable to do so, and some arrears must always consequentially be calculated upon and the average rentals, here stated, too high to form any data upon … under the present purchase on agricultural produce.[47]

Out of a total area of 4,785 acres surveyed in the 1846 tithe assessment, 2,247 acres was arable land. Grassland and meadow was generally to be found near to the farms and to the town and in all amounted to 1,276 acres. Woodland extended more than 873 acres, with the rest furze, gardens, orchards and waste. The two main estates of Hall Barn and Wilton Park had seven and four main tenants respectively, whilst Earl Howe, of Penn House, had one. Only one large farm, William Dawkins' 226-acre Whites Farm, was fully owner-occupied. John Rolfe, who farmed both Wattleton and Wiggenton Farms, had some freehold land, but this formed a solid block with his Hall Barn land. Only one farmer, Edmund Grove, rented land from both estates. He was also a coal merchant and lived at the former *Bull Inn*, London End. Grove also rented 51 acres of arable land in Coleshill from James Du Pre. Some of the grassland in the parish was held by those who were not primarily farmers, with the land used to pasture horses used in transport, or cows for local milk supply.

An 1877 return to the government providing a summary of the parish's agricultural statistics reveals a decline in arable farming. Although woodland, waste and parkland were not included, 3,341 acres were covered by the return. Of this,

FARM	TITHE AREA	ESTATE	ACRES				EMPLOYMENT: MEN AND BOYS			
			1851	1861	1871	1881	1851	1861	1871	1881
Woodlands	157	Hall Barn	150	200	200	1,000	na	3+2	3+3	20
Hyde	235	Hall Barn	136	200	210	214	3	9+5	1+4	5+1
Hillmotts	138	Hall Barn	147	147			6	2+2		
Overs	105	Hall Barn	163	299	298		8	8+2	8+3	
Harrias	82	Hall Barn	104		178	177	3		6	5+1
Holloways	150	Hall Barn	?160	156	190		6	3+2	8	
Wilton Park	245	Wilton Park	240	away	244	375	5		4+4	5+2
Davenies	159	Wilton Park	150	160	160	177	4	4	4+2	3+2
Oldfields	147	Wilton Park	147	167			6	3+1	3+3	
Gregories	310	Wilton Park	na	310	499	314	3	5+2	8+3	6+2
Wattleton	247	Owner/ H. Barn	370	270	120	122	18	12+4	5+1	3+1
Wiggenton		Hall Barn			120	147			3+2	4+1
Whites	226	Owner	160	na	160		6		5+1	
Seeleys	96	Howe	na	184		208		4+1		9
Bull	69	HB/WP	80				4			
Red Barn		Whites			100	124			3+1	3+2
TOTAL ACRES	2,367		2,007	2,093	2,479	2,868	72	74	88	75

Table 1   *Beaconsfield farm acreages and labourers employed, 1851-81.*

50 per cent was occupied by crops, like wheat, 14 per cent; oats, 10 per cent; barley, 10 per cent; turnips and swedes, nine per cent, with the remaining seven per cent being used for a variety of other crops. Permanent grass accounted for 23 per cent of the area, with 14 per cent down to grass from which a hay crop was taken, and 12 per cent to grasses for hay. Only 0.5 per cent was fallow. At this date orchards accounted for only 15 acres, a small figure considering the future development of extensive orchards at Seeleys Farm. There were 344 sheep, 285 lambs, 94 cows in milk and 151 other cattle, and 95 pigs. Of the 123 horses, 87 were used on the farms and 35 were unbroken. The proportion of horses was far higher than the average for Buckinghamshire, that of cattle was similar, but there were fewer sheep (58 per cent compared with 69 per cent).

Four

The Oxford Road

Prior to the 16th century, there was no statutory provision for the maintenance of English roads. It was left to local communities to fill the ruts and potholes left in their roads, although most wear and tear was caused by travellers passing through and tradesmen carrying goods to distant markets. So it was that the wealthier members of the community often included in their wills bequests for the repair of local roads and bridges. Thomas Knight of Beaconsfield left the generous sum of £1 6s. 8d. for the repair of Holtspur Lane in 1493. John Waller left 13s. 4d. for 'mending the highway between Margery Robins and Beaconsfield' in 1521, and in the same year Joan Waller of Beaconsfield left 20s. for 'mending the way from the Cross to the Stone' in London Way.

These bequests for road maintenance had all but disappeared by 1555, when an Act of Parliament made every parish responsible for the repair of its own roads. Churchwardens appointed surveyors who were to encourage every parishioner to spend up to four days a year working on the roads. In 1563, a further Act increased the number of days to six and made Justices of the Peace responsible for ensuring that parishes fulfilled their obligations. These Acts placed a particular burden on parishes like

Beaconsfield, which stood on the great road from London to Oxford. If their surveyors of highways were successful in mobilising the parishioners to improve the surface, it merely encouraged more travellers and carriers to use the road.

The Oxford road was never more significant than in the English Civil War. There was in theory little communication between the King in Oxford and Parliament in London. The rival armies were, however, constantly on the march along the road, and negotiators from either side travelled to seek a compromise with their opposite numbers. Oxford and London continued to draw in huge amounts of provisions and traders from Wycombe and Beaconsfield would continue to supply both cities. They became used to discretion as to the origin or destination of their goods. In 1686, when further upheavals threatened, the government drew up a list of the principal towns in the country where troops could be billeted and horses stabled. The list for Buckinghamshire shows Beaconsfield to be the sixth most important town, judged by the capacity of its inns.

Statute Labour

The records of the Justices of the Peace meeting in Quarter Sessions have been preserved from 1678 onwards. In 1689, the inhabitants of Beaconsfield

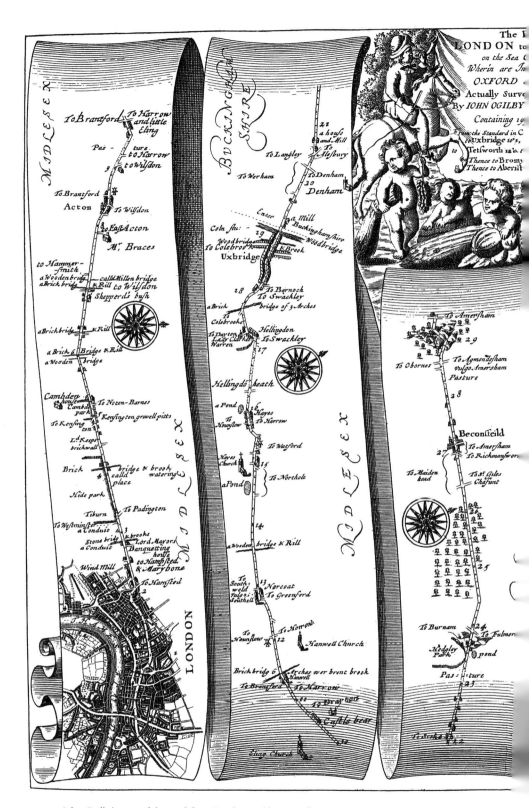

28   *John Ogilby's map of the road from London to Aberystwyth, 1675.*

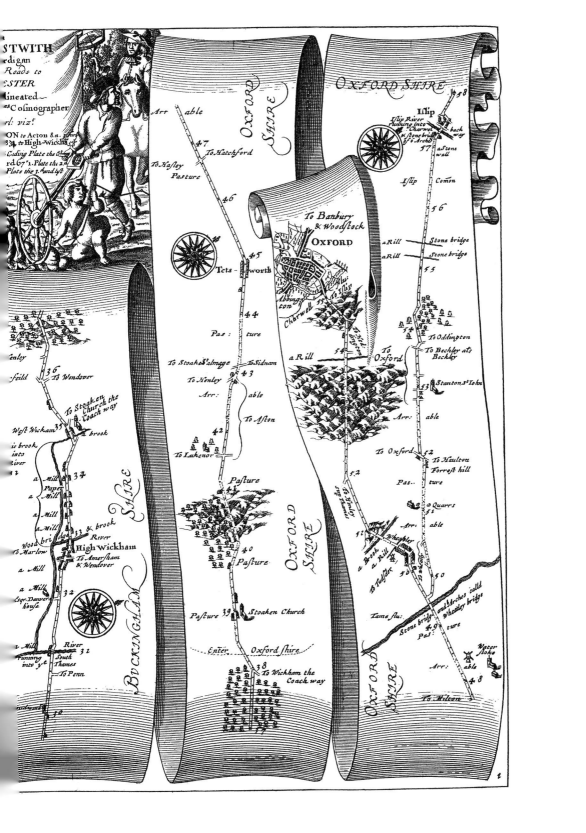

STWITH
rdigan
Roads to
ESTER
lineated
es Cosmographer
rl. viz.
ON to Acton 8.n. ...
... to High-Wickham ...
...ding Plate the 8...
...rd 67'1. Plate the 2d
...Plate the 3.and l.st

OXFORD SHIRE

58

Islip
Islip River
running into
Charwel
& stone bridg
of 6 Arch.d

back
way

57
a Stone
wall

Islip   Comon

56

a Rill   Stone bridge
a Rill   Stone bridge

55

To Banbury
& Woodstock

OXFORD

Abbing-
ton
Charwel
To
Oxford

a Rill   54

Arr   able   47   To Hatchford

To Hasley
Pasture

46

To Oddington

To Bechley ats
Beckley

45
Tets — worth
44

Stanton St Iohn

53

Arr   able

To Stoaken   S.'almage   To Sidnam
To Henley   43
Arr: able
To Aston

To Oxford   52   To Haulton
Forrest hill

Pas: ture

To Lukenor

42
To Lukenor

@ Quarrs
51

Arr: able

Pasture   41

Wheatley
a brook   a Rill
To Fulford

52

40
Pasture

51
50

Stoaken Church

Pasture   39

Tame flu: Stone bridge and Arches 'call'd
Wheatley bridge
Pas: ture

Enter   Oxford shire

48
Arr: able
Water
stoke

38
To Wickham the
Coach way

To Milcote

BUCKINGHAM

OXFORD SHIRE

OXFORD SHIRE

Henley
36   To Wendover
...feild

To Stoaken Church the
Coach way

West Wickam 35   a brook

...is brook
into
...river
...2

a Mill
a Paper
Mill
a Mill   34

a Mill
Wood bridge   33   & brook
To Marlow   River
High Wickham
To Amersham
& Wendover

a Mill

a Mill   32
Esqr. Danvers
house

a Mill   River   31
Running
into ye
South
Thames
To Penn

...ad ...   30

TOWN	BEDS	STABLING
Aylesbury	101	89
Stony Stratford	100	127
High Wycombe	82	171
Newport Pagnell	77	130
Buckingham	69	177
Beaconsfield	64	64
Fenny Stratford	45	64
Little Brickhill	45	62
Wendover	43	83
Olney	42	63
Winslow	36	87
Marlow	27	44
Amersham	26	51
Chesham	26	44[1]

Table 2 *Beds and stabling in Buckinghamshire inns, 1686.*

were presented for not repairing Aylesbury Way.[2] In the following year, they were given further time in which to produce a certificate that their highways had been repaired, owing to the unseasonableness of the weather. Failure to join in the communal activity of repairing the roads, or neglecting to contribute horses and wagons, could lead to an individual being named by the Justices of the Peace. In 1694, William Nash of Beaconsfield, farmer, was indicted for refusing to do his statutory work on the highways.[3]

Turnpike Acts

English trade increased dramatically during the 17th century, making the inadequacies of the road

network even more obvious. Tacitly admitting that forced labour was insufficient to repair the nation's roads, Parliament passed an Act in 1662 enabling parish surveyors to levy a highways rate to be spent on road maintenance. The first successful attempt to relieve parishes of the duty to maintain a major road, and make the carriers and ordinary travellers pay instead, came in 1663. In that year a private Act of Parliament was passed, enabling the Justices of the Peace of Hertfordshire to charge tolls and apply the proceeds to repairing a 15-mile section of the Great North Road near Royston. The success of this scheme led to the formation of other trusts, where local Justices of the Peace managed sections of major roads which passed through particularly difficult terrains. An even greater precedent was set in 1706 by the Act authorising the charging of tolls on a 15-mile stretch of Watling Street, from Fornhill in Bedfordshire to Stony Stratford in Buckinghamshire. The Act gave the power to charge tolls not to the Justices of the Peace, but to a committee of local gentry and tradesmen. This set the pattern for the formation of local trusts to maintain main roads across the country for the next 150 years. The toll roads became known as 'turnpikes', as the gates erected across the roads where tolls were to be collected resembled the spiked barriers, or 'turnpikes', more familiar at castle gates.

The first part of the road from London to Oxford to be turnpiked was the 15-mile section from Tyburn to Uxbridge, for which an Act of Parliament was passed in 1715. Two Acts passed in 1719 turnpiked the 12-mile section from Beaconsfield to Stokenchurch and a further 18 miles from Stokenchurch to Oxford. Maintenance of the eight miles of the Oxford road from Uxbridge to Beaconsfield remained the responsibility of the parish surveyors for another 30 years. The missing link in the local turnpike network was put in place by an Act of 1751, which turnpiked 'the road leading from the west end of the said town of Wendover to the end of a lane called Oak Lane, next to the great road called the Oxford Road, lying between the town of Beaconsfield in the said County of Bucks, and Uxbridge in the County of Middlesex, and that part of the said great road which leads from the west end of the said town of Beaconsfield to the River Colne near Uxbridge'. The Act claimed that these roads were 'very deep and founderous, and inconvenient and dangerous to persons and carriages passing the same'. The 1751 Act gave responsibility for maintaining these two sections of road to the Buckingham to Wendover Turnpike Trust, which had been in operation since 1720. To the list of existing trustees were added more than 80 gentlemen from the south of the county, including the Earl of Shelburne, then owner of Wycombe Abbey, Lord George Bentinck, brother of the owner of Bulstrode Park, Sir Francis Dashwood of West Wycombe, Edmund Waller senior, Harry Waller and Edmund Waller junior, all of Beaconsfield.

In the 1770s, responsibility for maintaining the roads from Wendover to Oak Lane and Beaconsfield to Uxbridge passed to separate turnpike trusts. An Act of 1777 created a new trust to repair the road from the west end of the town of Wendover to the end of a lane called Oak Lane, next to the great

29 *The Star Inn, Oxford Road.*

road called the Oxford road; and also half a mile of road from the River Colne towards Beaconsfield. Another trust was established by an Act of 1779 to repair the Oxford Road from the west end of the town of Beaconsfield to within half a mile of the River Colne, near Uxbridge. Curiously, the remaining half mile of road into Uxbridge was repaired by the Wendover to Oak Lane End Trust as late as 1852.

George Lipscomb, writing in about 1830, described the recent improvements made to the Oxford road by the Trustees of the Beaconsfield and Stokenchurch Turnpike:

> A considerable improvement has been effected in the line of road between Beaconsfield and Wycombe by the filling up of valleys, and reducing the height of the hills. In one part of the road, a valley has been filled up to the extent of near four hundred yards in length, and in some parts eighty feet in height; and a neighbouring eminence reduced, by cutting through it, to the depth, in some places, of forty five feet, and of a commodious width.[4]

Toll Collectors' Houses

Travellers on the Oxford Road passed toll gates opposite the *Dog and Duck*, Denham; at Red Hill, near the turn to Amersham; at Holtspur, west of Beaconsfield; and at the east end of High Wycombe. None of these toll houses remain in place today, although the toll house from London Road, High Wycombe has been rebuilt at the Chiltern Open Air Museum at Chalfont St Peter. Several of the milestones erected by the turnpike trustees have survived, including the milestone on the left-hand side of the road as it leaves Beaconsfield for Gerrards Cross.

The early turnpike Acts gave trustees powers to charge tolls and to repair roads for a period of 21 years only. There were five Acts for the Beaconsfield to Uxbridge Road; 1751, 1779, 1806, 1828 and 1852. The last Act of 1852 was known as the Beaconsfield and Red Hill Road Act and

30   *Toll collector's house, Chiltern Open Air Museum, 1990.*

BEACONSFIELD – STOKENCHURCH TURNPIKE TRUST
TABLE OF TOLLS

Payable at this Gate by virtue of an Act of Parliament passed in the Eighth Year of the reign of King George the Fourth

	d
For every horse. mule. ass or other beast of draught drawing any carriage. coach. landau etc. Six Pence.	6
For every horse. mule. ass or other beast of draught drawing any cart if the rollers be of a width or gauge of Six inches at the least. Six Pence.	6
For every horse or other beast of draught or burden laden or unladen but not drawing. Two Pence.	2
For oxen. cows etc Ten Pence the score and so in proportion for any greater or lesser number.	10
For every drove of calves. sheep or lambs. hogs or pigs Five Pence the score and so in proportion for any greater or lesser number.	5

By Order Thos. J. Reynolds
Clerk to the Trustees

31   *Beaconsfield to Stokenchurch turnpike tollboard, Chiltern Open Air Museum, 1990.*

moved responsibility for repairing the last half mile of road into Uxbridge from the trustees of the Wendover to Oak Lane End Road to those of the Beaconsfield and Red Hill Road. The powers conferred on the trustees by this Act were to continue in force for only 12 years, plus the time remaining in the Parliamentary session then in progress. This meant that the powers of the Wendover to Oak Lane Trustees and those of the Beaconsfield and Red Hill Trustees would expire in the same year.

With the opening of the London to Birmingham Railway, and part of the London to Bristol Railway in 1838, income from tolls on coaches and carriers' carts declined rapidly. In 1846, the Wycombe historian Kingston remarked:

> Much of the prosperity of the town has declined, in consequence of the almost total suspension which railway transit has given to the activity and excitement of the hourly influx of stage coaches and posting.[5]

The Beaconsfield to Stokenchurch road ceased to be a turnpike in 1867, and in November of that year the trustees auctioned the materials of the turnpike houses at the east end of High Wycombe and at Holtspur.[6] The site of the Holtspur toll collector's house was sold to James Du Pre of Wilton Park. The ornate toll house at High Wycombe was bought by the owner of Bassetbury Manor. The trustees of the Beaconsfield and Red Hill Turnpike closed their accounts in 1867. The toll houses at Denham and at Red Hill were sold in December 1867 to Benjamin Way of Denham Place for £25 each.[7] The Red Hill toll house was demolished for road widening in January 1929 and the Denham toll house was taken down in February 1931.[8]

Stagecoaches

The *Bucks Gazette* of 19 January 1833 reprinted an article on early stagecoach travelling taken from the *Quarterly Review*:

In 1742 the Oxford stage-coach left London at seven o'clock in the morning and reached Uxbridge at midday. It arrived at High Wycombe at five in the evening, where it rested for the night, and proceeded at the same rate for the seat of learning on the morrow. Here then were ten hours consumed each day in travelling 27 miles, and nearly two days in performing what is now done with the greatest ease in under six hours.

The *Universal British Directory* of 1792 gave a comprehensive list of the coaches passing through Beaconsfield:

> Two coaches go through the town; one, called the *Wycombe and Beaconsfield New machine* (performed by George Wright) sets out from the *Falcon Inn*, High Wycombe, every Monday morning at four o'clock, Wednesday and Friday mornings at seven; passes through Beaconsfield at eight, to the *Bull Inn*, Holborn; and returns from thence Tuesday, Thursday and Saturday afternoons at half past two. The other goes from High Wycombe to the *Bull and Mouth*, in Bull and Mouth Street, London; and returns about the same time.

> There are other coaches which pass daily, through Beaconsfield from and to London viz: the *Oxford*, from the *New Inn*, Old Bailey, arrives at Beaconsfield from London about twelve o'clock at noon; and at Beaconsfield from Oxford to London about one o'clock. The Oxford coach, from the *Black Lion*, Water Lane, Fleet Street, London, passes through Beaconsfield from and to London about the same time. The Gloucester, from the *Bolt and Tun*, Fleet Street, passes through Beaconsfield from London about four o'clock in the afternoon. The Worcester, from the *Bull and Mouth*, Bull and Mouth Street, London, passes through Beaconsfield about half past three.

Coach travel was not without its dangers. The fear of being robbed on the highway was very real. In January 1799, Edward Copleston, later Bishop of Llandaff, recorded in his diary, 'Robbed by two mounted highwaymen on my return to Oxford with Mr Woolcombe and Mr Mant (afterwards the bishop) between Uxbridge and Beaconsfield.'

Coach accidents also made the headlines. In January 1816 the Shrewsbury mail coach was reported to have overturned near the public house known as *Mother Red Cap's*, between High Wycombe and Beaconsfield. All the passengers were severely injured and two of them lay at the public house with little hope of life.

In an 1831 survey of the Hall Barn Estate, there is a highly illuminating reference to farms at Beaconsfield being attractive to stagecoach proprietors.

> The Hyde Farm, in the occupation of Daniel White, has frequently changed hands … I am inclined to think that Mr Sherman, the coach proprietor at the *Bull and Mouth*, London, who has many horses standing at Beaconsfield, would take this farm, as it is contiguous to the London Road.[9]

In 1836, Edward Sherman had 77 coaches based at the *Bull and Mouth*, near the post office in St Martins le Grand. No fewer than 30 of Sherman's coaches left the *Bull and Mouth* each day. Of these, the *Union*, the *Blenheim*, the *Sovereign* and the *Telegraph* all went through Beaconsfield. Sherman also provided the Royal Mail coaches which passed through Beaconsfield on their way to and from Worcester every day. The *Royal Mail* to Worcester stopped at the *George Inn*, Beaconsfield, at 11 p.m., whilst the London-bound Royal Mail stopped there at 4 a.m.

The following coaches passed through Beaconsfield on their way from London in 1836: the *Union*, to Birmingham; the *Berkeley Hunt*, to Cheltenham; the *Regulator* and the *Retaliator*, both to Gloucester; the *Champion*, to Hereford; the *Blenheim* and the *Age*, to Oxford; the *Thame Safety Coach* and J. Coles' *Omnibus*, both to Thame; the *Hope*, to Warwick; and the *Sovereign*, the *Telegraph*, the *Paul Pry* and the *Royal Mail*, all to Worcester.[10]

Wagons

The improvement of the Oxford road led to a great increase in the number of wagons running between Oxford and London. The Oxford carrier Edward Bartlett advertised in 1672 that he had removed his inn in London to the *Oxford Arms* in Warwick Lane, where he did trade before the fire. His wagons set out on Monday, Wednesday and Friday.[11] Wagons were rarely mentioned in the press unless they had caused an accident or been robbed. In 1691, £300 was stolen from a London wagon near Gerrards Cross. Joseph Perkyns, the ostler at the *Oxford Arms*, was fired at by the thieves. William Gray, the Beaconsfield surgeon, charged £20 to treat his injuries.[12]

In 1792, the *Universal British Directory* lists wagons passing through Beaconsfield on their way to London.

> One stage wagon sets out from Beaconsfield every Monday morning (Richard Healy) to the *Bell*, Warwick Lane, and returns from thence the next day. The *Woodstock* wagon (Bellinger) passes through Beaconsfield for London, Monday and Wednesday and on Wednesday and Friday on its return to Woodstock. The *Banbury* wagon (Judd) passes through Beaconsfield to London on every Sunday, Tuesday, and Thursday about 2am. and every Tuesday, Thursday and Saturday evening about 4pm. on its return to Banbury. The *Bicester* wagon (Phillips) passes through Beaconsfield to London every Wednesday and Sunday about 5pm. and on Tuesday and Friday about 3pm. on its return to Bicester. The *Brecon* wagon (Golding) passes through Beaconsfield for London every Wednesday evening about 5, and on Sunday morning about 8 on its return. Several other wagons pass through Beaconsfield.

In 1823, a tree was blown down across the turnpike road near Beaconsfield just as a wagon and eight horses were passing. Two horses were killed on the spot, and three seriously injured. The wagoner had both his legs crushed and his right hand smashed, with other injuries.[13]

Five

Inns and Innkeepers

The earliest list of public houses at Beaconsfield comes from a return of 1577. It gives the names of three innkeepers, who could provide overnight accommodation, one taverner, who could sell wines and spirits, and 12 alehouse keepers, who could only sell beer.

Innholders
William Netherton
Gabriel Redman
William Holman

Taverner
Margery Dabney

Alehouse Keepers
Thomas Hutchens
Nicholas Grace
Richard Eggells
Thomas Kempe
Lawrence Lyssy
Nicholas Grace
John Howe
Roger Francklyn
John Aldridge
John Holden
Nicholas Smewyn
Robert Idell.[1]

John Ogilby, who published his famous strip maps of England's principal roads in 1675, noted that Beaconsfield had 'several good inns' but mentioned only one, the *Swan*, by name. He was referring not to the present-day *Old Swan Inn* on the south side of London End, but to an earlier and altogether more prestigious *Swan Inn* which stood on the corner of London End and Shepherds Lane. Whilst not all of Beaconsfield's inns had such grand accommodation as the *Swan*, they all had extensive yards and stabling and a few acres of land nearby where the coach horses could be pastured. Local innkeepers were anxious to secure contracts with the Oxford and London stagecoach proprietors. When Edward Marshall of High Wycombe, an innkeeper, died in 1698, he was owed £8 by Mr Edward Bartlett of Oxford, coach master, and two sums of £20 and £40 by 'Mr Moore that keeps the Oxford stagecoach'.[2]

During the 18th century, the average speed of stagecoaches improved dramatically. This was due partly to improved road surfaces on the turnpike roads and partly to the introduction of steel springs on coaches in about 1750. With higher speeds, coach proprietors now found it more efficient to have more stages and therefore to use fresher horses. Travellers could now reach High Wycombe and even Oxford in one day, so fewer made an overnight stop at Beaconsfield, which was only 23 miles from London. This caused over-capacity in the local inns. The *Swan*

Inn was the first to close in 1700. It was followed by the *Crown* in 1760, the *Kings Head* in 1776 and the *Bull* in about 1798. The *Universal British Directory* of 1792 had this to say of the remaining inns at Beaconsfield:

> Here are two inns at which are good accommodations, viz, the *Saracens Head*, William Hall, where the excise office is kept; and the *White Hart*, Clifford William Phillips.

In 1796, the innkeepers of Beaconsfield protested to Parliament about the use of their inns for the billeting of troops. Their petition was countersigned by Edmund Burke:

> We the innholders and publicans of the parish of Beaconsfield, humbly beg your support in getting us relief of so heavy a burden for so small a place, which only consists of three small inns and eight little public houses. The town without trade or manufactory, the inns very little business except the stage wagons leading to and from London market, with which we are unable to support so large a number as 94 horses and 88 men that being the number now quartered on us ... which take up the great part of our stabling so much as we are obliged to turn away several wagons which comes regularly every week.[3]

In 1841, the census enumerator noted that 'at 7 o'clock on Sunday evening June 6, about fifty individuals were making through the town in wagons on the high road to London, but whether they slept on the wagons I know not, nor do I know whether they were enumerated the next morning'.

The Bull Inn

The *Bull Inn*, now numbered 49-53, London End, is a timber-framed building to which a brick façade and sash windows were added in the early 18th century. The tall coach entrance is still prominent. The *Bull Inn* is first mentioned by name in the will of William Bulstrode in 1520. He states that his wife Maud 'has an estate in

32 *Former Bull Inn, London End.*

my dwelling house in Beaconsfield and in the *Bull* with its lands'. Bulstrode may have changed the name of the inn to the *Bull*, which features on the coat of arms on his tomb in Beaconsfield church. Robert Waller, of Beaconsfield, witnessed the will of William Bulstrode and was also a beneficiary. He seems to have acquired much of the Bulstrode property and, in his own will of 1545, left to his son Ralph Waller his 'tenement with the appurtenances in Beaconsfield sometime called the *George* and now called the *Bull* in the occupation of Nicholas Cooke'. When there was a shortage of small coinage in the 1660s, the occupant of the *Bull*, William Willis, issued his own half-penny token. On the one side was the inscription, 'William Willis 1668 Bull'.

In 1691, John Barnes, tapster at the *Bull Inn*, married Anne Winter at Beaconsfield. In 1721, Carell Ramsden, innholder, insured his goods and merchandise in the *Bull Inn* with the Sun Fire Office.[4] In 1739, his successor, Thomas Barrett, innholder, insured his household goods and stock

in trade in the dwelling house of the *Bull Inn* for the large sum of £500.[5] The building was said to be brick and tiled, and there was mention of a vault and cellars.

Successive holders of the *Bull Inn* are listed in the annual alehouse recognizances from 1753.[6] These include Thomas Richmond (1753-71); Edward Hawkins (1772-3); Edward Rawlins (1776-81) and Thomas Collins (1782). Collins paid a very heavy land tax of £10 16s. on the *Bull Inn* and the farmland belonging to it in 1783. The occupant from 1784-94 was Richard Hester. The last man to run the *Bull Inn* was John Wood, who is listed as a victualler in the *Posse Comitatus* in 1798. The former *Bull Inn* then became a farmhouse and continued to belong to the Waller family of Hall Barn right up to the sale of their Beaconsfield property in 1832. It was later divided into three separate dwellings.

The Crown Inn

One of the earliest known Beaconsfield inns is the *Crown*, now numbered 20-2, London End. The original timber-framed building had two wings extending back from the street. Its appearance was transformed in the late 17th century by the addition of an elaborate cement-rendered façade, incorporating five bay windows. The central coach entry, with semi-circular window above, remains the chief architectural feature. When the *Crown* ceased to be an inn in the late 18th century, the building was divided into two gentlemen's houses. It has more recently been converted into offices.

The *Crown Inn* is first mentioned by name in 1510, when a neighbouring innkeeper, John

Dawbeney, left his wife Elizabeth 'my mansion with all that belongs thereto lying near the *Crowne* which late I had of John Browne'. A victualler called Gabriel Redman appears on the 1577 return of public houses. In 1599, possibly the same Gabriel Redman leased the *Crown Inn* from Thomas Waller of Gregories for 25 years at a rent of £14 per annum. During the 17th century, the *Crown* was occupied by the Rutt family, and Richard Rutt of Beaconsfield, an innholder, made his will in 1633. He was succeeded by his son, Michael Rutt, whose daughter, Martha, was baptised at Beaconsfield in 1637. In 1658, Michael Rutt bought another large house on the opposite side of the road and converted it into an inn called the *Kings Head*. He gave the tenancy of the *Crown* to his son Lawrence. When Lawrence married in 1669 he decided to move to the *Kings Head*, not before a room by room inventory was made of all his goods in the *Crown*. The 13 bedrooms all had romantic names, perhaps relating to famous inns in larger towns. They included the 'Crown', the 'Fleece', the 'Fox', the 'Fleur de Lys', the 'Rose', the 'Goat', the 'Half Moon', the 'Red Chamber', the 'Green Chamber', the 'White Horse', the 'Star', the 'Sun' and the 'Globe'. There were 24 beds, most of them four-posters, each with feather mattresses and tapestry hangings to keep out the draughts. The rooms had fire irons in the fireplace and curtains at the windows.[7]

After 1669, the *Crown* was continued by John Holmes and his widow into the 1680s. By 1692, the *Crown Inn* was occupied by Elias Birt, who left a will in 1709. John Willson was the tenant from 1720 until his death in 1735. Willson insured the contents of the *Crown Inn* with the Sun Fire Office in 1731.[8] The policy also refers to a barn near the *Chequers Inn* where he had some of his farming stock.

John Willson at the *Crown Inn* Beaconsfield innholder & farmer

33   *Former* Crown Inn, *London End, c.1890.*

34   George Inn, *Wycombe End, c.1900.*

	£
Household goods and stock in trade in the dwelling house drinking rooms lodging rooms and cellars of the inn brick & tiled	180
Stock in his stable & chambers over the same on the right hand of the yard brick timber & tiled	66
Stock in his brewhouse stables & chambers and granaries on the left hand the yard brick & tiled	50
Stock in the stable fronting the yard brick panelled & tiled	4
Stock of corn thrashed or unthrashed & utensils in his barn and granaries adjoining behind the house called the Chequer brick timber & tiled	100
Stock utensils & harness in his stable near the barn brick timber & tiled	100
	500

The last innkeeper at the *Crown* was Edward Turpin, who was listed in the rate books and alehouse recognizances from 1742-59. The building was then divided into two genteel houses, later called Burke House and Burke Lodge. The larger house was first occupied by Edward Fuller, whose family had owned Gregories. Then came William Harrison, who died there in 1780. The next occupant was the socialite Mrs Salisbury Haviland, widow of General William Haviland. She died in 1807. By 1810, the building was owned by James Du Pre of Wilton Park and the larger of the two houses was leased to a surgeon named Samuel Ferris. Later tenants included the Countess of Orkney; Lady Willoughby; John Parton, solicitor; Catherine Charsley

(widow of John Charsley); Francis Johnson, surgeon; and William Kennedy, also a surgeon. Burke House still belonged to the Du Pre family in 1910 when the tenant was again a doctor, Geoffrey Hobbs. Another prominent resident was Rear Admiral Sir Edward Fitzmaurice Inglefield, who was living at Burke House in 1939.

The George Inn

The *George Inn* is a timber-framed building, perhaps of the 17th century, with a late 18th-century brick façade. The front of the inn was altered in about 1900, but has recently been restored to its 18th-century appearance. The reference to a *George Inn* in the will of Robert Waller in 1545 is not to this building but to a forerunner of the *Bull Inn*, London End. The *George Inn*, Wycombe End, is not mentioned in documents until the 17th century, when it was kept by the Sills family. John Sills of Beaconsfield, an innholder, left a will in 1632. Perhaps the same John Sills paid tax on eight hearths in 1662 and Thomas Sills paid a 2s. chief rent for the *George Inn* in 1682.[9] A Thomas Sills, innholder, was buried at Beaconsfield in 1707. By 1743, when William Sills of Beaconsfield, a yeoman, insured the *George Inn* for £500, it was

35 George Inn, *Wycombe End, 1948.*

occupied by Edward Turpin, innholder.[10] In the alehouse recognizances of 1765, an Edward Mead is listed at the *Old George*, as if there was briefly a competitor, or there had been some break in its occupancy. By 1810, the *George* had been acquired by Samuel Salter, brewer, of Rickmansworth. This brewery continued to own the *George* well into the 20th century. The building has recently been converted into a very upmarket hotel and restaurant called the *Crazy Bear*.

The Kings Head Inn

The *Kings Head*, now numbered 15-17, London End, is yet another ancient Beaconsfield inn which went out of business in the late 18th century. It comprises two timber-framed buildings, one of five bays west of the coach entrance, and a six-bay house on the east side. Matching brick façades with sash windows were added to the two houses in 1714.

The earliest mention of a *Kings Head Inn* in Beaconsfield is in the will of John Gardner, citizen and grocer of London, in 1507. As Gardner made generous bequests to the church at Beaconsfield, he obviously had family connections there, but he chose to be buried in the parish of St Benet, London. He left his 'great cauldron … of 20 gallons and more now being within my messuage called the *Kings Head* at Beaconsfield' to his sister Margery Robins, widow. To Margery's daughter, Agnes, he left his 'greatest brass pot being within my said messuage and to the youngest daughter of my same sister Margery another brass pot of mine next in value to my great pot being within my said messuage'.

At the time of his death, John Gardner was evidently making alterations to the *Kings Head*. He left to John Hawdey of Beaconsfield, a tailor, his 'great pot of iron with the cupboard of iron belonging thereto at Beaconsfield and 20s. in money to the intent that the same John Hawdey be good overseer for me in the work and building done and to be done at my said messuage called the *Kings Head* and that he make and yield unto

36   *Former* Kings Head Inn, *London End, c.1930.*

my executors a true account of all the money spent and to be spent by his overseeing in and about the same'. His tenant at the *Kings Head* was probably William Barton, to whom he left 'as much as much of my household stuff being within my said messuage called the *Kings Head* at Beaconsfield most necessary for him after the discretion of my executors as shall amount to the yearly value of 20s'.

It would be unwise to assume that the *Kings Head* described in 1507 was on the same site as the house now called the *Kings Head*. The deeds to this house go back only as far as 1658, when George Gosnold of Beaconsfield, a gentleman, sold to Michael Rutt of the same place, innholder:

> All that capital messuage or dwelling house with the appurtenances wherein Thomas Haythorne gentleman now dwelleth, situate and being at Beaconsfield aforesaid in the said County of Bucks, adjoining to the messuage or tenement now in the tenure or occupation of John Waslington and Elizabeth Minor widow on the east, to the inn called the *Swanne* on the west, the street called London End on the south and the lane called Sheppards Lane on the north.[11]

Michael Rutt appears to have converted the house into an inn called the *Kings Head*. His tenant, John Holmes, paid tax on 12 hearths in 1662. In 1668, Michael Rutt gave the capital messuage called the *Kings Head* to his son Lawrence who then occupied the *Crown* on the opposite side of the road. This gift was in anticipation of Lawrence's marriage to Mary Browne in 1669, at which time Lawrence moved to the *Kings Head* and John Holmes moved to the *Crown*. Following the death of Lawrence Rutt in 1690, the *Kings Head* was let to William Smith and then to Stephen Chasemore.[12] The Rutt family continued to invest in the premises, however, and Richard Rutt, citizen and glover of London, refronted the house in 1714. He had his initials, RRE, moulded on to the drain-water head to the left of the coach entrance. His tenant, Sarah Englie, insured her goods and merchandise at the *Kings Head*, Beaconsfield, for £500 in 1723.[13]

Richard Rutt, son of the glover, finally sold the *Kings Head* in 1730.[14] It had a succession of owners until it was purchased by the sitting tenant, Matthew Davis of Beaconsfield, an innholder, in 1764.[15] In 1776, Davis sold the *Kings Head* to Edmund Basil of Wilton Park. He immediately insured the premises, which were valued at £1,000:

Edmund Basil of Wilton Park Esq	£
On his house at Beaconsfield in tenure of Matthew Davis Innholder brick & tiled	500
Stable & woodhouse adjoining brick timber & tiled	50
Great Stable separate timber & tiled	100
Front stable brick & tiled	150
Ballroom wine vault & granary under one roof brick & tiled	100
Three stables under one roof brick & tiled	100
	——
	1000[16]

Matthew Davis, now Basil's tenant, insured the contents of the buildings, including the ballroom:

Matthew Davis Innholder	£
On his household goods in his dwelling house brick & tiled	400
Utensils & stock	100
Utensils & stock in the ballroom wine cellar & granary under one roof brick & tiled	50
In a stable & woodhouse adjoining timber & tiled	10
In the Great Stable timber & tiled	10
In the front stable brick & tiled	20
In the three stables under one roof brick & tiled	10
House in two tenements in tenure Nathaniel Charsley & Ann Nash brick & tiled	100
	——
	700[17]

Edmund Basil did not own the *Kings Head* for long. Almost immediately he divided it in two, the western half being sold to Robert Charsley of Beaconsfield, a solicitor,[18] and the eastern portion to John Anthony of Beaconsfield, a draper. Each of them paid £325 for their half, and they built a dividing wall from the coach entrance to Shepherds Lane at the rear. A room called the 'Fountain', which formed part of the boundary between them, was allotted to John Anthony.[19] The last innkeeper, Matthew Davis, moved to a part of the former *Swan Inn*, now numbered 7-9 London End, where he was in business as a maltster and brandy merchant. Robert Charsley let his part of the *Kings Head* to a succession of wealthy tenants, starting with Charles Jenkinson, gentleman. During the 19th century, this half of the *Kings Head* became known as 'Essex House', but it was called by the old name of the *Kings Head* by 1929.[20] John Anthony let his half of the *Kings Head* to a Mrs Lawrence. In 1792, it was purchased by John Jackson of Beaconsfield, watchmaker, whose family continued to own the house until its sale in 1891. It was for a time known as 'Highway House'.

The Saracens Head Inn

The *Saracens Head* was a timber-framed house, which had been refronted, probably in the late 17th century. It had a cement-rendered façade with five gables on the north side facing London End. The building was completely remodelled and false half-timbering was applied in 1893. The common English inn sign of the *Saracens Head* evokes ideas of the Crusades, when English gentleman sought adventure, profit, and possibly salvation, in trying to recover the Holy Land from the Muslims. The *Saracens Head* at Beaconsfield may indeed be that old. It is mentioned obliquely in the will of John Dabney, or Dawbeney, of Beaconsfield, an innkeeper, in 1510:

> I give and bequeath to Elizabeth my wife my mansion with all that belongs thereto lying near

the Crowne which late I had of John Browne to her and to the heirs of her body lawfully begotten.

John Dawbeney was evidently a tenant of John Browne and refers to his house as a 'mansion', which can mean a *stopping place* as well as the better-known meaning of *large house* or *manor house*. According to his will, Dawbeney owned or leased another 'mansion' at 'Holme End' (Aylesbury End) in Beaconsfield. This may have been another inn but it has not been identified.

The inn is first mentioned by name in the inquisition post mortem of Robert Waller of Beaconsfield in 1545. Waller's property included:

> One messuage with appurtenances in Beaconsfield opposite the *Saracens Head* there in which the same Robert inhabited.

There is a similar mention of the house opposite the *Saracens Head* in the inquisition post mortem of Francis Waller in 1559. The Wallers had a close connection with the inn, for Margery, daughter of Robert Waller and sister of Francis, had married Robert Dawbeney, the innkeeper. Dawbeney died in 1575 and his widow, Margery, was included on the list of taverners of 1577. She died in 1578. A later occupant of the *Saracens Head* was Robert Idle, who died in 1624. He left the *Saracens Head* to his cousin Robert Idle. A Sarah Idle, widow of Beaconsfield, left a will in 1708.

The inn is mentioned in the 1710 will of Richard Rutt, citizen and glover of London, whose family also owned the *Kings Head* in Beaconsfield. He left his messuage called the *Saracens Head* in Beaconsfield to his daughter Elizabeth Rutt until his son Thomas Rutt reached the age of twenty-one. Thomas Rutt's tenant at the *Saracens Head* was John Martin, who died in 1724. Martin's executors prepared a meticulous inventory of the contents of the inn.[21] Just like the *Crown* in 1669, the *Saracens Head* had evocative names for the principal bedrooms, such as the 'Down Steps Room', the 'Chamber over the Ostry', the 'Crown',

37   *The* Saracens Head, *rebuilt 1893.*

the 'Little Crown', the 'Rose and Crown', the 'Fleur de Lys' and the 'Dolphin'. In the brewhouse were 'two brass furnaces and wooden lids, one mash tub, tap wast, stirrer and stand, one cooler, one jett, five kivers, one strainer, three drink tubs and one stand, and some other odd things' worth £5. In the cellar were seven hogsheads full of beer, two empty hogsheads, one working tub, two half firkins, two brass corks, two drink stands, one bucket, one little kiver, one hand bowl, three dozen glass bottles and some other odd things valued at £18. There was also wine and brandy worth £1 10s. In total, Martin's goods were valued at £226 15s. 8d.

Thomas Rutt, of St Andrews Holborn, a yeoman, sold the *Saracens Head* in 1738 to William Basil of Wilton Park, Beaconsfield, for £576.[22] In 1777, the Wilton Park Estate, including the freehold of the *Saracens Head*, then in the occupation of Joseph Jagger, was purchased by Josias Du Pre.[23] The inn was to remain in the hands of the Du Pre family well into the 20th century. The alehouse recognizances give the names of successive licensees of the *Saracens Head*. These included James Davis, 1754-68, and Joseph

Jagger, 1769-87. Jagger is mentioned in the Sun Fire Office policy of 1781:

	£
Rebecca Du Pre of Beaconsfield gentlewoman	
For her house & brewhouse adjoining situate as aforesaid in the tenure of Joseph Jagger innholder	500
Three stables under one roof	150
Three stables under one roof	150
Another stable	100
	————
	900[24]

Later licensees included William Hall, 1788-96; Alice Hall, 1797-1804 and William Hall, 1805-28.

Cordelia Wright, a teacher at the Church of England School in Windsor End from 1910, claimed to remember the Oxford coach changing horses at the *Saracens Head*. In fact she was probably relating a story told to her by someone older:

First you would hear the horn blaring out to warn of their approach. Then you would see the coach rounding the bend at the top of London

End in a cloud of dust. At the *Saracens Head* four fresh horses would be waiting in the yard under the archway, and as the coach arrived they were led out – there was no delay; the weary steaming arrivals were quickly un-harnessed and the others took their places between the shafts. In no time, it seemed, they were on their way again, to another blast of the horn.[25]

During the 19th century, the Du Pre family leased the *Saracens Head* to Lucas's Brewery of High Wycombe and later to Whitbreads Brewery. None of the licencees remained at the *Saracens Head* for long. Their names are taken from *Pigot's* and *Kelly's Directories*: William Hall, 1830; John Westbrook, 1842; George Green, 1850; William Jeffs, 1864; Mary Jeffs, 1877; Thomas Collins, 1883; John Joseph Kent, 1887; James Woodcroft, 1899; Anne Chapman, 1903; William H. Latilla, 1907; William George Still, 1911; Henry J. McSorley, 1925 and M.W. Stafford, 1931.

In 1874, the *Saracens Head* was the venue for a large meeting promoting the cause of the London, Beaconsfield and High Wycombe railway. The meeting was attended by Arthur Riversdale Grenfell, a relative of the Du Pres of Wilton Park, and Thomas Wheeler, the brewer and banker from Wycombe.[26] The *Saracens Head* was rebuilt in 1893 to the design of the High Wycombe architect, Arthur Vernon. The name of the architect and the builder, G. Gibson, is cut into the woodwork of the west gable. The style is similar to that of nearby Butler's Court, designed in 1891 by the same architect. From 1887-95 the inn was described as the 'Royal Saracens family and commercial hotel and posting house', and in 1899 as having 'livery and bait stables; good accommodation for tourists; good stables for hunters; patronised by royalty'.

The Star Inn

A new coaching inn was built at Beaconsfield in the late 18th century, just as several long-established inns were going out of business. This was the *Star Inn*, built some time after 1784 on a strip of land formerly part of the Oxford road. In the mid-19th century it was leased to Langton's Brewery of Maidenhead.

Sir Frank MacKinnon, who lived at Wiggenton Farm, next door to the former *Star Inn*, recalls a conversation with Robert Rolfe in 1919:

> One Oxford Coach had stables for its fresh horses at Wattleton Farm, when occupied successively by his uncle and his father. The horses were changed outside the farm. The next stages towards London were at Uxbridge and Southall. Westward was a short stage for they always changed at the *Red Lion* at Wycombe and next he thinks at Tetsworth.

The coach passengers would have enjoyed refreshments across the road at the *Star Inn*. In 1846 the *Star Inn* was leased by John Edwards Langton, an Maidenhead brewer, and occupied by James Halsey. Sir Frank MacKinnon relates another of Robert Rolfe's stories:

> Mr Rolfe tells me that when he was a boy *The Star* was occupied by Mr Langton a brewer from Uxbridge. On the north wall of the house was a board painted white with black letters 'Langtons Ales'. Mr Rolfe's home was then at Wattleton Farm opposite: he had a small rook rifle and he used to aim with this at the White centre of 'O' in 'Langtons'. He also says that in front of the inn (where is now the front garden with lawn and a monkey puzzle tree, it was open to the road with a horse trough … The last publican was one Halsey, who also used to stuff birds, which he kept in a long room (now the dining room) and sold. He also had a stuffed tiger there.

The *Star Inn* closed in about 1860 and is not to be confused with the beerhouse in Aylesbury End which later took the name of the *Star*. This was a common lodging house where 10 tramps were sleeping on census night in 1871.

The Swan Inn

The *Swan Inn* stood opposite the *Saracens Head* and comprised all the buildings now numbered

38   *The* Swan Inn *comprised all the building now numbered 1-13 London End.*

1-13 London End. It was therefore the largest of the Beaconsfield inns. Elegant wall paintings of the 16th or 17th century were found in 1966 at no. 1 London End, and removed to the county museum.[27] These would have been in the bedrooms in the west wing of the inn, overlooking the crossroads. Although the *Swan Inn* closed in 1700, much of its structure survives in the present-day shops on London End.

The earliest deeds to the *Swan Inn* go back to 1611 when Richard Gosnold of Beaconsfield, a gentleman, leased it for 21 years to Thomas Cossam of Beaconsfield, an innholder. Cossam assigned the lease to John Whitefield of Beaconsfield, a vintner, in 1615.[28] Whitefield bought the freehold in 1623 and sold or mortgaged the inn for £105 to Adrian Scrope of Wormsley, Oxfordshire, a gentleman, in 1625.[29] Scrope may have sold it on to the Waller family. At the manor court in 1645, Michael Edgerley, then landlord of the *Swan*, was ordered to scour and cleanse the ditch in Shepherds Lane, and the ditch lying against his own garden. During the Civil War, Michael Edgerley's son, Thomas, was imprisoned for

carrying messages from Oxford to London. In 1660, the *Swan Inn* was mentioned in a Waller family settlement of that year:

> All that messuage or inn commonly called or known by the name or sign of the *Swan* with the appurtenances now or late in the tenure or occupation of Michael Edgereley.[30]

39   *Wall paintings found at the former* Swan Inn, *1966.*

Subsequent tenants of the *Swan Inn* were Arthur Turner, who left a will in 1690, and Robert Jones, who paid 11s. 2d. poor rate for the *Swan* in 1692. When Edmund Waller the poet's son died in 1700, much of his Beaconsfield property was sold. The 1701 conveyance of the *Swan Inn* to John Fawsett shows that the inn had already closed and was being divided into shops and houses:

> All that messuage or tenement with the appurtenances as it was then made or laid or intended to be made into several tenements and being then or lately called or known by the name of the *Swan Inn* situate in Beaconsfield aforesaid in the County of Bucks (being part of the freehold estate of the said Edmund Waller and being by order of the Court of Chancery ordered to be sold) heretofore in the occupation of Arthur Turner deceased and then partly untenanted and part in the occupation of the said John Fawsett.[31]

John Fawsett died in 1720, leaving his Beaconsfield property to his nephew, John Hartley of High Wycombe, a draper. Hartley insured the premises for £1,000 in 1725:

John Hartley of Wycombe Co Bucks draper

For his two tenements with the outhouses thereunto belonging in Beaconsfield in Co aforesaid	£
Dwelling house only of Woodbridge a barber	100
Dwelling house only of Elizabeth Cherry widow	300
Stable thereunto belonging	50
Dwelling house only of John Young collar maker	100
Stable thereunto belonging	50
Dwelling house only of Henry Fellows maltster	100
His malting office only	150
His barn and stables only	50
Dwelling house of John Harding a baker	100
	——
	1000[32]

The *Swan Inn* was thus converted into five very respectable houses and shops. The best house,

that of Elizabeth Cherry, was valued at three times any of the others. It is not clear whether Henry Fellows's malting was a recent addition, or whether it had belonged to the *Swan Inn*. John Hartley's grandson, Charles Hartley, sold the row of shops to Robert Charsley in 1786.[33]

The White Hart Inn

The *White Hart* was perhaps the smallest of the inns catering for the traveller. A horseman or coach passenger coming from London might not notice the building, as it was set back in Aylesbury End and would be masked by the *Swan Inn*. At the manor court of 1622, the innkeeper, Nathaniel Aldridge, was fined for setting out his signpost further than before. A later innkeeper, William Woods, was at least wealthy enough to leave a will in 1699. His successor, Robert Bates, was no doubt embarrassed in 1713 when his son John was named as the father of an illegitimate child by Hester Izord. Robert Bates was in turn succeeded by John Crockett, who was at the *White Hart* from 1715-45.

At some point in the 18th century, the *White Hart* was purchased by the Wallers of Hall Barn. Their tenant from 1750, Joseph Millward, supplemented his income by working a malting in Windsor End belonging to the Waller estate. Joseph Millward insured his household goods in 1760:

> Joseph Milward at the *White Hart Inn* Beaconsfield Co Bucks innholder

On his household goods & utensils & stock in the dwelling house & brewhouse adjoining only brick & tiled	£200
Utensils & stock hay straw & horses included in the stables only adjoining in the yard brick & tiled	100
Utensils & stock in his malthouse in Beaconsfield distant from the aforesaid brick & tiled	100
	——
	400[34]

40 *The* White Hart, *c.1900.*

Subsequent tenants entering the *White Hart* included Thomas Gregory, 1767; Samuel Chapman, 1777; Clifford William Phillips, 1782 and Isaac Mills, 1795. Mills was still at the *White Hart* in 1831, when the agent on the Hall Barn Estate noted that:

> The inn is well situated in Beaconsfield and capable of doing more business than at present in the hands of an active man and a large club room has lately been built by the tenant the landlord allowing £30 towards it and finding rough timber.[35]

Both the *White Hart* and *Saracens Head* were regularly named in newspaper adverts as places where sale particulars could be inspected, relating to houses for sale or to let, all over South Buckinghamshire and West Middlesex. The facilities of the *White Hart* can be judged from the fact that in 1841, 180 members of the Bucks Agricultural Association, including the Duke of

Buckingham, could sit down to lunch there. By 1846, Wellers Brewery of Amersham had leased the *White Hart* from Sir Gore Ouseley. At a manorial court held at the *White Hart* in 1881, the jury urged the new owners, Thomas Williams & Co. of Wooburn, to call the inn the *Manor Hotel* and not to erect their signpost in the street. The brewery added fake half-timbering to the façade and called the inn the *Royal White Hart Hotel*. In 1891 the tenant, Thomas F. Lane, advertised the inn as a 'family and commercial hotel and posting house' and, in 1895, as 'caterer to the cricket club and HQ of the cyclists' touring club and lawn tennis club at Beaconsfield'. After he retired, Thomas Lane was chairman of Beaconsfield U.D.C. He had some role in the development of Horseshoe Crescent on land belonging to the brewery.

In 1872, a list of the licensed premises in the county was drawn up and printed. It is surprising how few pubs had survived in Beaconsfield:

Public House	Occupier	Owner	Leaseholder
Cross Keys	Thomas Wood	Neville, Reid & Co., Windsor	
Elm Tree	George Ford	Salter, Rickmansworth	
Farriers Arms	James Aldridge	Weller, Amersham	
George	Henry Manley	Salter, Rickmansworth	
Greyhound	Henry Welch	George Harman, Uxbridge	
Old Hare	Charles Evans	Salter, Rickmansworth	
Old Swan	Richard Atkinson	Wethered, Marlow	
Saracens Head	William Jeffs	C.G. Du Pre, Beaconsfield	Lucas
White Hart	William Child	J. Hargreaves, Beaconsfield	Weller
White Horse	George Hare	Neville, Reid & Co., Windsor	
Beerhouse			Licenced
Alexandra	Frederick Carter	Ratcliff, Harefield	1844
Plough	John Sheal	Chapman, Farnham Royal	1830
Prince of Wales	John Jennings	Wethered, Marlow	1837
Queens Head	John Snapes	Wethered, Marlow	1846
Star	Edward Bowler	J. Harding, Beaconsfield	1830
No Sign	Uriah Day	Uriah Day, Beaconsfield	1870
No Sign	Edward Morford	J. Owen, Beaconsfield	1870

Table 3   *Beaconsfield public houses in 1872.*

Six

Professional Men

Attorneys

From the late medieval period, right up to the present day, Beaconsfield has been the home of a succession of wealthy lawyers, who practised both in Buckinghamshire and in London. The Waller family began as lawyers, and Robert Waller was acting for Burnham Abbey at the time of its dissolution in 1538. Waller died in 1545, but his granddaughter married Richard Tredway, who was to become the leading attorney in Beaconsfield. He lived at Gregories and acted for the Wenmans as lords of the manor. In 1603, Richard Tredway was an overseer named in the will of Edmund Waller of Coleshill, who made a bequest to Tredway's son, Walter. Richard Tredway died in 1604, his son having died earlier that year. Another grandchild of Robert Waller, Thomas Waller of Gregories, was one of the Prothonotaries of the Court of Kings Bench.

The Wallers made other alliances with prominent legal families. In 1618 Elizabeth Waller, daughter of Edmund Waller, married Maximilian Petty, whose family had established themselves as the leading attorneys at Thame, in Oxfordshire. Two of the couple's children were baptised at Beaconsfield and Elizabeth, wife of Mr Petty Esq., was buried at Beaconsfield in 1628.[1] Their daughter, Anne,

married Thomas Smith, a member of a legal family based at Dinton, west of Aylesbury.[2]

In 1604, Richard Tredway's legal practice at Beaconsfield passed to his son-in-law, Richard Gosnold, who had joined the family firm by marrying Sarah Tredway in 1594.[3] Richard Gosnold died in 1621, leaving Overs and Waddenton Farms and the *Swan* and the *Chequers* inns to his sons, Richard, George and Thomas. His son George Gosnold took over his legal work and had chambers at Clements Inn. He not only acted for the Wallers and the other prosperous families of Beaconsfield, but he was also steward to the Packingtons, the Worcestershire family who owned the valuable manor of Aylesbury. Amongst George Gosnold's properties in Beaconsfield was a capital messuage in London End which he sold in 1658 to Michael Rutt of Beaconsfield, an innholder, for £340.[4] This house was then used as the *Kings Head Inn*. George Gosnold was closely associated with the Petty family, for Gosnold and Edmund and Maximilian Petty were all parties to the complex family settlement made in 1660 by Edmund Waller the poet.[5]

When George Gosnold died in 1675, Thomas Smith soon took over the practice. Thomas Smith had married Gosnold's daughter, Mary, at Wooburn in 1670. Smith was clerk to the County

Justices from 1689-1702, the period when Thomas Lord Wharton of nearby Wooburn was *Custos Rotulorum* for Buckinghamshire. Thomas Smith lived at Wattleton Farm, on the north side of the Oxford road, and had chambers at Clements Inn. He was a witness to the will of Edmund Waller in 1686 and was left a legacy of £20 in the will of Edmund Waller of Hall Barn in 1699. He also acted as solicitor to Montague Drake of Shardeloes. Thomas Smith died in 1709, leaving a large portfolio of property including Wattleton and Wiggenton Farms and the capital messuage called Hall Place, which was let to the Presbyterian minister Samuel Clarke. Smith's clerk, Samuel Tripp, appears to have continued the practice, but had moved to High Wycombe by 1722, when he was made Town Clerk. Tripp was appointed a Coroner of Buckinghamshire in 1736.[6]

There followed a period of about thirty years when there was no resident attorney in Beaconsfield. This left an opening which was eventually filled by John Charsley, whose family had long been established at Amersham as farmers, millers and land agents. John Charsley was Steward to Montague Garrard Drake and William Drake of Shardeloes from 1738-47. He married Alice Birch at Chesham Bois in 1733 and moved to Beaconsfield in about 1760. Mr John Charsley was buried at Beaconsfield in 1767, and Mrs Charsley, widow of the late Mr John, was buried there in 1771. His brother, William Charsley, became a doctor and lived at The Grange, Chalfont St Giles.

John Charsley, son of John and Alice Charsley, was born in Amersham in 1735. He became a lawyer and was Town Clerk of Chepping Wycombe in 1784. His brother, Robert Charsley, was born in Amersham in 1742. He married Elizabeth Parker at Chalfont St Giles in 1771 and was established as an attorney at Beaconsfield by 1772. He built Wycombe End House but preferred to live at the former *Kings Head* in London End. His brother, Nathaniel Charsley, was a baker with premises in London End, near the *Saracens Head*. Robert Charsley insured his Beaconsfield property with the Sun Insurance Company in 1786.

Robert Charsley of Beaconsfield Bucks gent	£
On his now dwelling house only	350
Household goods	120
Plate & printed books	40
Stable granary & chaisehouse	50
House only in tenure Peter Mitchell Esq.	400
Wash house chaise house stable & loft over	100
Tenement only near in tenure … Harris private	30
Stable & shed adjoining timber & tiled	30
Five tenements adjoining no hazardous trades brick timber & tiled	80
Six tenements adjoining no hazardous trades	350
Malthouse stable woodhouse coach house & outhouse adjoining in tenure of Davis	100
The above situate at Beaconsfield.[7]	

The house occupied by Peter Mitchell is Wycombe End House. The six tenements are the former *Swan Inn*, then divided into six shops.

Robert Charsley's principal client was Edmund Waller of Hall Barn. Charsley drew up a detailed list of deeds to the Hall Barn Estate in 1788. Curiously, he did not include the 1624 conveyance of the manor of Beaconsfield to Edmund and Anne Waller.[8] Robert Charsley died in 1812, leaving his house, formerly part of the *Kings Head*, to his son John.

John Charsley was in partnership with his father by 1798. He married Catherine Eliza Gilbert of Tettenhall, Staffordshire, in 1815. The couple moved from the former *Kings Head* to The Elms, 21 London End, which was bought from the Anthony family. John Charsley acted as Coroner for South Buckinghamshire from 1820 until 1855. On the eve of the destructive Swing Riots in November 1830, John Charsley was made secretary of a committee set up to represent the interests of the noblemen, magistrates, gentry, clergy and farmers in the Hundreds of Stoke and Burnham. On 29 November, Charley was at

Wycombe Marsh, along with other magistrates from Beaconsfield, when the rioters destroyed the papermaking machinery at W.R. Davies' mill. A rioter called John Sarney was prevented from striking Charsley over the head with an iron bar only by the timely intervention of a special constable.[9] Sarney was sentenced to death for his part in the riots, but reprieved at the last moment. In February 1831, John Charsley drew up a claim for rewards on behalf of the special constables from Beaconsfield who had helped apprehend some of the rioters.[10]

For many years, John Charsley was in partnership with James Randall, who lived at Church Cottage, Windsor End, and died in 1836, aged 76. A subsequent partner was John Parton, who married Charsley's daughter, Dorothy, at Beaconsfield in 1840. John Parton retired from the partnership with John Charsley in 1853.[11] John Charsley's eldest son, William Henry Charsley, was destined for a career in the Church, going in 1837 to St Mary's Hall, Oxford, aged seventeen. W.H. Charsley founded Charsley's Hall, a private college in Parks Road, which took on idle or incapable students removed from other colleges.[12] Another son, Robert Harvey Charsley, was Chaplain to the Radcliffe Infirmary. Two of John Charsley's sons became solicitors. Frederick Charsley established a practise in Amersham and then moved to Slough. He was Coroner for South Bucks from 1855-82. John Charsley's youngest son, George Allington Charsley, took over the Beaconsfield office and was Coroner for South Bucks from 1882. John Charsley died at Beaconsfield in 1855.

George Allington Charsley was born in 1831, and in 1856 he married Catherine Elizabeth, daughter of Henry Hough, Coroner for Rutland. G.A. Charsley was a typical country solicitor, who knew everyone of consequence in the county, was a good shot and rode to hounds. He played cricket with the Drakes of Shardeloes and the Hearns of Buckingham. He was involved in the foundation of the Beaconsfield Local Board of Health, for which he was Clerk from 1865. He

41 *The Charsley family occupied The Elms, 21 London End, from about 1815 until 1913.*

42   *Church Cottage, 2 Windsor End, the home of James Randall, solicitor, 1810-36.*

was a member of the Beaconsfield U.D.C. from 1898-1901. He acted as an agent for the Earl of Beaconsfield and for Caledon George Du Pre at successive Parliamentary elections. He retired from his practice in 1905 and died at The Elms, 21 London End, in 1913.[13] Two of his sons also became solicitors. George Henry Charsley, born in 1858, joined his uncle, Frederick Charsley, at Slough, whilst his younger son, Arthur Edmund Webster Charsley, born in 1864, became a partner with his father in Beaconsfield.

A.E.W. Charsley lived at Gregories Farm and succeeded his father as Coroner for South Bucks and as Clerk to the Local Board of Health and to Beaconsfield U.D.C. He was in partnership with James Bailey Gibson until 1913.[14] A.E.W. Charsley retired as Coroner for Buckinghamshire in 1935 and died in 1951. James Bailey Gibson was born in Nottingham in 1877. He was Deputy Coroner for South Bucks from 1906 and took over from A.E.W. Charsley as Coroner in 1935. He lived at Burke Lodge, 20 London End.

Doctors

Just as Beaconsfield's attorneys had clients all over South Buckinghamshire, the town's doctors were called upon to attend patients over a wide area. One of the earliest known surgeons to have practiced in the town was William Gray, who paid 4½d. chief rent on his house in Beaconsfield in 1682.[15] 'Mr Grey the surgeon' attended a soldier injured during the march of Colonel Cambon's Company from Beaconsfield to Marlow in 1693.[16] William Grey, 'chirurgion', was buried at Beaconsfield, 21 January 1703. Another early surgeon was Thomas Read, who came to Beaconsfield in about 1750. He lived in the large house now known as the Old Post House, 18 London End. In 1775, he was paid a salary of 10 guineas to provide medical attendance at the parish workhouse.[17] Thomas Read died in 1780, leaving the interest on £100 three per cent bank annuities to be laid out in bread and distributed to the poor. Thomas Read's practice was taken over by Thomas Grove. He insured his house near the *Saracens Head* in 1781:

Thomas Grove of Beaconsfield in Bucks surgeon & apothecary	£
On his now dwelling house only situate as aforesaid brick & tiled	400
Household goods therein	200
Printed books therein	10
Utensils & stock therein	100
Wearing apparel therein	100
Plate therein	50
China & glass	40
	900[18]

The sum of £100 for wearing apparel is high, even if this reflected the value of his wife's wardrobe rather than his own. Mr Thomas Grove, apothecary, was buried at Beaconsfield in 1809, aged sixty-three.

Another long-serving Beaconsfield surgeon was Nathaniel Rumsey. In 1798, Rumsey was serving an apprenticeship with James Rumsey, the leading surgeon in Amersham. A monument in Amersham church records that James Rumsey died on 27 February 1824 in his 71st year 'after exercising his profession in this place with great ability and indefatigable earnestness and benevolence fifty years'. Nathaniel Rumsey came to Beaconsfield in 1806 when he married Lavinia, daughter of Robert Crook, of Hall Place. The couple had eight children baptised at Beaconsfield. Dr Rumsey's house and surgery, later numbered 27 London End, formed part of the sale of the Hall Place estate in 1815.[19] The Countess of Orkney lived on the opposite side of the street at Burke House. When she died in 1831, she was attended by Dr Rumsey.[20] In 1830, Nathaniel Rumsey was sworn in as one of the special constables who helped break up the papermakers' riot at Wycombe Marsh. Nathaniel Rumsey, along with William Robarts of Burnham and Robert Ceeley of Aylesbury, presented a petition from 115 medical practitioners in and near Buckinghamshire to Lord John Russell, about section 25 of the First Report of the Poor

43   *The Old Post House, the home of surgeons Thomas Read and Thomas Grove from about 1750-1809.*

Law Commissioners. He eventually retired to Remenham Hill, near Henley-on-Thames, and died there in 1845. His practice was taken over by his son, John Crook Rumsey, who was in partnership with William Atkinson.[21] John Crook Rumsey was later in partnership with John Smith, one of the promoters of the Church School in Beaconsfield.[22] Rumsey retired to Solihull and died in 1856. He was succeeded by his assistant, Harding Rees, who in 1854 had purchased the large house in London End now known as Wendover House.[23] Rees became a member of the Local Board of Health and died at Beaconsfield in 1867.

The Rumseys did not have a monopoly of medical services, for several doctors appeared in the town during the 19th century. William Hickey, who leased Little Hall Barn in 1807, struck up a friendship with Dr Samuel Ferris, who lived at Burke House on the south side of London End.

> Dr Ferris must be an acquisition to any place wherein he resided, and it is to be lamented that his abilities are confined to so trifling a place as Beaconsfield, and its vicinity, which however is his own choice. He is a man of deep erudition and in every way accomplished, yet of the most mild and unassuming manners. Mrs Ferris, his wife, is likewise a most amiable woman, and I cannot but consider myself as peculiarly fortunate in meeting with so estimable a pair.[24]

Another opulent surgeon was Frederick Petersdorff, who rented Burke Lodge, 20 London End, in the 1820s. In 1821, James Rymer of Beaconsfield, a surgeon, was advertising for an apprentice. He claimed to have 15 years' experience and was a member of the Royal College of Surgeons. The position advertised would provide the youth with an 'opportunity of acquiring a perfect knowledge of the sciences connected with medicine: and moreover should he be deficient in classical learning attention will be given to forward him in the Greek and Latin languages.'[25]

A Dr John Hutchinson practised in Beaconsfield during the 1840s and acted as registrar of births,

marriages and deaths. Although his family extended to seven children he had no servants, which places him well down the social hierarchy compared with Dr Rumsey, who in that year, even with no children, had one male and two female servants. In 1861, Rumsey's successor, Harding Rees, had three female servants and a groom.

In 1861 a doctor who does not fit readily into the local scene was resident at Hall Place. Seth B. Watson was aged 50 and described himself as 'M.D. Oxford, practicing medicine' and had indeed practiced there in 1841. At Hall Place his household included a pupil and three boarding scholars, six female and two male servants. In the last 30 years of the century no doctor kept as many servants as Rumsey or Rees. This indicator, plus the frequent changes in names, suggests that servicing the gentry in the surrounding countryside became increasingly difficult, given their proximity to London specialists. The lack of access to hospital facilities would have added to the difficulty of keeping doctors in the town.

For much of the 20th century, the best-known Beaconsfield doctors' surgery was Sunnyside, 51 London End, later called London End House. The doctors practising from this address included Dr Arthur George Pocock, Dr George Victor Bakewell, Dr Charles Walter Simpson and Dr Hugh Smith. Another respectable doctors' surgery was at Leigh House, 53 Wycombe End, home of Dr Arthur Herbert Turner, Medical Officer of Health to the U.D.C. and Dr Rupert Harry Kipping, Medical Officer to the Amersham Area Guardians Committee.

Veterinary Surgeons

The veterinary profession only fully developed in the second half of the 19th century. At Beaconsfield it was in the hands of two families. Christopher Williamson, a farrier, lived at Wycombe End, but his widow, Mary, was a blacksmith and veterinary surgeon in Aylesbury End by 1841. Their son

44 *Leigh House, 53 Wycombe End, the surgery of Dr A.H. Turner, c.1925.*

Christopher Williamson moved to the elegant house later known as Old Bank House, 25 London End, where he had three servants in 1851. When he died in 1869, he was followed by his son Christopher, who was a Member of the Royal College of Veterinary Surgeons (M.R.C.V.S.) by 1877.

John Hatch, who described himself as a castrator, was also in business in Aylesbury End by 1841. Hatch moved his business to Windsor End, but his son, also John Hatch, qualified as an M.R.C.V.S. and was living next door to the Rectory in Wycombe End in 1881, with one servant. For a small town to have two vets was unusual and in 1861, there may have been three, for Charles Allnutt, chemist of London End, had also qualified as an M.R.C.V.S.

Estate Agents

Beaconsfield was often listed in advertisements as a place in which auctions were held and house particulars deposited at the major inns. Thomas Everett, a cooper in London End, combined his business with that of an auctioneer from 1822-51.

In 1822, James Wassell described himself as an auctioneer and architectural surveyor. He died in 1833. Murray & Son tried to establish their business in the town but probably did not live in the town, as their home base was Uxbridge. Samuel Wells was listed in the 1863 *Directory*, but this may simply have been an attempt to extend his High Wycombe business.

The most important surveyors and land agents in 19th-century Beaconsfield were the family of James Rolfe, one-time agent to Edmund Burke at Butler's Court. James Rolfe prepared the valuation of Butler's Court prior to its sale to James Du Pre of Wilton Park in 1812.[26] His son, John Rolfe, was one of the special constables from Beaconsfield who intervened in the riots at W.R. Davies' mill at Wycombe Marsh in 1830. He was a leading tithe map surveyor and prepared the plans for the enclosure of Latchmoor Field, near Gerrards Cross, in 1846. John Rolfe died in 1850, but his brother William's two sons, Hubert John and Robert Henry Rolfe, continued the family tradition by setting up as auctioneers and surveyors in the

1870s. The brothers lived at the former *Star Inn*, next to Wiggenton Farm, and were prominent members of the Local Board of Health and the U.D.C. When the railway was about to open, they bought Knotty Green Farm, over the border in Penn, and sold off the land adjoining Penn Road for building. John Rolfe died in 1907, but his brother Robert was in business as an estate agent in the New Town until his death in 1928.

The Board of Heath had no full-time surveyor. Richard Hedges, previously the master of the National School, was the assistant overseer and registrar of births, marriages and deaths by 1879 and also described himself as a land surveyor. By 1896 the U.D.C. had appointed Herbert Watson as assistant surveyor and collector. By 1901, Watson was an auctioneer and estate manager for Wilton Park. His son, Charles Herbert Watson, became a partner in Burgess, Holden & Watson, developing the New Town.

The two main estates both employed agents, although they were sometimes called stewards or bailiffs. At Hall Barn, John Hargreaves promoted his gardener, George Smith, to be his agent, a move that was not popular with the local community. Smith seems to have acted for Hargreaves' successor, Allan Morrison. John and Robert Rolfe became agents for the Lawsons after their purchase of Hall Barn in 1881. Continuity was important for the Du Pres, perhaps reflecting their moderate interest in Wilton Park. The Hare family acted as their agents over the period 1847-71, when they were succeeded by Thomas Perryman.

James Gurney

James Gurney was the most entrepreneurial of all the Beaconsfield estate agents. He was born in 1845, the son of James Gurney, a Chalfont St Giles farmer and miller. He acted as a land agent for several local families. His brother William Gurney was chairman of the Amersham Board of Guardians, and became chairman of the newly formed Amersham Rural District Council. He was to chair its development committee throughout the period when the two brothers' property in Amersham on the Hill and the Chalfonts was being developed for housing.

In 1905, James and William Gurney bought the Orchehill Estate at Gerrards Cross, for £20,000, and laid out the land near the new railway station in building plots. In 1907, they paid William Baring Du Pre £58,690 for 293 acres of building land at Gregories Farm, Beaconsfield. They raised this huge sum by mortgaging the land partly to Du Pre's uncle, Francis Baring Du Pre, and partly to H.M. MacKusick. They divided the land into 200 building plots and marketed it as the Burke's Estate. James Gurney spent some of the proceeds of these land sales buying the Ireby Grange Estate in Cumberland, a 52-room mansion with 1,876 acres of land. He died at Ireby in 1933.

Norman William Gurney

James Gurney's son, Norman William Gurney, born in 1880, was also an estate agent. His offices were at Burke's Chambers, Station Approach, Beaconsfield, and he lived at Woodlands, Burke's Road, which has recently been redeveloped. He served in the Boer and First World War. He was Chairman of Beaconsfield U.D.C. and a County Alderman. Norman William Gurney was Sheriff of Buckinghamshire in 1952 and died at Beaconsfield in 1973.

Vernon & Son

Arthur Vernon, land agent and architect, was five times Mayor of High Wycombe. He designed Butler's Court for Arthur Riversdale Grenfell in 1891 and supervised the rebuilding of the *Saracens Head* in 1893. As an estate agent, he acted for Earl Howe in the sale of the Ledborough Lane and Penn Road, building plots in 1903 and 1906. He also acted for the Du Pre family in marketing the Baring Road and Reynolds Road sites in 1905.

45 *Norman William Gurney.*

Alfred Cardain Frost

Alfred Frost originally worked for Wetherall, Green & Co., auctioneers and land agents, 22 Chancery Lane, London. He set up on his own in 1906, possibly with suburban development in mind. In 1908 he built the tall red-brick building beside the railway bridge in Beaconsfield, from which his firm still operates. This was next door to the architects Burgess, Holden & Watson, with whom he worked closely in the development of the Burke's Estate. Alfred Frost lived at 'Manawatu', Burke's Road, Beaconsfield.

Frost not only acted as agent for vendors and lessors of the new houses, but also developed houses himself, particularly on the Burke's Estate. He also sold a large number of houses for more prestigious London firms, sharing the commission on each deal. He died in December 1942, leaving £65,689. A.C. Frost & Co. was taken over by The Prudential in 1986, but the freeholds of the local offices were retained by the partners, including the founder's grandson, Alan Frost. He later started a new business called A.C. Frost, using many of the original offices, including the premises at Beaconsfield, which celebrated their 100th anniversary in 2008.

Architects

Percy Charles Boddy was born in London in 1881, although his father was from Beaconsfield. In 1908 he formed a partnership with John Graham Johnson, who designed at least 50 houses at Gerrards Cross, whilst Boddy lived in Baring Road, Beaconsfield, where the partners were equally busy. When Johnson left the firm in 1912, he was replaced by Charles Davis. After Herbert Green joined the partnership in 1913, the firm continued as Davis, Boddy & Green. When Percy Boddy applied to become a Fellow of the Royal Institute of British Architects (F.R.I.B.A.) in 1925, his list of architectural works included houses at Beaconsfield, Fulmer and Gerrards Cross. Percy Boddy later lived in Ruislip and is particularly known for his designs on the Grange Estate, Northwood. He died on 1 January 1964.

Julian Gulson Burgess was born in Leicester in 1876 and was articled to his uncle, Edward Burgess, architect, of Gray's Inn, London. He moved to Beaconsfield in about 1906, and formed a partnership with the local surveyor, Legender Myers, who surveyed the Burke's Estate for James and William Gurney. The firm designed most of the houses on the north side of Ledborough Lane, including Cestria, built for Edward Norcross in 1913. They also designed the larger houses on either side of Penn Road for the builders G. & F. Bagley, including Upton Leigh, 46 Penn Road, in 1914. The firm carried out numerous alterations and additions to buildings on the Hall Barn Estate and designed the new Harrias Farm in 1913. Julian Burgess built his own house, Netherlands, at Penn Road, Knotty Green, in about 1907. When Legender Myers joined the Ford Motor Company in 1914, Walter Holden, who had been with the firm since 1907, was made a partner. The gap left by Myers in the surveying area was filled by C.H. Watson. Burgess, Holden & Watson took on several council housing schemes for Beaconsfield U.D.C. and Eton R.D.C. The firm also designed the Church of England Secondary School at Beaconsfield and Oakdene School. Julian Burgess designed several branch premises for Lloyds Bank, in particular that at Watford. He became an F.R.I.B.A. in 1925. Burgess died at Netherlands, Penn Road, in 1933.

Stanley Hinge Hamp was born in 1877. He was in partnership with Thomas Edward Collcutt, architect of the *Savoy Hotel*. Hamp was president of the Architectural Association in 1922 and a vice-president of the R.I.B.A. from 1935 to 1937. He designed several chalet-style houses in Burke's Road and Grove Road for the estate agent N.W. Gurney. One of these houses appears in an advertisement for the Burke's Estate in *Where to Live Round London* in 1910. In 1911, Hamp was living with his mother at Davenies Farm, where he linked the house to a large barn. The conversion featured in the *Studio Yearbook of Decorative Art* in 1921. He also designed Beaconsfield Golf Club. Stanley Hamp is perhaps best known for the starkly modern flat-roofed houses he designed for sites in Gregories Road and Cambridge Road in the 1930s. He died in 1968 at the age of ninety-one.

Walter Frederick Clarke Holden was born in Edinburgh in 1882, but his family moved to Cambridge where he gained his first experience as an architect. He joined Burgess & Myers at Beaconsfield in 1907 and designed their offices over Lloyds Bank in 1910. He personally carved the date on the timber over the bank and the dog at the apex of the gable. He was probably the architect of Overroads, Grove Road, built in 1909 and rented by G.K. Chesterton. He certainly designed Top Meadow for G.K. Chesterton in 1921 and Corner Cottage, Stratton Road, for the photographer R.N. Speight in 1921. He also designed his own house, Salter's Acre, 116 Gregories Road, in 1920. His daughter, Brigit Gale, still lives in the house. Walter Holden

served with the Royal Engineers in the First World War and won the Military Cross. He was one of the first officers to work on camouflage and his daughter has preserved several excellent drawings of French towns near the front. After the war, Walter Holden became the chief architect for the National Provincial Bank, so his work can be found all over the country. He died at Beaconsfield in 1953 aged 71.

John Graham Johnson was born in London on 26 January 1882. He obtained his architectural training in London in the 1890s, first as an articled pupil to Charles Forster Hayward, and then as improver and assistant to J.E.K. & J.P. Cutts. In 1907 he worked with Percy Hopkins at Gerrards Cross, but in 1908 he began a fruitful partnership with Percy Boddy of Beaconsfield. Although Johnson lived at Gerrards Cross, he was perhaps the most prolific of the Beaconsfield architects and designed many of the small villas in Baring Road built by T.W. Hanson and Y.J. Lovell. He designed larger houses on the Burke's Estate, including Heatherdene, 30 Burke's Road, in 1911; Fairlawn, 34 Burke's Road, in 1910; Wyngates, 42 Burke's Road, in 1912; and Orchard Dale, Gregories Farm Road, in 1912.

J.G. Johnson dissolved his partnership with Percy Boddy in 1912 and moved to British Columbia. After service during the First World War, he returned to Canada, becoming resident architect for the Canadian Pacific Railway. He died in Victoria, 27 July 1945, aged sixty-three.

Legender William Myers was born in London in 1879, but was brought up in Beaconsfield, where his mother was a lace dealer. He was articled to Arthur Vernon, architect and surveyor at High Wycombe, and later worked in architects' and surveyors' offices in Cambridge. In 1905, he was engaged by James and William Gurney to lay out the Orchehill Estate at Gerrards Cross and and in 1907 he worked on the Burke's Estate at Beaconsfield. He was in partnership with Julian Burgess at Beaconsfield until 1914, when he joined the Ford Motor Company. He died in 1958.

Seven

Trade and Industry

The Market

In 1255, the new lord of the manor, Richard Earl of Cornwall, secured a charter from Henry III to hold a Tuesday market at Beaconsfield:

> For Richard Earl of Cornwall, the King to the Archbishops etc. Know ye that we have granted and hereby confirm to our beloved brother, Richard Earl of Cornwall, that he and his heirs shall have a market on Tuesday of every week in his manor of Beaconsfield, so long as that market be not to the detriment of other markets in the neighbourhood. For our will is etc.
>
> Given under our hand at Westminster 6th day of February in the 39th year of our reign.[1]

The clause about the new market not being 'to the detriment of other markets in the neighbourhood' was hardly necessary, as both Wycombe on the west and Uxbridge to the east were very well-established markets, unlikely to notice competition from Beaconsfield.

By 1269, Richard Earl of Cornwall had assigned the lordship of Beaconsfield to his newly founded Abbey of Burnham. In that year, the Abbess of Burnham obtained a charter for an annual fair to be held at Beaconsfield on the eve of, the day of, and the six days following Ascension Day. This charter has been translated:

> For the Abbess and Nuns of Burnham, the King to the Archbishops etc. Greeting. Know ye that we have granted, and hereby confirm, to our beloved in Christ the Abbess and Nuns of Burnham that they and their successors shall hold a fair in their manor of Beaconsfield every year, which shall last for eight days, to wit, on the vigil, on the day, and on the morrow of the Ascension of Our Lord, and on the five following days. Provided that the said fair be no nuisance to neighbouring fairs. Our will is, and for ourselves and our successors we command that the Abbess and Nuns and their successors shall for ever hold the said fair, and shall have all privileges and free customs such as pertain to fairs of this kind. Provided that etc.
>
> Given under our hand at Windsor, 10th May in the 53rd year of our reign.[2]

In 1271, the Abbess obtained a similar charter for a market and fair at Burnham. In 1414, the Abbess of Burnham secured a new charter from Henry V, confirming Beaconsfield's market day as Thursday. The Ascension Day fair was reduced from eight to two days. The charter did, however, authorise another fair at the feast of St Mathias (24 February). This continued as a cattle fair, held on Candlemas Day (2 February) right up to the time of the First World War. In 1551, the new owner of the manor of Beaconsfield, Sir John Williams, procured a royal grant to change the market day to Wednesday.[3] The market was held

46 *The natural place for the market and fairs was the crossing point of the Oxford and Windsor roads. By 1920, the fair was a serious hindrance to the passage of traffia*

in the road at the junction of the Oxford and Windsor roads.

There was evidently an ancient market house in Beaconsfield. At the Court Baron of 1778, the jurors presented:

That Beaconsfield Market House is very much out of repair and a nuisance to the public, and that Edmund Waller Esquire, the Lord of this Manor, the owner thereof hath the sole right to repair it, and for the encouragement of the market there to be weekly held, they do recommend the Lord of this manor forthwith to put the same in such repair as he shall think proper.[4]

It seems that the recommendation of the court was acted upon for in 1781, Henry Turrell of Beaconsfield, a carpenter, insured the Market House in Beaconsfield for £100. The building

was brick-panelled and tiled.[5] It was mentioned in the *Universal British Directory* of 1792:

In the middle of the town is a market house, which is a low building. A market is held weekly on Wednesday; and two fairs, chiefly for cattle, viz. on Candlemas-eve and day, and on Ascension-day.

The tolls from the fairs and markets are listed in the schedule of a private Act of Parliament of 1812 settling the lands of Edmund Waller, late of Hall Barn. They were let to Isaac Mills, along

47 *(Opposite) The market house and Uriah Day's drapery and grocery shop, c.1890.*

with the *White Hart Inn* and 54 acres of land, at the annual rent of £195.[6]

George Lipscomb, writing in about 1830, stated that the market was 'almost wholly discontinued'. James Sheahan, in his 1862 *History and Topography of Buckinghamshire*, said that the market 'has fallen entirely into disuse by the superior traffic of the neighbouring towns of Wycombe and Uxbridge'. The market tolls were reviewed at a Court Baron in 1876, when it was agreed that the tolls and market dues, which had been immemorially payable to the lord of the manor on the sale of animals and for the holding of stalls in the open market, should continue to be collected by the bailiff. The tolls were:

Animals
One sale of every horse, mare, pony,
  gelding, donkey or mule each   6d.
One sale of every ox, cow, bull, heifer,
  stirk or calf   6d.
One sale of every cow and calf   6d.
One sale of every score of sheep or
  lambs or any quantity less than a
  score   6d.
One sale of every score of ewes with
  lambs or any quantity less than a
  score   6d.
One sale of every sow, pig or boar   2d.
On sale of each store pig   1d.
Standings
For every standing or stall   1s.
For every show caravan, cart or
  carriage   2s. 6d.
For every implement of husbandry   6d.[7]

At the same court, Uriah Day was ordered to throw open the old market house of which he had unlawfully taken possession. If he failed to do so, the Bailiff was ordered to knock off the lock and take possession for the lord of the manor. The market house was part of a group of buildings in the centre of the road at Aylesbury End, dominated by Day's drapery and grocery shop. The buildings were demolished in 1952. Beaconsfield's market was, however, revived in 1982, and the stalls, sited in Windsor End, have appeared there every week since then.

In 1863, the Ascension Day fair was fixed at 10 May. It was seen by some as an encouragement

of bad behaviour and by others as a serious obstacle to the passage of traffic. In 1969, however, Beaconsfield celebrated the 700th anniversary of the charter with a fair from the 2-10 May. The last day was more like a carnival, with floats representing every organisation in the town.

Millers

Beaconsfield is unusual in not having a river or stream adequate to turn a waterwheel. Local farmers therefore had to grind their corn either at one of the mills on the Wye at High Wycombe or Wooburn, or rely on the modest windmill near the corner of London End and Lakes Lane. In 1716, John Burt left the *White Horse Inn* and a piece of land called the Windmill Platt to his son John. The Windmill Platt was still in the family's possession in 1782.[8] A new windmill was built on the same site in about 1811 by James Rance, who is listed in later directories as both a miller

and bricklayer. The mill was of brick and flint, octagonal at the base, but merging into a circular tower about two-thirds of the way up. There were two stones, each 4ft 6in in diameter. James Rance's son George was tenant of Oldfields Farm and became chairman of the Local Board of Health. Another son, Joseph Rance, was a builder in the town. James Rance died in 1845, but his tenant, James Sibley, miller, who died in 1850, and his son George Sibley continued to operate the mill into the 1870s. One sail fell off in about 1880 and another some years later. The remaining sails were removed in 1898. Milling continued with a small steam engine, located in an outhouse and connected to the mill by a belt drive.

Maltsters

Most Buckinghamshire farmers, especially those in the Chilterns, grew barley, the basic ingredient of beer. The barley was sold to maltsters, who stored it in their maltings, which were long barn-like buildings with a kiln attached. The grain was spread on the upper floor of the malting and moistened to promote germination. As soon as the grain began to sprout, it was moved to the kiln where the moisture was removed and further growth stopped. The resulting 'malt' was then ready for brewing, which was done by the innkeepers in their own brewhouses.

Most maltings were located near to a farmhouse. James Boddy of Wilton Green insured his house and malting with the Sun Insurance Company in 1778:

48 *Beaconsfield Windmill c.1930.*

James Boddy of Wilton Green, Beaconsfield, maltster	£
On his now dwelling house and malthouse communicating situate as aforesaid	240
Household goods therein	50
Utensils and stock therein	250
Tenement separate in tenure of Zachariah Worley labourer	60
	600[9]

James's son, also James Boddy, sold the family farm and malting to James Du Pre of Wilton Park in 1812 for the substantial sum of £2,839.[10] The buildings were demolished and the site became part of the parkland surrounding the big house.

Some maltings were near to the principal inns in the town, suggesting that the tenants, who were often farmers as well as innkeepers, also involved themselves in the malt trade. The *Swan Inn*, which comprised most of the buildings now numbered 1-11 London End, had a malting accessed from Shepherds Lane. The *Swan Inn* had closed by 1700, but the malting was continued by Henry Fellows. He was fined £69 at the Quarter Sessions in 1712 for 'mixing together 276 bushels of corn of several wettings which had been wetted and was making into malt for sale' contrary to the statute. The fine had already been reduced by the Justices to £50. Fellows' appeal was dismissed and orders were given to the officer of excise at Beaconsfield to distrain.[11]

When Michael Rutt of Beaconsfield, an innholder, made a settlement of the *Kings Head* in 1668, the property included barns, stables, malthouses and brewhouses.[12] Subsequent occupants were therefore both innkeepers and maltsters. Matthew Davis was the last innkeeper at the *Kings Head*. By 1777 he had moved to the former *Swan Inn* where he was a maltster and brandy merchant. He insured his household goods in his dwelling house, brick, plaster and tiled, for £300. He insured his utensils and stock in his malthouse, brick and tiled, for a further £300.[13]

There was a substantial malting near to the *Crown Inn*, which seems to have belonged to the property now known as the Old Post House. The occupants' names appear in the rate books from the 1690s, when Charles Idle, innkeeper at the *Saracens Head*, rented the malthouse.[14] He was followed by William Grove, maltster, who died in 1707, when the business was continued by his son, also William Grove. The house and malting was later occupied by Henry Fellows' son, John Fellows, who owned another malting in Windsor End. The malting in London End seems to have ceased operation in about 1750 when Thomas Read, surgeon, came to live at the house.

There was also a malting behind the *Saracens Head*, accessed from Windsor End. This belonged to Richard Clarke of Beaconsfield, a maltster, who made the following bequest in his will of 1715:

> Item I give and bequeath unto my loving wife all my stock of malt and all such sum or sums of money as shall be due to me for malt at the time of my decease and all the barley which I shall have bought to be malted only and also my malt mill screen and other utensils and materials belonging to my malting trade she paying such sum or sums of money out of the said malting stock as may happen to be due at the time of my decease for barley.

Clarke's malting was taken over by William Carter, whose father Francis Carter had yet another malting further down Windsor End. By 1752, the malting was occupied by Joseph Millward, landlord of the *White Hart Inn*. In 1760, Millward insured his household goods and stock in trade in his dwelling house and brewhouse, brick and tiled, for £200. He also insured the 'utensils and stock in his malthouse in Beaconsfield, distant from the aforesaid, brick and tiled', for £100.[15] The malting was later purchased by Joseph Jagger, who was innkeeper at the *Saracens Head* from 1769-87. His tenant, James Clifford, maltster, bought the freehold some time before 1820. In his will of 1826, James Clifford, maltster, left to his son, William Clifford:

All that my freehold messuage cottage or tenement with the malthouse, garden barn, yard and appurtenances thereto belonging, together with the pump, cistern, kilns, implements and fixtures in about and to the said malthouse belonging … situate in the Town of Beaconsfield in the county of Bucks in a street or end there called Windsor End and now occupied by me … and also all that stable with the granary or loft over the same, with the appurtenances, situate at the back of the said messuage and premises at Beaconsfield aforesaid, and in the occupation of Mr William Hall, all which said premises I purchased of Mr Joseph Jagger.

James Clifford died in 1829. The malting was continued by William Clifford and his partner, James Lee Williams. In 1851, James Lee Williams, then aged 72, described his occupation as 'brewer and maltster'. Following his death in 1863, his property was auctioned, including a 'freehold messuage and premises known as the Brewhouse and Malthouse with the brewery plant and fixtures situate at Windsor End, Beaconsfield'.[16] John Williams was still in business here as a maltster in the 1880s.

Perhaps the most opulent maltster in Beaconsfield was Francis Carter, who held the lease of Seeleys Farm but lived in the house now known as Prospect Place, 19-23 Windsor End. When he died in 1723, his inventory revealed a fortune of £2,064, including £374 worth of malt at Westrup in Little Marlow. His book debts amounted to £186 and he was also owed £760 on bonds and mortgages.[17] His business in Beaconsfield was continued by his grandson, William Carter junior, until about 1735. In 1729, the freehold of Carter's house and malting was purchased by John Fellows of Beaconsfield, a maltster, for £660. The property included outhouses, malthouses, malting rooms, kilns and cisterns.[18] In 1786, Christopher Fellows of Beaconsfield, mealman and maltster, insured the household goods in his dwelling house for £200, but the utensils and stock in an adjoining malthouse were valued at £450.[19] Fellows also had

49　*Prospect Place, home of Christopher Carter, maltster, and later of John Stransum, brickmaker.*

utensils and stock in a corn loft over a stable at the *Swan Inn*, High Wycombe, valued at £100. The malting at Windsor End was purchased by John Stransum, bricklayer, who rebuilt Prospect Place. This house and the former malting later became the property of Joseph Marshall, a grocer in London End. The industrial buildings behind the houses are still known as Marshall's Yard.

Francis Carter of Beaconsfield, maltster, also owned a malting on the land in Windsor End, next to the *Greyhound Inn*. Shortly before his death, Francis Carter sold the freehold of this malting to Edmund Waller of Hall Barn. The malting was then occupied by Benjamin Birch, next by James

that Beaconsfield U.D.C. built the council houses called Malthouse Square in 1919.

If the Beaconsfield maltsters had any surplus malt after supplying the local inns, it was sold at the local market or transported to London to fulfil contracts with 'common brewers'. These brewers produced beer in industrial quantities to serve their chains of inns, taverns and alehouses across the capital. Few market towns had their own common brewers before the 19th century, but an exception was Amersham, where the brewery near the church certainly dates back to 1600.

Carriers

Given the number of carriers' carts which passed along the Oxford road to London, it was hardly necessary for the town to provide carriers of its own. Joseph Grove, however, is shown in this role from 1851-4, when he went to London two days a week, staying for a day and returning on the next. A similar arrangement was adopted by William Jeffs, who was also publican at the *Saracens Head*, but by 1864 he was returning the next day. His widow had taken over the service by 1877. In 1883, Horace Roberts was offering a service four days a week, an arrangement that was continuing in 1907. From 1895 to 1903 he had competition from William Hare. The carriers were prominent in the community. Grove sat on the Board of Health and Hare was a member of a very respectable family in the town. Roberts was the son of a Saunderton hay dealer and, as a Congregationalist, was easily accepted within the close-knit, non-conformist business community in Beaconsfield.

Garland and later by Samuel Rolfe, farmer and maltster, who lived on the corner of Windsor Road and Hedgerley Lane. By 1777, the malthouse was run by Edward Rawlins, innholder and maltster, who kept the *Bull Inn*, London End. He insured his utensils and stock in his malthouse and loft adjoining at Windsor End for £200.[20] The last mention of this malting is in 1820 when it was occupied by Isaac Mills, landlord of the *White Hart*. The tithe map shows a cellar, just to the north of the *Greyhound Inn*, rented from Sir Gore Ouseley by George Harman of Uxbridge, a brewer. This structure seems to have been the only part of the malting still standing in 1844. The site was used in 1870 for the construction of the new police station. The land behind was still known as Malthouse Mead and it was here

Wheelwrights

In a town offering overnight accommodation to travellers and carriers to London, there was plenty of work for those who could repair carriages and carts. As early as 1541, the aptly named William

Axtell of Beaconsfield bequeathed to his son William 300 of 'ashen timber as it lies', 1,000 spokes, two axes and three augers. Francis Axtell, making his will in 1598, hoped that his son would follow his occupation and left him 'one tool of every sort for it' at the age of twenty-one. Not all the work was linked to the coaching or carrying trades. Richard Clarke of Beaconsfield, a maltster, who held the lease of Davenies Farm, mentioned in his will of 1715, the 'sums of money as I shall happen to owe at the time of my decease to the smith, wheelwright and collar maker'. The collar here referred to must be the leather-covered roll worn by a draught animal, to which the shafts of a cart or plough were attached. From about 1700, John Young of Beaconsfield, a collar maker, rented a workshop near to Henry Fellow's malting, behind the *Swan Inn*, London End.[21] There were two collar makers in Beaconsfield in 1798, James Clifford and Andrew Silcock.[22]

Blacksmiths

Blacksmiths in particular benefited from Beaconsfield's passing trade. Richard Nedham of Beaconsfield, a smith, made his will in 1567. His business was to be taken over by his nephew, John Nedham, to whom he left his best anvil, a pair of bellows, his second vice, a nail hammer, a shoeing hammer and a pair of pincers. His nephew, William Nedham, received the second anvil, whilst Christopher Nedham of New Windsor was left 60 horseshoes and 400 horse nails. William Lacke of Beaconsfield, a blacksmith, left his son Henry his bellows and anvil in 1632. Edward Boulton of Beaconsfield, a cutler, left his son John his working

tools, swords, daggers and other weapons in 1624. The *Posse Comitatus* of 1798 list two members of the same family, William Thompson and his son William, who were edge-toolmakers.[23]

The town was too small for its blacksmiths to emerge as machinery manufacturers, but George Symth Gower, who described himself as an 'agricultural implement maker and engineer', had premises on the north side of London End, near the former *Chequers Inn*, from 1861. His son Albert had taken over the business by 1901.

Potters

Up until the end of the 19th century, several potters, brick and tile makers worked near Beaconsfield. Part of the parish of Penn is known as Tylers Green and the *Potters Arms* still stands at Winchmore Hill. When James Du Pre moved the road from Beaconsfield to Chalfont St Giles away from Wilton Park, the new road cut through a close belonging to William Wellings of Beaconsfield, a brickmaker and potter.[24] The new road became known as Pot Kiln Lane. Several of the potters brought their children to be baptised at the parish church of Beaconsfield. Wellings was succeeded by John Swallow, whose son Robert was baptised at Beaconsfield in 1827. In the 1864 and 1869 directories, John Swallow, brick and drainpipe maker, gave his address as at Pitlands Wood, again on the edge of the Wilton Park Estate. Robert Swallow, potter, was employing 10 men at his pottery in 1861. Robert Swallow of the Beaconsfield Pottery was made bankrupt in 1878.[25]

50 *The premises of J.H. Watkins, carriage builder, Wycombe End.*

Lace Making

Lace making was a common occupation for women in most Buckinghamshire towns. As early as 1624, William Borlase, the founder of the grammar school in Marlow, also set up a school 'for 24 women children of the Borough of Great Marlow to make bone lace'. The same idea of employing the poor in making lace was applied in Beaconsfield in the 18th century. In 1774, Beaconsfield's overseers of the poor received £7 4s. 6¼d. for lace made by girls at the workhouse.[26] Indeed, one of the storerooms in the workhouse was known as the 'Silk Room'. Although the lacemakers were mostly female, the trade was usually organised by men like Stephen Woodbridge, lace merchant, who was renting a house in London End in 1779.[27] Although Stephen Woodbridge earned his living selling Beaconsfield lace at the London lace markets, he called himself a gentleman in his will of 1815. In 1818, Eleanor, daughter of James Why, lace dealer, and his wife Mary Anne, was baptised at the parish church. The editor of *Pigot's Directory*, describing Beaconsfield in 1830, stated that 'its lace trade too, which is the only manufacture here (with the exception of some paper made in the neighbourhood), is in a most depressed state'.

There was still money to be made however. In 1846, George Withall was occupying the three-storey brick house in Windsor End now known as Hall Barn Cottage. He was listed in the directories as a lace manufacturer, but in fact he supplied yarn and patterns to a number of outworkers who made lace in their own cottages. In 1891 he described himself as a lace trimmings manufacturer. He had retired to Scarborough by 1901.

In the 1880s, many of the Beaconsfield lace makers found beading a better source of income. This was the process of sewing tiny glass beads onto dresses, particularly to the collars. Elizabeth Myers, who lived at Essex House, 15 London End, started a workshop where this fancy beadwork was carried out for London dressmakers.[28] She was the mother of Legender Myers, a partner in Burgess & Myers, who laid out the Burke's Estate in 1907. Another agent for beadwork was Anne Oakley, who lived in one of the houses in the Broadway, backing on to the churchyard. Her house was later known as Oakley Cottage.

Silk Weaving

During the 19th century, several Buckinghamshire towns were unable to provide employment for their growing populations. Some parishes tried to keep down the poor rates by encouraging entrepreneurs to bring new industries to the area. In about 1818, Isaac Peet, who had a connection with James and Charles Peet, silk weavers, of Derby, set up a ribbon factory on the north side of Wycombe End. This locality is still known as Factory Yard. Ellen, daughter of Isaac Peet, silk weaver, and his wife Mary was born in Beaconsfield in 1818 and Isaac Peet, ribbon manufacturer, Wycombe End, is listed in the 1822 *Pigot's Directory*. Eight families of silk weavers had children baptised at the parish church during the 1820s. Isaac Peet's enterprise soon ran into trouble, for in November 1823, a commission of bankruptcy was issued against George and Isaac Peet of Gutter Lane, Cheapside, City of London, ribbon manufacturers. Isaac Peet, late of Beaconsfield, now of Derby, a weaver, sold part of the ribbon factory as a Wesleyan Chapel in 1824.[29]

Isaac Peet's successor at Beaconsfield, George Mills, also ran out of money. In 1826, a commission of bankruptcy was issued against George Mills of Wood Street, Cheapside, City of London, and of Beaconsfield, Co. Bucks, silk manufacturer, dealer and chapman. The factory seems to have closed down completely by 1830. In 1846, parts of the former ribbon factory were used for a girls' school. The Wesleyan Reformers continued to use another part of the factory as their chapel until they moved to Shepherds Lane in 1900.[30]

Chair Factories

Given its proximity to High Wycombe, it is surprising that more of Beaconsfield's businessmen did not set up chair factories. In fact, there was no substantial chair manufacturer in the town until the late 1850s, when William Harding, who had a chair factory in Easton Street, High Wycombe, moved to Beaconsfield. Harding lived at Wycombe End, near to the *Cross Keys Inn*. His factory was across the road in 'Harding's Yard', near to the former Presbyterian Chapel. William Harding and his son John were employing 34 men and eight boys in their factory by 1861. By the time William Harding died in 1879, he had transferred the business to his sons John and William Harding. The partnership of Harding Brothers was dissolved in 1880.[31] By 1881, the number of employees had declined to 29 men and three boys. William Harding junior continued the business at 13 Windsor End until his death in 1895. His widow Sarah Harding was still living there in 1910.

Perhaps as a result of the closure of William Harding's chair factory, the Beaconsfield Chair Manufacturing Company was formed with offices in Aylesbury End. Sir Edward Lawson of Hall Barn was the principal investor and the secretary was Henry Johnstone. Amongst the Hall Barn papers is a manuscript report on the Beaconsfield Chair Manufacturing Company, written by Johnstone in 1900, recommending the purchase of new machinery to fulfil existing orders. By 1903 a new secretary, Edward MacDermott, was in charge, but the company was officially wound up in 1905.[32] The workshops at 42 Aylesbury End were listed on the 1910 valuation of the town. A new Beaconsfield Chair Company was formed in 1915, but by 1920 the premises were occupied by the Beaconsfield Sanitary Laundry.

Another attempt to promote local industry was the Beaconsfield Machinery Company, which built the Station Works in about 1920. The firm was

51 *The entry on the left gave access to the Beaconsfield Chair Manufacturing Company, Aylesbury End.*

wound up in 1924, but Messrs Wilson & Pearce continued to manufacture woodworking machinery in Post Office Lane until the 1950s. The premises were adapted for Perkin Elmer in 1957.

Gas Works

The Beaconsfield Gas Light Company started in 1865 with works on the Penn Road, near to Davenies Farm. The first secretary was the solicitor G.A. Charsley, but a variety of local businessmen were involved, including Charles Smith, harness maker, Herbert Fowler, grocer and John Rolfe, estate agent. The company was taken over by the Uxbridge and Hillingdon Gas Consumers Company in 1908 and closed down in 1912. The two small gasholders on Station Road remained in use until 1922. The site was cleared in 1955.

Builders

In the 18th century, builders often described themselves as brickmakers, bricklayers, timber merchants and carpenters. Thomas Briars, carpenter, registered his house for religious meetings in 1693. It was his son, John Briars, who built Hall Place for John Crook, and left considerable property in the town in his will of 1751. He was the brother-in-law of Samuel Clarke, minister of the Presbyterian Church in Beaconsfield, and his daughter had married John Anthony, another leading figure in the church. Another prosperous carpenter and timber dealer was Henry Turrell, who lived in the Broadway and owned the old Market House in Aylesbury End. He died aged 80 in 1822, when a fine monument to his memory was erected in the churchyard. In 1786, John Stransum of

F. Froude.

Telephone
No 19.
Beaconsfield

Builder & Contractor

Station Parade

Beaconsfield

Houses erected on delightful and
convenient sites to suit Purchasers
£400 to £1500

52 *Advertisement for Frank Froude, builder, 1910.*

Beaconsfield, a bricklayer, insured his dwelling house and two houses adjoining in the occupation of Elizabeth Fellows, shopkeeper, and William Haynes, chandler, situated opposite the church, for £300.[33] The *Universal British Directory* of 1792 lists John and Joseph Stransum, both bricklayers. The will of Joseph Stransum of Beaconsfield, brickmaker and farmer, was proved in 1794 and John Stransum of Beaconsfield, a builder, left a will in 1842. His business in Windsor End was continued by John Spring, a member of the Local Board, and Henry Sexton, who employed nine men and two boys in 1871.

During the 19th century, the one of the leading builders was William Child of Aylesbury End, who employed four carpenters and two sawyers in 1851. He built the National School in Windsor End in 1872. His sons Frederick and Robert were also carpenters and builders. Various members of the Bagley family were also builders in the town. Benjamin Bagley of Wycombe End was followed by his sons, George and Francis. They bought several building plots from Earl Howe in 1903 and built most of the houses on the north side of Ledborough Lane. They also built several large houses in Seeleys Orchard, Penn Road, in 1914. Edward William Tilbury, born in Penn but living in Wycombe End, built cottages in Shepherds Lane in 1911. He was later a chairman of the U.D.C. Jesse Reeves, formerly a shopkeeper in Aylesbury End, had a yard near the corner of Aylesbury End and Mill Lane. He built several houses in Horseshoe Crescent. Alfred William Nash, builder, Priory Avenue, High Wycombe, also built several houses in Horseshoe Crescent.

The local builders were joined in 1906 by several firms new to the district, like Y.J. Lovell & Son of Marlow and Gerrards Cross who set up a yard in Baring Road. Thomas William Hanson, a builder from Ealing, lived at Bridge House, Baring Road, and Charles Edwin Gibbings, a builder born in Chelsea, lived at Nevona, Cruzon Avenue and built several houses for the London estate agents

Robinson & Roods. Frank Froude, a builder and sanitary engineer from Hemel Hempstead, lived at Red Cottage, Baring Road, and had a yard on Warwick Road. He built several small houses in the Baring Road area, but his most prestigious work was Kingswear House, Burke's Crescent, designed by James Ransome. Edward Goodyer, from Lower Norwood in Surrey, lived in Candelmas Lane and had a yard in Baring Road. Other established builders, like Henry Brown and Claude Baldwin, who were already building houses at Gerrards Cross, developed a few houses here. William Edmund Vare, a builder and sanitary engineer from London, came to live at Burke's Cottage, Burke's Road and built some very large houses on plots near the site of Edmund Burke's house. He also built the Council Chambers on the corner of Burke's Road and became chairman of Beaconsfield U.D.C.

Film Making

A new industry came to the town in 1921 when the film producer George Clark built the Beaconsfield Studios on Station Road. Clark wanted clean air and rural locations, but needed to be in easy reach of his contacts in London. In 1927, the studios were taken over by Sam Smith's British Lion Film Corporation, which made its first 'talkie', *The Clue of the New Pin*, at Beaconsfield in 1929. In 1939, the studios were requisitioned by the Ministry of Works and adapted for the manufacture of aircraft parts. In 1947, Alexander Korda's London Films bought the freehold of the site. He soon sold the studios and the Crown Film Unit moved in, producing films for the Central Office of Information.

The National Film Finance Corporation then sold the studios to Beaconsfield Films Ltd, and films were made right up until 1966. The site was purchased in 1971 by the National Film School and from 1983 was called the National Film and Television School.

53 *The Rotax Factory, Maxwell Road, c.1950. Note Station Works on Post Office Lane.*

Rotax Ltd

The British Lion film studios at Beaconsfield were requisitioned in 1939 for Rotax Ltd of Willesden, to increase the production of magnetos for aircraft engines. Rotax soon became the largest employer in the area and a new factory was built on the south side of Maxwell Road. After the war, Rotax remained at Maxwell Road and 500 employees went on strike at the factory in 1956.[34] By 1959, however, there was greatly reduced demand for military aircraft, and much of the remaining production was moved to the Rotax plant at Hemel Hempstead. The factory was eventually purchased by Perkin Elmer.

Scientific Instruments

In 1957, the Station Works, Post Office Lane, was taken over by Perkin Elmer, an American manufacturer of optical instruments, founded in Connecticut in 1937 by Richard Perkin and Charles Elmer. A.R. Gibson and a staff of 20 began making instruments under licence from the American company. Many orders were for export, some back to the U.S.A. The firm expanded into the old Rotax factory on Maxwell Road and was employing 500 people in 1967.[35] The company supplied scientific laboratories around the world with precise measuring instruments. Perkin Elmer won the Queen's Award for Export in 1987. By 1991, however, a world-wide restructuring of Perkin Elmer brought about the closure of the Beaconsfield plant and the removal of production to the firm's factory at Llantrisant, South Wales. The Maxwell Road factory was purchased by Sainsbury's, who opened a new supermarket on the site in 1994.

Eight

Shops and Shopkeepers

In the 18th and 19th centuries, most of Beaconsfield's shops would look like private houses or cottages. The distinction between craftsmen and retail shopkeepers was small and in many cases non-existent. Bread would come fresh from the oven and no separate 'shop' would exist. A butcher would hang his meat and turn his carcasses into joints in a building with no display. Saddlers, tailors and shoemakers would use their workshops for selling. Only grocers, drapers, chemists and ironmongers, although far more craft orientated than they were to become, would have had shops in the modern sense. One guide to the relative prosperity of their businesses was their ability to employ sons, daughters and live-in assistants and the number of domestic servants they kept.

Many of the better-off shopkeepers lived on the north side of London End, where Shepherds Lane provided a convenient rear access to their premises. The closure in 1700 of the *Swan Inn*, on the corner of London End and Shepherds Lane, provided a particularly good development opportunity and the building was converted into five upmarket shops. In 1726, the whole row was insured by the High Wycombe draper, John Hartley, for £1,000. It comprised the premises (from west to east) of John Harding,

baker; Henry Fellows, maltster; John Young, collar maker; Elizabeth Cherry, widow; and Stephen Woodbridge, hairdresser.[1] When the Hartley family sold the property to the local solicitor, Robert Charsley, in 1786, the shops were occupied by Thomas Everett, cooper; Arthur Tredway, shoemaker; Isaac Field, tailor; Matthew Davis, maltster; Lucy Grove, widow; and William Williams, hairdresser.[2] Charsley sold most of the shops to the sitting tenants, but by the 1850s the local butcher, William Mead, had purchased most of them.[3] Although proprietors changed over the years, certain shops continued to sell the same products. The single-storey shop on the corner of Shepherds Lane was for many years a grocery, whilst the premises on the corner of London End was occupied by a family of shoemakers and later by a succession of corn merchants. Number 9 London End was a chemist's from the 1840s until modern times and 11 London End was owned and run by an ironmonger from the 1780s, developing into a cycle dealer's by 1910 and more recently into a toy shop. At the turn of the 20th century, most of these shops were bought up by Sir Edward Lawson, later Lord Burnham, and remain part of the Hall Barn Estate.

54   *The former Swan Inn, 1-11 London End.*

Tallow Chandlers

Before the days of gas and electricity, candles were a vital commodity and the tallow chandler was often the wealthiest man in an English market town. In 1681, William Cole, chandler of Beaconsfield, was made a trustee in the will of Hugh Butler, the former puritan minister. William Cole lived on the north side of London End in the house later called The Elms, 21 London End, where his business benefited from the rear access from Shepherds Lane. Cole was a non-conformist and registered his house for religious meetings at the Quarter Sessions in 1693. A disproportionate number of Beaconsfield's shopkeepers supported the Congregational Church, suggesting the existence of an informal network of non-conformist businessmen.

William Cole insured his premises with the Sun Insurance Company in 1730:

> William Cole of Beaconsfield Co Bucks
>   tallow chandler and draper   £
> On his dwelling house only brick panelled
>   timber & tiled   100
> Household goods and stock therein only 300
> Workhouse & warehouse adjoining
>   in the yard behind the house brick
>   & tiled   50
> Utensils & stock therein   50
>   _____
>   500[1]

When he died in 1732, William Cole's business passed to William Anthony, who married Susanna Cole in London in the same year. In 1755, William Anthony of Beaconsfield, tallow chandler, was an executor of Joseph Davis, Protestant Dissenting

Minister of Beaconsfield. William Anthony died in 1763, leaving to his eldest son, John Anthony, his 'messuage or tenement with the appurtenances in which I now dwell in London End'. John Anthony probably rebuilt the house. The increase in its value can be seen by comparing the fire insurance of William Cole in 1730 with that of John Anthony in 1777. What is most notable is the increase in the value of the stock in trade, from £350 to £1,100:

John Anthony of Beaconsfield in Co Bucks	
draper & tallow chandler	£
On his now dwelling house situate	
as aforesaid	400
Household goods therein	100
Utensils & stock therein	900
Warehouse candle house & stable	
adjoining separate	100
Utensils & stock therein	100
Warehouse separate	100
Utensils & stock therein	100
House adjoining & untenanted	150
Stable washhouse adjoining	50
	2000[5]

John Anthony did not have the market all to himself. Also in 1777, Thomas Green of Beaconsfield, a tallow chandler and soap boiler, insured his dwelling house, candle house and stock in trade for £900.[6] Green lived near to Anthony in that part of the former *Kings Head* east of the coach entrance. John Anthony appeared in the 1792 *Universal British Directory* as a draper, but when he died in 1800 he described himself as a gentleman, leaving the handsome sum of £3,000 to his unmarried daughter, Elizabeth. He left his house in London End to his son, William Anthony. This house was briefly let to William Hickey before being purchased by the solicitor John Charsley.

Drapers

John Anthony's drapery business passed to Thomas Anthony, who lived next door to The Elms at 23 London End. His draper's shop at London End was taken over in about 1825 by James Neighbour,

who also acted as an undertaker. The partnership of James and Edmund Neighbour, drapers, was dissolved in 1838.[7] By 1851, their premises were occupied by Thomas and Mary Perrin, a brother and sister from Kent, who ran the drapery shop until 1871. In 1881, the business was run by John Cawsay Lee, draper, with his wife, son, an assistant and one servant. He had come from Shrivenham, where he had been a commercial traveller in the iron trade. By 1891, the shop was occupied by Archibald Cheale, the son of a commission agent from Littlehampton. He maintained the drapery business at London End until 1920 and also opened a branch at Penn Road in the New Town. The draper's shop at 23 London End was continued by C.J. Buxton until 1939, ending a period of 200 years of continuous trading as a drapery.

Thomas Anthony had some serious competition. John Newell, a draper living in Wycombe End, had several children baptised at Beaconsfield from 1809. In 1819 he moved to larger premises at 39 London End, which were later to become Edward Morford's grocery shop. When Newell went bankrupt in 1824, his stock was perhaps too elaborate for a small town:

Genuine and valuable stock of linen and woollen drapery ready made clothes, haberdashery, hosiery and silk goods, by Tarrant and Carter at No 23 Ironmonger Lane, Cheapside, tomorrow, Sept. 7, and following day, at 10 each day, by order of the assignees in bankruptcy of John Newell of Beaconsfield, linen and woollen draper, a bankrupt, removed for the convenience of sale. The linen drapery stock comprises Irish lawns, lawns, French cartibricks, diapers, huccabacks, sheetings, muslins, printed cambrics and furniture, brown hollands, home bleached linens, jeans, handherchiels, shawls, and various other goods. The wool drapery stock consisting of broad cloths, and seconds, coatings, kerserymeres, velveteens, fustians, toilinets, flannels, balnkets, ready made clothes; a general assortment of haberdashery and hosiery, valuable silk goods in sarcents, satins, poplins, Persians, and lustres, Barcelona handkerchiefs, ribands, silk shawls and numerous other articles.[8]

Newell was succeeded as a draper at 39 London End by George Osborne, and then by Thomas Constable who, in 1841, had an assistant and one servant. By 1851 the former draper's shop was occupied by Joseph Owen, grocer.

In 1851, a Charles Jones, born in Wendover, was running a linen and woollen drapery and clothes warehouse at 5 London End. Living with him were his wife and brother and one servant. The brother was later a draper in London. He and his successors did not stay in the drapery business for long. The shop was later occupied by Theophilus Soundy and later by Charles Richard Haslam. The drapery was then taken over by Walter Blackwell from Princes Risborough, who had previously worked in a large drapery store at Chipping Norton. Blackwell ran the business until the late 1890s. Early photographs of London End show his advertisement, painted onto the white cement render of the building. He was a draper, tailor and outfitter and also sold boots and shoes. From 1911-15 this shop was occupied by Charles Giles, outfitter.

There was certainly a trend in the 19th century for shopkeepers to diversify. From the 1840s, George Hatton and then William Neve ran a drapery and grocery store in the island premises in the Market Place. Neve was from Wittersham in Kent, and in 1861 was helped by his mother and two live-in assistants. By 1871 he had taken his business to the larger market afforded by Richmond, Surrey. In the late 19th century it was Uriah Day who took over the island shop at the head of Aylesbury End, who emerged as the most successful grocer and draper.

Tailors

Until the late 19th century, when mass-produced clothes became available, most respectable families bought material from the draper and made their own clothes. Only the better-off would have their clothes made by a tailor or dressmaker in the town. The poor probably wore second-hand clothes, altered or repaired by seamstresses living in cottages away from the centre of the town. The leading Beaconsfield tailor in the 18th century was Isaac Field, who occupied part of the former *Swan Inn*. He appeared in the rate books in the 1760s, and brought his son James Field into the business in 1789. In that year, James Field purchased the freehold of the shop from the solicitor Robert Charsley for £250. The transaction also included the shop on the west, occupied by Arthur Tredway, shoemaker.[9] Isaac Field, tailor, died in 1803 at the advanced age of ninety-six. When James Field died in 1826, aged 77, his widow Anne carried on the business as a milliner and dressmaker.

Another upmarket tailor was William Stevens. He was from Gloucestershire but his wife was born in Beaconsfield. In 1841 Stevens was living in Aylesbury End, near to the *White Hart Inn*. He formed a brief partnership with John Snell but by 1851 his son Charles was in the business and Snell had his own shop in the Broadway, opposite the *George Inn*. In that year, Stevens was living in a part of the former *Kings Head Inn*, later numbered 17 London End. Some time before 1861, William Stevens moved to 37 London End, where his sons Charles and Henry were also tailors. The business did not thrive and the two sons moved away, one becoming a railway clerk and the other a gardener. Stevens died before 1881, when his daughter Catherine, a dressmaker, had the shop. When she moved on to cheaper premises, this shop was incorporated into Morford's grocery store. In 1891, Catherine Stevens was living in part of the former *Bull Inn* at the far end of London End. She was still a dressmaker but took in lodgers, two of whom were teachers at the National School. By 1861, John Snell had taken over the premises of his former partner at 17 London End. Snell was from Cornwall, but his wife, Eliza, herself a dressmaker, was born in Beaconsfield. He was a trustee of the Wesleyan Church in Wycombe

55   *Edward Morford's grocer's shop, 39 London End, c.1908.*

End. Their son Edward was also employed in the business, before setting up as a tailor in Clerkenwell. John and Eliza Snell remained at 17 London End until the 1880s, when they moved to a smaller shop on the opposite side of London End, near the *Old Swan Inn*. Snell's business probably suffered as Uriah Day and Walter Blackwell developed what were essentially small department stores.

Shoemakers

When boots and shoes were made entirely by hand, there were several shoemakers in a market town. In Beaconsfield in 1792 there were Richard Hare and George Slatter, as well as Arthur Tredway, who was also a draper. Few shoemakers had such imposing premises as Tredway, who lived on the corner of London End and Shepherds Lane from 1787. He was able to raise £140 in 1789 to buy the freehold of this house, and the newly built shoemaker's

workshop, from the solicitor Robert Charsley.[10] When Arthur Tredway died in 1834 the business passed to his son William, but the freehold of the shop was sold in 1836 to William Mead, butcher. No Beaconsfield shoemaker established a shoe factory of the sort that were developing in Chesham at this time. Indeed, only three shoemakers are recorded in 1851 as employing journeymen, one man in each case. As mass-produced shoes came on the market, they were sold by outfitters like Walter Blackwell and Uriah Day.

Grocers

Provisions were normally bought at the market, but during the 19th century, specialist grocers emerged to sell the wider range of branded goods now becoming available. The better grocers would stock particular lines to the taste of their more prosperous clients and deliver to their houses. Josiah Wade ran a high-class grocery business from the shop later numbered 5 London End from about 1800. After his death in 1811, the business was continued until the 1840s by his widow, Mary Wade.

Another prosperous grocer was John Crick, who started his business at 28 London End in about 1800. He died in 1837, but the grocery store was taken over by his son John, and then by their former assistant Joseph Marshall. Joseph Marshall died in the 1890s and his widow Emma ran the shop. The yard behind their shop, accessed from Windsor End, is still called Marshall's Yard.

Another respectable grocery store was run by Joseph Owen at the house later numbered 39 London End. There is a memorial at the Congregational Church to his wife, Martha, who died in 1861. In 1869, Owen became Beaconsfield's postmaster and moved to 5 London End, employing Edward Morford to run the grocery shop in his place. Morford was also a Congregationalist and came from Staines, where his father had a draper's business. In 1871, Morford was still in Staines, but his young wife Emma was running the Beaconsfield shop with an assistant and one servant. After Emma's death in 1877, Edward Morford married Annie Eliza Platt, formerly a milliner at Theophilus Soundy's drapery at 5 London End. In 1891, when Morford's son Frank needed training, he was apprenticed to Messrs Carrick and Coales, drapers and outfitters in Uxbridge, a shop that dwarfed any in Buckinghamshire. By 1901, Edward Morford had four sons working in his business. He was a member of Beaconsfield U.D.C. and a supporter of the Congregational Church. When Edward Morford died in 1914, the grocery shop was continued by his son Edward.

56   *Warren's grocery shop, Aylesbury End, 1908.*

William Fowler was born in Kingsey in Buckinghamshire and established his grocery business north of the *White Hart Inn*, Aylesbury End, some time before 1841. By 1851 he employed one assistant and one domestic servant. Fowler was a Congregationalist and chairman of the Local Board of Health. His son George Fowler joined the business, but it was his younger son, Herbert Fowler, who took over from his father in about 1883. Herbert Fowler was chairman of the Beaconsfield Gas Company and an early member of the U.D.C. By 1907, the Fowlers' grocery shop had been taken over by Archibald Warren. When the shop was extended in 1913 it took in the former stable block belonging to the *White Hart Inn*. The original 18th-century façade of the shop was faithfully copied on the extension to the south.[11]

Perhaps the most successful grocery business was that established in the island premises in the Market Square. In 1841, part of this shop was run by a locally born hairdresser named George Hatton. By 1851, Hatton described himself as a draper and grocer and had two live-in assistants and one servant. By 1861, Hatton had been replaced by Jane Neve and her son William, both born in Kent. They described themselves as drapers and grocers, and employed two assistants. In 1862, the Neves were succeeded by Uriah Day, a Congregationalist who came from Shrivenham in Berkshire, and had been a grocer in Wallingford. In 1864, Day described himself as 'grocer, draper, clothier and dealer in British wines'. In 1895, he was a 'a general draper and outfitter, family grocer and agent for W. & A. Gilbey, wine and spirit merchants. His sons Henry, Augustus and Frederick all worked in the grocery business. His wife was a milliner and his daughters Florence and Evelyn worked as dressmaker and drapery assistant respectively. In 1871, Day employed two female domestic servants, who probably released members of the family from domestic duties whilst the business expanded. His shop was continued by

Augustus Day, who was a member of the U.D.C. and secretary of the Reading Room. A sign of things to come was the establishment by 1907 of a branch of the International Tea Company in part of the former boys' school in London End. By 1920, it had moved to the New Town, where the multiple stores were to have a much bigger impact.

Butchers

Meat was usually sold from covered areas in market places, sometimes called butchers' shambles. This was probably the origin of the island premises at the head of Aylesbury End, which later housed Uriah Day's grocery store. Many butchers raised their own animals and therefore rented or owned farmland. Robert Bates occupied the large house at 27 London End, later called Norfolk House or The Yews. In 1736 he was the tenant of the grazing land

57 *Warren's Grocery Store after restoration in 1913.*

58   *The butcher's shop of K. Blinko & Son, 33 London End, 1908.*

between Hall Place and Hall Barn.[12] He probably had connections in London and drove his cattle to market in the capital. When he died in 1754, his business was taken over by Jonathan Druce. In 1779, Druce insured his property with the Sun Insurance Company for £450. His adjoining slaughterhouse was valued at £70.[13] The butcher's house was later bought by Robert Crook of Hall Place and passed to his son-in-law, Dr Nathaniel Rumsey.

From 1790-1850 another prosperous butcher, George Gregory, occupied a large timber-framed house on the corner of Windsor End, backing on to the churchyard. This building was later rebuilt by Sir Edward Lawson and for many years housed the Capital and Counties Bank, later Lloyds Bank. Gregory's main competitor was William Mead, who from 1792 occupied the shop later numbered 9 London End. These premises included a slaughterhouse on Shepherds Lane. Mead died in 1801 at the early age of 33, but his business was continued by his widow Mary until her death in 1825. In 1836, their son

William Mead bought the neighbouring shops of Arthur Tredway, shoemaker, and John Field, tailor.[14] Like his father, William Mead died young in 1841. There is a monument to him at the Congregational Chapel, Aylesbury End. By 1842, his shop in London End was occupied by William Thomas Butler & Son, chemists, druggists and stationers. Butler was an old-established chemist from High Wycombe and had been party to Mead's purchases of 1836. William Mead's widow Mary sold her Beaconsfield property in 1857, by which time her son William Mead was farming in Abingdon.

In the second half of the 19th century the leading butchers in Beaconsfield were the Blinko family. William Blinko rented a butcher's shop and slaughterhouse at 33 London End from the 1820s. It was later run by his son Henry Blinko, who died in 1901. When Henry's son William died in 1905, the business was continued by his widow Kate, and sons Alfred and Bertram. By 1925 their butcher's shop had been taken over by Beale & Froude, who also had a shop in the New Town.

Perhaps the best-remembered butcher's shop is that of the King family, who opened their shop at 3 London End, in about 1877. William Garrett King was a member of the Local Board of Health. He was succeeded at London End by his daughters Janet and Sarah and the business continued right through into the 1950s.

Bakers

Given the capacity and efficiency required of a baker's oven, bakeries tended to remain in the same premises, despite changes of ownership of the business. Bakers often came from milling families or coupled their businesses with that of a corn chandler. When the former *Swan Inn*, London End, was converted into shops, in about 1700, one of the units was taken by a baker named John Harding. His landlord, John Hartley, insured the building for £100.[15] John Harding continued in business at London End until the 1760s.

Another well-to-do baker was Nathaniel Charsley, brother of the solicitor Robert Charsley, whose premises in Aylesbury End were insured for £100 in 1777.[16] He later moved his bakery business to the house now numbered 16 London End. When he died in 1831 he left a large portfolio of property in the town, including the bakery then occupied by his grandson, Thomas Weedon. These premises are now occupied by Pizza Express.

Part of the Market Place, the island premises at the head of Aylesbury End, was for many years a bakery. This was occupied successively by Thomas Brooks, Stephen Tredway and William Blinko. By 1901, George Blake, baker, was living over this shop in the Market Place with two journeyman bakers. His bakery was fondly remembered by Kathleen Day, whose father Augustus Day had the grocery business next door.[17]

Eli Chapman had set up as a baker at 11 Windsor End, by 1861. His premises were taken over by William Blake, another supporter of the Congregational Church. After his death in

59 *E. Blake & Sons, Church Side Model Bakery, 1908.*

1893, his widow Louisa ran the shop in Windsor End. Blake's premises were rebuilt in 1908 as the Church Side Model Bakery.

Bakers were generally locally born and few had assistants or kept domestic servants. One exception to this was Berkshire-born Arthur Brookman, who in 1881 was baker's man to Arthur Stevens in Wycombe End. By 1883 he had set up on his own at 41 London End, in premises formerly occupied by George Lawrence, baker. In 1891 Brookman advertised as a corn dealer, wholesale and retail confectioner (wedding cakes etc.) at The Restaurant, High Street. He had two live-in assistants and two servants and, in 1901, one assistant and two servants. The business was later run by George Goddard, and then by G. Newman. In 1958 the shop was called Ye Old Beaconsfield Bakery by the proprietor, Arthur Newman.

Chemists

Beaconsfield supported only one chemist for most of the 19th century. In 1830 Jesse Dutton, chemist and druggist, was in business at Wycombe End, but did not stay in the town. In 1841 Henry Soulby, a 25-year-old chemist, was living in London End. He was probably an employee of William Thomas Butler, chemist, of High Wycombe, who established a branch at 9 London End, at about this time. Butler had a business relationship with William Mead, the former owner of these premises. By 1847 the business was in the hands of Henry Allnutt, whose father was a grocer in High Wycombe. In 1854, Allnutt & Co. were described as booksellers, stationers, printers, bookbinders, chemists and druggists, a mix of trades common to chemists in most market towns. By 1861, Allnutt had a live-in assistant, Arthur Devereux, who was to run the business for Allnutt from 1869-91. Allnutt himself moved to Windsor, where in 1871 he was a veterinary surgeon with four servants. Devereux was succeeded after

1891 by Charles Edward Hanslow, who ran the business until 1907. In that year Beaconsfield enjoyed the services of two chemists, for Arthur White, chemist, was living in Windsor End. By 1911, however, White had moved into 9 London End, Hanslow having set up as a stationer in Wycombe End. The chemist's shop was later run by Edward Stonnell and Albert Tidy, but from 1911 there was competion from Rupert Brooke, chemist, in the New Town. The former chemist's shop in London End is now a superior audio shop belonging to Martin Kleiser.

Ironmongers

The ironmonger was vital to the market town, providing the spades, mattocks, hoes, scythes and other implements of husbandry upon which the agricultural community depended. When George Floyd, ironmonger, died in 1786, his business was continued by John Floyd. That same year, John Floyd, ironmonger, insured his house at Beaconsfield for £200.[18] John Jackson was listed in the directories as both a watchmaker and ironmonger. He bought the shop later numbered

60 *Joseph Jackson's cycle shop, London End, 1908.*

11 London End, and had several children baptised at Beaconsfield in the 1780s. His son John Jackson continued the business and died at Beaconsfield in 1843. The ironmonger's shop was then taken over by Charles Newland who, in 1854, described himself as a furnishing ironmonger, cutler, locksmith, whitesmith and bellhanger. Newland's shop later became a branch of William Down and Co., furnishing and general ironmongers, of 1 Cobourg Place, Bayswater. In 1871, it was run by William Down, a widower, aged 73, and his nephew John, aged thirty-two. The shop was later occupied by Joseph Jackson, cycle dealer and remained a cycle shop until the Second World War.

The Post Office

The *Universal British Directory* of 1792 gives the times of opening of Beaconsfield's post office, but gives neither its location, nor the name of the postmaster. By 1822, the post office was at the house of Thomas Everett, on the north side of London End, near the former *Chequers Inn*. Everett was a cooper and auctioneer as well as postmaster. The mail from London arrived at his house at 11.30 p.m. and departed at 3.45 a.m. A cross-post to Amersham, Chesham and Missenden left at 6 a.m., and returned at 10.30 p.m. In 1842, letters were received from Uxbridge at 6.55 a.m. and despatched to there at 7.45 p.m. When Thomas Everett died in 1846, his widow Margaret Everett took over as postmistress.

By 1850, the post office had moved to the south side of London End, next to the *Saracens Head*. The postmistress was Anne Cox, who, with her sister Mary, ran a dressmaker's business there. In 1854, letters from London and Uxbridge arrived at 6 a.m. and were despatched at 7.15 p.m. Letters from all parts (that is, from the Northern parts of the country) arrived at 1.40 p.m. and were despatched at 3.45 p.m. In 1864, letters from London, Wycombe, Maidenhead and Exeter arrived at 5.41 a.m. and were despatched at 8 p.m., whilst letters from all parts arrived at 4.41 p.m. and were despatched at 6 p.m. Letters were delivered to houses in the town at 7 a.m. and 4.15 p.m.

In 1869 the grocer, Joseph Owen, became Postmaster and moved to 5 London End. He sold up in 1874.[19] The post office then moved to the

61   *The Old Town Post Office, Wycombe End, c.1920.*

home of Robert Henry Robens, further up the street at 30 London End. Robens was succeeded by his daughter, Henrietta, but in the 1890s, the post office was taken over by Mary Elizabeth Whitfield at 18 London End, the large house now known as the Old Post House. In 1899 there were three deliveries to houses in the town, at 7 a.m., 12 p.m. and 7.40 p.m. Miss Whitfield was the postmistress until 1910, after which the post office moved yet again, this time to a shop at Wycombe End near the *Cross Keys Inn*, where the postmaster was Albert L. Gower. A sub-post office was established at Station Parade in the New Town by 1911 and a purpose-built post office was opened near the station in 1926. The Old Town post office was then downgraded to a sub-post office and moved to Windsor End.

The U.K. Electric Telegraph Company began to serve the town in the early 1860s, much to the annoyance of the solicitor John Charsley. He paid a group of labourers to cut down the telegraph pole which had been erected opposite the *White Hart*, claiming that it was a dangerous nuisance. The magistrates did not agree, and fined the workmen 1s., plus £5 for the damage to the post.[20] In 1862, the U.K. Electric Telegraph Company was successfully prosecuted at Aylesbury for obstructing the highway in the parishes of Denham, Iver, Chalfont St Peter and Beaconsfield. It is interesting to note that photographs were used in court. The company soon came to an arrangement with the G.P.O. that telegrams were sent and received from local post offices.

Shops in the New Town

The presence of a full range of shops in the Old Town did not discourage newcomers from opening stores in the New Town. The first commercial development in the New Town was the *Railway Hotel*. The land on the north-east side of the railway bridge was leased by Earl Howe in 1902

for 99 years to Weller's Amersham Brewery. The building had nine bedrooms, and in 1909 concert and billiard rooms were added. There was stabling for five horses, a carriage house and garage, as well as beer and coal sheds. In all it was valued at £4,000 in 1910. The stables were quickly converted to a riding school. In 1911, the publican was Thomas Borlase, aged 47, who was born in Cornwall. He had five servants.

Next to the hotel there were two shops, the Rolfe Brothers' estate agency and the South Bucks Hardware Company on the corner of Warwick Road. On the opposite corner of Warwick Road, two further rows of shops became known as the Broadway, despite the fact that the upper part of Wycombe End in the Old Town was also known as the Broadway. The first was a block of five purpose-built units and the second consisted of six semi-detached houses, built in 1908 and almost immediately converted into shops. In the corner shop was the drapery of Archibald Cheale, a branch of his old-established business at 23 London End. He was to retain the two shops in the town until 1920. By 1925, Cheale's shop had been acquired by a Harold Coad, who boasted that it was 'the nicest shop in Bucks'. The next-door dairy of John Robarts claimed that its milk came from Grange Farm. The next two shops were occupied by Rupert Brooke, chemist, and John Kenneth Flemons, confectioner. The final one of the original six units was occupied in 1911 by Algernon Joiner, fishmonger.

Before the First World War, the houses which had been converted into shops included a florist who had relocated, probably from a hut on the Station Approach, an electrical engineer and a house furnisher. By 1925 there was a ladies outfitter, a florist, an ironmonger (with a branch in Gerrards Cross), a tailor (with a branch in Farnham Common), a grocer, another ladieswear shop and a shoe shop. Of these seven traders, three were from local families. Overall there was little duplication of premises between the Old

62 *The Railway Hotel, c.1910.*

and New Towns. Furthermore there were few traders who had a branch elsewhere.

On the north-west side of the railway bridge, Station Parade was developed by the London estate agents Robinson and Roods and the builder C.E. Gibbings on two of the plots sold by William Baring Du Pre in 1905.[21] They built six shops, each 19ft wide and having a gable end facing east towards the station. The shop by the bridge was occupied by Chapman and Davis, architects. This shop was later taken by Rita, dressmaker, and then by Alfred W. Hitchcock, a builders' merchant.

63 *New shops in Penn Road, 1912.*

64   *Station Parade, 1910.*

Number 2 was occupied by William Poole, greengrocer, but he was soon replaced by Thomas and Frank Froude, builders and ironmongers. Number 3 was rented by Rupert Weller, butcher. The tenant of number 4 was Mrs S.A. Holland, newsagent and sub-post office. Number 5 was Samuel Thorpe, grocer and number 6 was Joseph Nichols, draper. Both Thorpe and Nichols were living above their shops in 1911. Some of these shopkeepers traded for many years, suggesting that the growing population was creating a good demand for their services. At the end of Station Parade, a much larger 43ft-wide site was taken by the London and South Western Bank (later Barclays Bank). Their premises in Gerrards Cross, which are almost identical, were built in 1907. The London and County Bank (later the National Westminster Bank), vacated their premises at 25 London End and opened a new branch on the corner of Reynolds Road and Penn Road in

FRONT ELEVATION .

65   *New offices for A.C. Frost, Burke's Parade, 1908.*

about 1915. This was built on a triangular plot left vacant since the sale of the Du Pre land 10 years earlier. Station Parade features in the early sequences of the 1945 film *Brief Encounter*.

To the south-west of the railway bridge, James and William Gurney gradually developed Burke's Parade, comprising 10 plots extending to the turning into Gregories Road. Development seems to have been in three phases. The first to be built was the premises of estate agent Alfred Cardain Frost, which bear the date '1908' on the drain-water head. Frost was living on the premises in 1911 with his wife, daughter and one servant. The shop is still occupied by the Frost Partnership today. Next was Horace Roberts, haulier and furniture remover, who was also living above the shop in 1911. Then came the Capital and Counties Bank (later Lloyds Bank), a three-storey half-timbered building, designed by Walter Holden, who personally carved the date 1910 on a prominent beam. Holden was to become a partner with the architects Burgess, Holden &

Watson, who had their offices above the bank. Holden also designed the next building in the row, the Burke's Estate Office, built in 1910 for the estate agent Norman William Gurney.[22] He was the son of James Gurney, one of the promoters of the Burke's Estate, and was to become chairman of Beaconsfield U.D.C. Burke's Parade can also be seen in *Brief Encounter*.

N.W. Gurney continued to build elegant three-storey shops designed by Walter Holden all along Station Road, as far as the corner with Gregories Road. These were occupied by Francis Moss, tobacconist, F. Batte, fishmonger, Sidney Holdaway, draper, International Tea Company (relocated from the Old Town by 1920), Eastmans, the multiple dry cleaners and, prominent on the Gregories Road corner, R.W. Mayne, cycle dealer. There were thus the first signs that the shops south of the railway would become more important than those north of it.

On the corner of Gregories Road and Burke's Road, a town hall was built in 1911. Later known

66   *The Capital and Counties Bank and the offices of N.W. Gurney, Burke's Parade, 1912.*

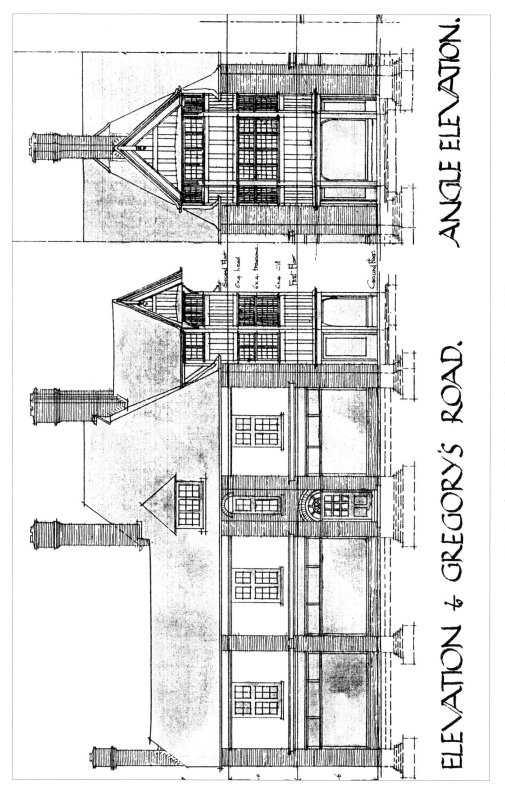

ANGLE ELEVATION.

ELEVATION + GREGORY'S ROAD.

67   New shops in Burke's Parade, designed by Burgess & Myers, 1912.

68 *The Town Hall and Constitutional Club, c.1915.*

69 *Station Road, c.1939.*

70   *The* Beech Tree, *Maxwell Road, 1950.*

as Burke's Hall, this was built as a commercial enterprise, with seating for 300 people. It also had offices for professionals like Hugh Blockley, estate agent, and Percy Hopkins, architect. Also on this corner was Burke's Furnishing Co., later occupied by Edwin Crome, house furnisher. The building with the curved window in front of Burke's Hall was later occupied by WH Smith and then by the Five Ways Café. An elegant Council Chamber was built on the corner of Station Road and Burke's Road in 1915.[23] This was promoted by the developer W.E. Vare and designed by Burgess, Myers & Holden. The same architects designed the shops adjacent to the Council Chamber in 1915.[24] A new picture house was opened in 1927, further south, between Burke's and Grove Roads, with some shops, but not the complete run that

was to appear. Even in 1958 a private house stood at the southern end of this group.

The next element of the shopping centre was the development of the east side of Station Road, starting with a new post office in 1926, and was followed by 'The Highway', a typical London suburban parade, with multiple retailers like Boots the Chemists, which opened in 1933. The development also included the National Provincial Bank, the last bank to arrive in Beaconsfield. The presence of four different banks in the New Town by 1930 is a good indication of the affluence of the area. There were few relocations into these shops from elsewhere in the town, although WH Smith and the International Tea Company moved across the road and a hairdresser moved from Gregories Road.

	NEW TOWN	OLD TOWN	TOTAL
1911	15	35	50
1915	22	31	53
1924	36	29	65
1928	35	29	64
1931	44	32	76
1935	52	34	86
1939	56	37	93

Table 4 *Numbers of shops in the Old Town and New Town., 1911-39.*

In the 1920s and 1930s, the Old Town continued to exploit its position on the Oxford road. A passing trade was valuable for hostelries, garages, cycle dealers and tea rooms. In 1935 the bakers E. Blake & Sons, Windsor End, advertised, 'teas and refreshments'. There was also the Oak Tea Rooms in Market Place and Old House Tea Rooms in London End. Louis Brown, a long-established furniture trader at 26 London End, began to list himself as an antiques dealer in 1924. His shop was visited by Queen Mary. The presence of the hand-weaving workshop of Marie E. Marques in 1935 was a further sign of a visitor-related trade. A simple count of the number of shops and professional and other businesses listed in subsequent directories shows that it was not until the early 1920s that there were more shops in the New Town than the Old Town.

Of the 15 shopkeepers and tradesmen who had moved into the New Town by 1911, none were local and only three were born in Buckinghamshire. Other than the national multiples mentioned above, who saw the town as another London suburb, only a few were part of a West London network, with branches for instance in Northwood. None have been identified with an origin in the nearest Buckinghamshire town of High Wycombe, which was irrelevant to the life of the town, as London and perhaps Uxbridge became increasingly the focus of attention.

It was not until the 1950s that shops extended beyond the Station Road frontage into Maxwell Road. The amount of extra space so added was limited, although names such as Woolworths and Home & Colonial were to appear in the town. A new public house called the *Beech Tree*, designed by Desmond Hall of Burgess, Holden & Watson, was built by Wethereds Brewery on Maxwell Road in 1950.

In the 1960s, the spending power of the employees of Rotax Ltd in Maxwell Road, later replaced by Perkin Elmer, helped the development of the shopping centre. In about 1960 a large house called Penn Croft, 18 Station Road, was demolished and replaced with a row of new shops and flats. At the junction of Gregories and Burke's Road, Burke's Hall was demolished and replaced with a large block of shops and flats called Cardain House, named after the estate agent Alfred Cardain Frost.

It was only with Waitrose's development of the old *Railway Hotel* site in 1982 and Sainsbury's, who had traded in Gregories Road in the 1930s, building their supermarket on the former Perkin Elmer site in 1994, that substantial units were added to the town.

71 *New shops and flats built on the site of Penn Croft, 18 Station Road, c.1960.*

72 *The large block of shops and flats called Cardain House was designed by Desmond Hall in 1960.*

Nine

Churches and Chapels

The parish church of Beaconsfield was so heavily restored in the Victorian period that it is necessary to refer to earlier writers and old prints to get an idea of its original architecture. Sir Stephen Glynne described the church in 1849:

> Beaconsfield Church has a tower with a small spirelet upon it. The church is built of flint and stone like the Abbey of Burnham, which gives its name to this Hundred. In the chancel are some Early English features and in the north aisle some Decorated windows. In the south chapel is an altar tomb of freestone of good design, and there is some excellent woodwork.[1]

An 1855 drawing of the church shows the nave, with three clerestory windows under a shallow-angled roof. The chancel, lit by a five-light lancet window, has a steeply pitched tiled roof. The north aisle is continued alongside the chancel and has three 'decorated' windows on the north wall, and a similar window at its east end. It has a shallow-angled lead roof. The north porch must have had a flat lead roof for it is hidden behind shallow battlements. The buttresses of the tower are faced with alternate blocks of chalk and inlaid flint, in chequerboard fashion. At the top of the tower is a small pointed spire, surrounded by an iron balustrade.[2]

A plausible building sequence can be worked out from this description and the Victorian print. The 'Early English' nave and chancel probably dated from about 1250. The 'decorated' north aisle was perhaps built before 1350 and the north porch and the tower appear to have been added in about 1500.

The Windsor family, who owned Beaconsfield from the Conquest until about 1250, probably built the first church here. Nothing of this period remained by the 19th century, suggesting that the original church was a modest one, gradually replaced by later proprietors. At the division of the Windsor's estate, responsibility for maintaining the church at Beaconsfield descended to the owners of Huntercombe in Burnham. To their credit, they did not give away the right of presentation to any nearby religious house, thereby ensuring that the valuable income from tithes remained at the disposal of the rectors they appointed. What remained of the church before the drastic Victorian restoration must have been largely to their taste, although local families such as the Bulstrodes and Wallers may have extended the side aisles alongside the chancel to provide private burial places.

The rectors of Beaconsfield were often wealthy men in their own right. Richard Capel, rector from

73   *Beaconsfield church, 1855.*

1485-1500, left 40s. in his will 'to the building of the house of the Church of All Hallows'. George Lipscomb took this to be a reference to the rebuilding of the Rectory itself, and he or his typesetter gave the amount of the bequest as £40. In fact Capel made a modest contribution towards building the Church House, which still stands on the north-west side of the churchyard.

This building is remarkably similar in design to the surviving church houses at Haddenham and Long Crendon. It was meant as a public meeting place, a purpose now served by the recently built Fitzwilliam Centre. It was evidently not a success, for it became the stables to Hall Place, Beaconsfield's Rectory from 1869-1975. It has now been converted into two dwellings called Old Timbers and Capel House.

In 1522, John Parye, rector of Beaconsfield, had an income of £25 13s. 4d., making him one of the wealthiest men in the town.[3] The lucrative tithes (a tenth of the parishioners' crops payable to the church) were rarely collected by the rectors themselves. They tended instead to auction the right to collect the tithes to the highest bidder. The 'tithe farmer' would have a fair idea of the value of a given parish's crops and make a bid low enough to ensure a profit. Richard Rawson, incumbent of Beaconsfield from 1525-43, was wealthy enough to rebuild the Rectory. His coat

74   *Capel House, once the Church House of Beaconsfield.*

of arms is carved on one of the original fireplaces. The Rectory was comprehensively restored at the expense of Sir Edward Lawson in 1901.

During the 15th and 16th centuries, the leading residents of the town began to share the burden of maintaining the parish church with the lord of the manor and the rector. Thomas Knight of Beaconsfield made his will on 24 May 1493, making several bequests to Beaconsfield and neighbouring churches:

First I bequeath my soul to Almighty God and to the Blessed Mary his Mother and to all the Saints, my body to be buried in the parish church of Beaconsfield. Item I give to the Cathedral Church of Lincoln 6d. Item to the High Altar of Beaconsfield aforesaid 6d. Item to light of the Holy Cross 4d. Item to the light of St.Nicholas 4d. Item to the light of St.Anne 4d. Item to the light of All Saints 4d. Item to the light of Holy Trinity 2d. Item to the light of Our Lady of Pity 2d. Item to the light of the Resurrection 2d. Item to the light of St.Margaret 2d. Item to the light of St. John the Baptist 2d. Item to the light of the Chapel of St.Mary in the churchyard of the parish church of Beaconsfield 4d. Item to the light called the Torch Light 3s.4d. Item to the light of St.Catherine 2d … Item to Burnham church 13s.4d. Item to the churches of Wooburn and Little Marlow each 3s.4d, Item to Hedsor church 2s.6d.

Normally, candles were lit in front of the altars in the church at the festivals associated with the relevant saints. It is difficult to imagine this number of altars in Beaconsfield church. Thomas Knight made a particularly generous bequest for the maintenance of the 'Torch Light', perhaps lighting the path to the church in winter.

The Chapel of St Mary in the churchyard may have been a chantry chapel, supported by local tradesmen, where a priest could be employed to say masses for departed members. Joan Waller made provision for her own salvation in 1522, leaving £6 for a priest 'to sing for my soul and my husband's one whole year'. Similarly, Walter Bulstrode in his will of 1526 left 10 marks a year 'to be taken from my lands for 80 years for a chantry for my wife and myself in Beaconsfield'.

The Bulstrode family had their own burial place within the parish church. Sir William Bulstrode made his will in 1520, desiring to be buried in St Anne's aisle, near his father and mother. 'Whereas my brother was minded to bestow £20 on our tomb in St Anne's aisle, I will that £20 be bestowed for me.' He added a codicil to his will in 1526, reserving £20 out of his goods 'to the building of the aisle of Trinity in the Church'. In the south

75 *The Old Rectory, 1889.*

Old Rectory House, Beaconsfield, 1889.

chancel aisle is a large table tomb with the arms of Bulstrode carved on the base. The top slab has indents of brasses of a man in armour, a woman and three sons and two daughters. There is an earlier tomb with a stone canopy, probably of a Bulstrode, which once stood on the south side of the chancel. It was later moved to the north wall of the chancel where it takes the place of an Easter sepulchre. It is enthusiastically described in the report of a visit to the church by the Bucks Archaeological Society in 1907:

> By far the finest work in the church is the Bulstrode monument of the 15th century, now recessed in the north wall, but which would seem to have been formerly in the south chapel. This is an altar tomb with canopy, in Purbeck marble, which has been robbed of its brasses. The matrices indicate that on the dexter side was a man praying, a label issuing from his mouth, and four sons. On the sinister his wife and three daughters, a label also from her mouth. Below them, on another plate, an inscription. Above the figure was what may have been the Blessed Virgin with the Infant or the crucified Saviour. Four detached shields.[4]

The Waller family also took an active interest in the church. In 1522, Joan Waller of Beaconsfield left 20s. towards building the steeple. At this date the terms 'tower' and 'steeple' were interchangeable. The project to rebuild the tower had obviously stalled for, in 1545, Robert Waller of Beaconsfield also left 20s. towards the repair of the steeple, 'to be paid when the workmen work on it'. The Wallers had the right of burial in the north chancel aisle where there are several fine floor slabs to their memory. By the 17th century, only the Wallers of Gregories had access to this burial place. The branch of the family from which sprang the poet Edmund Waller did not have automatic access to this vault. Robert Waller, the poet's father, who died in 1617, requested to be buried 'in the churchyard among the poor, deeper than usual'. In 1631, Margaret Waller of Beaconsfield, spinster, desired 'to be buried at nine o'clock at night in the little chancel or chapel within the church of Beaconsfield which belongeth to my cousin Waller'. Even the poet, Edmund Waller, who died in 1687, was buried in the churchyard, his family delaying building a monument over his grave until 1700.

The Rector at Loggerheads with his Congregation

As well as regarding the parish church as their private mausoleum, Beaconsfield's leading families were determined that their family pews should also be as comfortable and prominent as possible. At an inspection of Buckinghamshire parish churches in 1637, it was reported that the pews in Beaconsfield church belonging to 'Mr Waller of the Town' and 'Mr Waller of Gregories' were too high.[5] Surviving correspondence from this time between the rector of Beaconsfield, Dr John Andrewes, and the Diocesan authorities, shows that the Wallers and other prominent families were resisting the reforms then being introduced by Charles I and his Archbishop of Canterbury, William Laud. In a letter of 14 July 1634, Andrewes complained that:

> They use to keep brabblings and janglings in our church, about the election of officers, and their accounts, and every base matter. Yea and to keep musters or (at the least) showing of arms in our churchyard, contrary to the canons … Divers use to gad from our service on Sundays to hear puritanical sermons in other parishes, contrary to the laws … Few or none come to church any Holy Day in all the year. Nay, the churchwardens themselves are seldom there, on those days … Many sit at Divine Service with their hats on and some lye along in their pews, their heads covered, even at the Litany and the Ten Commandments … Many do not kneel at prayers; nor bow at the Glorious Name of our Lord Jesus, nor stand up at the Creeds, nor at Gloria Patri … The churchwardens, though I have read the statute of Prim. Eliz. (which commands them to take 12d. a piece of all such as absent themselves from Divine Service), and though I have publicly charged them to put it in execution, yet they neither will nor dare to do it …[6]

The reference to keeping musters in the churchyard refers to John Hampden, one of the wealthiest men in Buckinghamshire and later to be a prominent voice in Parliamentary opposition to Charles I. In a letter of 27 October 1634, Sir Nathaniel Brent, Vicar General to Archbishop Laud, reported that:

> Mr Hampden of Hampden hath been with me who was presented in the Metropolitan Visitation for holding a muster in the churchyard of Beaconsfield and for going sometimes from his own parish church. He hath given so much satisfaction for that which is past and so much assurance of his willing obedience to the laws of the Church hereafter that I desire no presentment against him.[7]

John Andrewes died in 1636. It is doubtful whether his successor, the Rev. George Ashton, was such an enthusiast for the established church. Ashton was appointed by his father, William Ashton, with the approval of the patron, Sir Sampson Dayrell. This suggests that William Ashton, even before the death of John Andrewes, had paid the Dayrells a sizable sum of money for the right to make the next appointment to the Rectory.

The English Civil War

George Ashton must have been alarmed when, in January 1642, the trained bands again mustered at Beaconsfield, for on this occasion it was a prelude to civil war. Although protagonists like John Hampden had political ambitions, they drew their support from ordinary people by championing the Protestant religion, supposedly under threat from a King with a Catholic wife. Most of the residents of Beaconsfield would have approved of the muster, sanctioned as it was by both houses of Parliament, but Nathaniel Tomkins, brother-in-law of Edmund Waller the poet, thought differently. He wrote from Beaconsfield on 18 January 1642 to a friend in London:

> Here is tomorrow a meeting in this town of the Justices and of the trained bands (with their supplies) from several Hundreds in these Chiltern parts, by order from the two houses of Parliament, which is not only readily obeyed, but officiously, though it be the first (I think) that hath so come in many ages not issuing from his Majesty nor his Privy Council. That both houses should thus agree in these new ways I cannot but marvel …[8]

As the nation stumbled into civil war, the puritans amongst the population of Beaconsfield at first welcomed the Parliamentary soldiers who passed through the town. They relished their tales of removing altar rails and ripping up priests' vestments in each parish church on their march. Indeed, it is highly likely that the more zealous townsmen of Beaconsfield had already banished these symbols of Laudian policy before the soldiers arrived. As the Civil War progressed the rector, George Ashton, must have found his position in Beaconsfield increasingly difficult. With ever more Parliamentary soldiers in the town, excited by red-hot preachers promising a new route to salvation, only the need to protect his tithe income would have induced him to stay in the Rectory. Finally, in 1646, his living was sequestered by Parliament and he was replaced by Hugh Butler, who remained the minister until 1660.

The Restoration

In 1660, Charles II was restored to the English throne and many of the ministers who had 'intruded' during the Civil War were removed. Hugh Butler was 'ejected' from the Rectory of Beaconsfield, but he evidently stayed in the district. Richard Baldwin of Wiltons, a gentleman, making his will in August 1661, left to 'Mr Butler, lately minister of Beaconsfield, £10 to buy him mourning'. Hugh Butler was one of three ejected ministers licensed to preach in private houses at Uxbridge under the Declaration of Indulgence in

1672. Butler's daughter Elizabeth married Henry Child of Coleshill. Coleshill was a detached part of Hertfordshire and therefore an attractive place to live for non-conformists who might otherwise be persecuted by the Buckinghamshire J.P.s. When Hugh Butler died at Winchmore Hill in 1682, he appointed three notable non-conformists as his executors. These were George Swinhow, another ejected minister who was living at Woodrow High House; John Biscoe, a member of a strongly puritanical family from West Drayton in Middlesex, and William Cole, the tallow chandler from Beaconsfield, whose descendants were prominent supporters of the Congregational Church in Beaconsfield in the 18th century.

At the Restoration in 1660, the Rev. George Ashton, who had been forced to leave Beaconsfield in 1646, was reinstated as rector of Beaconsfield. He died there in 1668. His successor, Samuel Gardner, was appointed by the patron, Walter Hanford, but he was forced to resign in 1673 when Hanford sold the right to appoint the rector to Richard Robinson of Maidenhead.[9] Robinson immediately appointed his son, Philip, to the Rectory. In 1701, Robinson sold the Rectory to Christopher Newell, son of William Newell of Stokenchurch.[10] Christopher Newell was appointed to the Rectory on Robinson's death in 1704. This cycle of nepotism was finally broken when the right to appoint the rector

was purchased in 1707 by the President and Scholars of Magdalen College, Oxford.[11] At this time, Oxford colleges were buying up livings in order to provide an adequate income and suitable status for their Fellows.

The Religious Census of 1851

During the incumbency of John Gould, 1818-67, some significant alterations were made to the church. He took down the galleries and removed the old triple-decker pulpit, which had 'a bulky canopy, and a most capacious reading pew, with a corresponding enclosure for the parish clerk'. John Gould made a commendably thorough return for the Religious Census of 1851. He gave his income from tithes and glebe land as £871 19s. 8d. This was a first-class living and placed the rector amongst the richest men in the town. His congregation on the morning of 30 March was 250, exactly the same as the Congregationalists in Aylesbury End.[12]

In 1857, Magdalen College, possibly looking for an alternative Rectory, bought Hall Place, the large house to the west of the churchyard. This house had been a boys' school for more than 50 years and was purchased by the college from Edward Thomas Bradford.[13] John Gould and his family, however, remained at the existing Rectory. In 1863 his sister, Hussy, who probably taught at the Free School, instructed the schoolmaster to close the school on hearing that smallpox had broken

	Morning	scholars	Afternoon	scholars	Evening	Total
Church of England	250	70	100	70		490
Congregational	250	30	200	34		514
Methodist	84	70	136	68	176	534
Total	584	170	436	172	176	1538

Table 5 *Numbers attending religious services in Beaconsfield, 30 March 1851.*

76   *Beaconsfield church after its restoration in 1869.*

out nearby in Factory Yard. The treasurer, G.A. Charlsey, wrote formal letters of objection to the rector and got the school board to censure her. The school nevertheless moved for the summer to a large building in John Spring's builder's yard in Windsor End.

When John Gould died in 1867, he was replaced by Samuel Bowles, a veritable new broom. Bowles wrote to the President of Magdalen College in September 1867, demanding a new Rectory and funds for improvements:

> That which appears to me to be in the whole the best plan and one which I thought had your certain approval and the consent generally of the College meeting in May: that Hall Place be the new Rectory subject to the payment of a certain amount of quit rent and the old Rectory and premises remaining as now the Rector's freehold, to be adapted as he sees fit to purpose a school and other objects of parochial usefulness. Taking into consideration all the circumstances of the place – the state of ruin and decay everything has been allowed to fall into – a house neither wind or water tight requiring a very large outlay to make it really tenantable; the church absolutely demanding immediate restoration; no school building whatsoever and no dilapidations recoverable. It seems that the

Rector coming to this state of things may fairly ask for an unusual amount of liberal dealing from the College as patrons of the living.[14]

The Rev. Bowles employed his brother-in-law, the architect Henry Woodyer, to address these problems. Woodyer had designed several new buildings at Eton College and had already 'restored' Hambleden church.[15] All but the tower of Beaconsfield's medieval church was taken down and rebuilt. The nave was extended by two bays, pushing the chancel eastwards beyond the north and south aisles. Above the arcades, the clerestory was rebuilt with five pairs of 'decorated' windows on either side. The new windows in the north and south aisles were in the 'Perpendicular' style. The only portions reused were three bays of arcading at the west end of the nave and some of the window jambs in the south aisle. A 15th-century piscina was reset in the south chapel. Most of the monuments to the leading families were saved and repositioned in the new church.

Despite his responsibility for the state of the old church, the Rev. John Gould was commemorated by a stained glass window at the east end of the chancel. This fine window depicts the crucifixion and was supplied by John Hardman & Co. of Birmingham. Hardman also supplied the glass in the east window of the south aisle, given in memory of Henry Reginald Sykes of Harrias Farm. The pulpit and font were carved by Matilda Charsley and given in memory of her parents, John and Catherine Eliza Charsley.

As the work of restoring the church progressed, the rector and his architect turned their attention to Hall Place. The third storey, probably added in about 1800 to provide dormitory accommodation for the school, was removed and replaced with a hipped tile roof. A row of five dormer windows was provided to light the attic rooms. The south-facing room chosen as the rector's study was lined with 17th-century panelling, possibly using wood from the box pews removed from the old church. The

77   *The interior of the church after the 1869 restoration.*

78   *Hall Place, purchased by Magdalen College, Oxford, as a replacement Rectory, 1857.*

former schoolroom in the west wing was divided into a servants' hall and a butler's pantry.

The third part of the Rev. Bowles' improvement plan was the building of a new National School. The site immediately south of the old Rectory was given by the rector and partly by John Hargreaves, owner of Hall Barn. The new buildings, designed by Henry Woodyer, were opened in 1873. It was not until 1884 that Bowles turned his attention to the restoration of the church tower. The small spire and the surrounding iron railings were taken down and the prominent pinnacles built up from the existing octagonal buttresses. The wooden south porch was added in 1886, after Bowles' death. An inscription inside the porch explains:

> This porch was set up in the year 1886 to the glory of God and in loving memory of his servant Samuel James Bowles, Priest M.A., some time Fellow of Magdalen College Oxford, Rector of Beaconsfield, by whose care this church was restored and for the most part rebuilt.

Another interesting rector was George Albert Cooke, 1896-9, who had been a curate in Oxford and lecturer in Hebrew before coming to the town. Cooke left a diary giving an account of the church and the town in the period of his incumbency.[16] He resigned in 1899 to become private chaplain to the Duke of Buccleuch, and hold various appointments in Scotland, before being appointed Oriel Professor of the Interpretation of Scripture in 1908 and, in 1914, Regius Professor of Hebrew at Oxford. Cooke was succeeded in 1900 by Archibald Commeline, whose wife set up a branch of the womens' suffrage society.

The Congregational Church

Given Beaconsfield's strategic position during the Civil War and the number of soldiers passing through and billeted in the town, the residents must have been exposed to the full range of religious and political ideas which were debated at the time. The rector, George Ashton, was forced to

leave and was replaced by Hugh Butler, described by Calamy as 'a solid divine and very grave person'. This is probably a code for a good Presbyterian but an uninspiring preacher. When George Ashton regained the Rectory at the Restoration in 1660, Butler remained in the district. His daughter married Henry Child of Coleshill and he was preaching in Uxbridge in 1672. Butler died at Winchmore Hill in Coleshill in 1682.

There were several ejected Presbyterian ministers in the district besides Butler. Edmund Terry, who had been minister at Amersham, lived at the house of Mrs Fleetwood at the Vache, Chalfont St Giles. George Swinhow, formerly minister of St Leonards, lived at Woodrow in Amersham. As several Beaconsfield men were regularly fined at the Quarter Session for not attending church, they were probably frequenting the services given by these ministers. There were also Baptist meetings in the neighbouring parishes, and several leading Quakers lived in the Amersham hamlet of Coleshill. This was a detached part of Hertfordshire and therefore beyond the jurisdiction of the Buckinghamshire authorities who might have enforced Charles II's growing body of legislation against non-conformists.

Following the 'Glorious Revolution' of 1688 and the accession of William of Orange to the English throne, religious toleration was secured. Many dissenting groups who had kept a low profile during the reigns of Charles II and James II now met openly. In the Quarter Sessions of 1693, the homes of William Cole, grocer, and Thomas Briars, carpenter, both of Beaconsfield, were listed as public meeting houses. In 1697, the house of Samuel Clarke of Beaconsfield, a gentleman, was similarly registered and the homes of William Woods and John Anthony were added to the list in 1698 and 1701.

At the visitation of 1706, the rector of Beaconsfield, Christopher Newell, admitted that there was a Presbyterian meeting house in the town, 'but few or no dissenters, except a Quaker or two'. At the next visitation in 1709, his curate, George Cave, was more candid. He estimated the population of Beaconsfield at 550, or 146 families, of which two families were Quakers, and five were Presbyterians. 'These meet every Lord's Day, about 100 in number (many from the neighbouring parishes) Samuel Clarke teacher'.[17] Samuel Clarke was a well-educated and wealthy man who lived only a stone's throw from the Rectory at the house now known as Hall Place. There is some evidence that Clarke ran a school here, possibly a college for Presbyterian ministers. Clarke's congregation met at the Bell Barn, which he leased in 1712 from Margaret Woods, widow of William Woods, once the proprietor of the *White Hart*. The *Bell* had, by that date, closed as an inn, but it was situated in London End, east of the *Kings Head*. Samuel Clarke died in 1727, leaving his capital messuage in Beaconsfield to his wife, Rachel. When she died in 1730, she left 40s. a year for 10 years 'to such dissenting minister of the Gospel in Beaconsfield aforesaid for the time being as shall belong to the Christian dissenters called Presbyterians'.

The original aim of the Presbyterians was to build a national structure through which individuals might have a say in the direction of the Church. With the restoration of the Anglican Church in 1660, this aim became increasingly unrealistic and congregations necessarily went their own way. Presbyterians eventually had much in common with the Independents, who also had a meeting house in Beaconsfield by 1725. With the departure of Samuel Clarke, they appear to have joined the Independents, led by the Rev. Joseph Davies.

The Independents, or Congregationalists, met in a barn at Wycombe End belonging to the Wallers of Gregories. The land on which the barn stood was conveyed to trustees in 1730 and additional ground was acquired in 1741.[18] Joseph Davies had powerful support in the town. When he made his will in 1755 he appointed William Anthony of Beaconsfield, a tallow chandler, and

William Collett of Beaconsfield, a gentleman, as his executors. He died in 1763, to be succeeded by the Rev. Abraham Darby, a native of Dudley in the Black Country.

The Rev. Darby was an impressive preacher and attracted good congregations. The meeting house was extended to accommodate the new members. Perhaps the funds came from wealthy backers like James Gallopine, citizen and cooper of London, who owned Whites Farm in the Hertfordshire portion of Beaconsfield. He made his will on 16 December 1763, leaving the following bequest:

> I give unto the minister and elders of the Dissenting Congregation at Beaconsfield in the County of Bucks the sum of £100 to be by them placed out as a fund and the interest thereof from time to time paid out and applied to and for the benefit of the minister of the said Congregation for the time being.

Whites Farm was left to James Gallopine's son, Daniel, but it eventually passed to his son in law Joseph Stevenson, a London grocer. When Abraham Darby died in 1782, the congregation appointed a young man named John Geary as their new pastor. With the support of John Anthony of Beaconsfield, a friend of Robert Raikes, he opened a Sunday School attached to the meeting house. John Geary is said to have had a speech impediment, unusual in a dissenting minister, yet in 1790 he married Joseph Stevenson's daughter, Elizabeth, at Beaconsfield church. The fruitful relationship with the owner of Whites Farm continued, for when Joseph Stevenson himself died in 1799 he left a further sum of £100:

> to the trustees of the Congregation of Protestant Dissenters of Beaconsfield in the County of Bucks whereof my son-in-law John Geary is now pastor on the same terms as the legacy left to the said Congregation in the will of Mr James Gallopine deceased the father of my late dear wife.

79 *The Congregational Church, Aylesbury End, c.1920.*

Not everyone approved of John Geary. In about 1797, some of the congregation left to form a new group meeting at a house in Aylesbury End. This proved so successful that in 1800 they built a new meeting house called Bethesda Church behind cottages on the east side of Aylesbury End. In 1812, the Rev. John Harsant was appointed minister and remained for 46 years. John Geary was left to preside over a dwindling congregation at 'The Old Meeting House'. His son, John Stevenson Geary, also became a dissenting minister, and some members of the 'Old Meeting' hoped that he would succeed his father. In fact, when John Geary died in 1830, the son was passed over and Francis Watts became the minister. Although Watts left in 1838 to teach at Springhill College, he maintained contact with Beaconsfield and eventually advised the congregation to unite with the Bethesda Church in Aylesbury End. In 1851 the rector, John Gould, stated that the chapel was formerly used by the Unitarians, but was now only occasionally used by dissenters of various denominations.[19] The Old Meeting House was later purchased by Sir Edward Lawson and the 'site of Chapel' is listed on the 1910 valuation.[20]

The original Bethesda Church in Aylesbury End is a plain building, 44ft by 22ft with three round-headed windows in each side. Judging from the monuments inside, the Boddy family of schoolteachers were particular supporters. Their memorial plaques include those of Elizabeth Boddy, 1823; Laura Elizabeth Boddy, 1823; William Henry Boddy, 1825; Selina Margaretta Boddy, 1825; and William Boddy, 1832. When he made his return for the Religious Census of 1851, the Rev. John Harsant stated that on the morning of 30 March he had a congregation of 250, plus 30 in the Sunday School. In the afternoon he had the suspiciously round number of 200, plus 34 in the Sunday School, and he claimed to have addressed a further 300 in the evening. Harsant lived at the little house now known as Chapel Cottage, 4 Windsor End, until his death in 1858. The influence of later Congregational ministers was limited as a result of the policy of moving them around the country. Harsant's successor, David Mossop (1858-62), went to Australia and founded Congregational Churches in Queensland. James Duthie (1862-71) bought the land in Aylesbury End in front of the existing church. It was Matthew Henry le Pla, who became the minister in 1871, who built the present Bethesda Church which was opened in 1875 at a cost of £1,500. William Summers (1883-95) was an historian of non-conformity in South Buckinghamshire.[21] John Stay (1895-1908) was the first to occupy the new manse in Lakes Lane. He was Chairman of Beaconsfield U.D.C. in 1907.

Wesleyan Church

The Wesleyan Church at Beaconsfield dates from 1824, when £140 was paid to Isaac Peet, silk weaver, for part of the former ribbon factory in Wycombe End. The original trustees were mostly from High Wycombe, but the list included Thomas Bowler Bovingdon of Penn, who built the Wesleyan Chapel at Winchmore Hill.[22] The Wesleyans at Beaconsfield were determined on a democratic structure and held full meetings of the congregation every three months. In March 1851 their steward, John Snell, reported that the

Wesleyan Reformers' congregation numbered 84, plus 70 Sunday School children. John Snell was a tailor living in the Broadway, in one of the houses backing on to the churchyard. He was one of the trustees appointed under a new trust deed of 1868. He was joined by George Lawrence of Beaconsfield, a grocer; John Vear of Beaconsfield, a gentleman; Edward Spicer of Beaconsfield, a farmer; William Watkins of Beaconsfield, a saddler; John King of Beaconsfield, a husbandman; and John Vear the younger, a chairmaker.[23]

The Wesleyan Reformers remained in Factory Yard, Wycombe End, until 1900, when the present church was built in Shepherds Lane. The Wesleyan Reformers remained independent, even in 1932, when the Wesleyan Methodists and the Primitive Methodists combined to form the Methodist Church of Great Britain.

Primitive Methodist Church

In 1862, a Primitive Methodist Church was built behind the cottages on the west side of Windsor End. The trustees were mostly from High Wycombe and included several chairmakers. The chapel is marked on the Ordnance Survey map of 1880. By 1893, the numbers attending were so reduced and the debt so large that the surviving trustees decided to close the chapel. The building was sold to Sir Edward Levy Lawson.[24]

The Baptist Chapel

As the New Town expanded, the Bucks Baptist Association formed a sub-committee to found a church. They held their first meetings in a garage and then hired the newly built town hall on the corner of Gregories Road and Burke's Road. Their new church in Baring Road was designed in 1914 by Thomas Thurlow, architect, High Wycombe, and opened in 1915. Thurlow also designed the Baptist Chapel in Easton Street, High Wycombe, in 1908.

80   *The Baptist Chapel.*

The Catholic Church

Some wealthy Roman Catholics came to Beaconsfield after 1906, of whom G.K. Chesterton is the best known. Catholic services were held in the concert hall of the *Railway Hotel* during the First World War, partly to meet the needs of Belgian refugees. A church dedicated to St Teresa was started in Warwick Road in 1926. The architect was A.S.G. Butler, best known for his book on Lutyens. He designed the chancel and part of the nave. This was completed and the west tower added in 1939 as a memorial to Chesterton, who died at Beaconsfield in 1936. The architect for the extension was Adrian Gilbert Scott, grandson of the famous Victorian architect.

Ten

Schools

During the 18th century, many well-to-do families sent their children to private boarding and day schools in Beaconsfield. In 1785 James Puddifunt of Beaconsfield, a schoolmaster, insured his house and contents in Beaconsfield for £200.[1] The town was easily reached by coach and was relatively near Eton, for which many of the young men were being prepared. It was perhaps the presence of these private schools which delayed the establishment of a National School in Beaconsfield until a comparatively late date.

One of the earliest of the private boarding schools occupied a large house at the east end of the town, later called The Old House, 68 London End. It was run for many years by John Dubber, schoolmaster, who died in 1815 aged seventy-five. He was succeeded by William Boddy, who was descended from an old-established family of farmers and maltsters in the town. When William Boddy, schoolmaster, died in 1832, his family erected a monument to him in the Congregational Church in Aylesbury End. William Boddy's school was continued by his widow, Elizabeth Boddy, and her assistants Septimus Boddy and Charles Johnstone. There were 31 pupils living there in 1841. Only four had been born in Buckinghamshire and of these

two were farmers' sons. The other 30 had been born outside the county and came from trading or farming backgrounds. By 1851, four former pupils were listed on the census as a tailor's son, a grocer's apprentice, a tea dealer, and a carver and cabinet maker.

In 1854, the school was run by Edward Milner, who advertised it as a 'Classical & Mathematical Boarding and Day School for Gentlemen, High Street'. He had 28 pupils in 1861. By 1867, control of the school had passed to Arthur Denman. He was the son of a sculptor of West Hill Grove, Battersea, and had been an assistant at a school in Braintree before coming to Beaconsfield. His establishment was advertised as the 'Middle Class School'. For 25 guineas a year he offered instruction in reading, writing, arithmetic, bookkeeping, algebra and all else required for a liberal English education. Denman extended the premises in about 1878 and advertised the school in local and national newspapers:

Beaconsfield School, Bucks.
The premises are extensive and have recently been considerably enlarged. The dormitories are spacious and well-ventilated. There is a noble schoolroom, heated by hot water. A large and thoroughly drained gravel play ground, and a level well-kept cricket ground of several acres.[2]

81   *The Old House, London End. The schoolroom is the single storey building on the right and the dormitories are in the tall Victorian wing on the far right.*

In 1881, Denman had no fewer than 57 pupils and employed four assistant masters, a matron and four servants to run the school. Denman found time to enter into local society and was for many years a member of the Local Board of Health. His school closed in the 1890s when part of the house was taken over by the International Tea Company. The building later housed the Old House Tea Rooms and the yard is now the home of Beaconsfield Motors. The schoolroom still stands to the left of the rear yard.

One of the leading schools occupied the large house in Wycombe End called Hall Place. It was run by William Mussage Bradford, rector of nearby Hedsor, who had purchased the house from the executors of Robert Crook in 1818.[3] Lord Granville came to the school in 1823:

At eight years old I was sent to a private school kept by Mr Bradford at Beaconsfield, where I remained five years; a very bad school, and I remember no merit in the master; but it was

very fashionable, and called at the time, as others have been called since, the little House of Lords. A Queen Anne house, with a charming garden, and a broad gravel walk ended by a ha ha, which separated it from the pretty park of Hall Barn … Mrs Bradford was Irish and a virago, but more as with her husband and servants than with us, whom she fed well – not a usual thing in those days – and whom she nursed, when ill, with absolute devotion. The present Duke of Northumberland was at the head of the school, held in much awe by the boys … it was a great mark of favour being called on to clean the master's bird cages, and also to be taken occasionally to Hedsor on Sunday; when he was invited to preach there …[4]

William Mussage Bradford gave evidence in 1836 to a commission in lunacy of Viscountess Kirkwall. He stated that he was tutor to Lord Kirkwall from the year 1795. He lived in Lord Kirkwall's house when the then Earl of Orkney was born. He had taught the Earl of Orkney and his brother at his school at Beaconsfield. He explained that Lady Kirkwall, although living apart from her husband, was in constant communication with her children and, during part of the time took lodgings in Beaconsfield in order to be near them.[5]

William Mussage Bradford died in 1840 and was succeeded both as rector of Hedsor and as master of the school by the Rev. Abraham Youldon. In 1851, Youldon, his wife and one assistant master were running the school with the help of three servants. There were 13 pupils. Rev. Youlden, in an advert appearing in December 1841, indicated that the school prepared young gentlemen for Eton and other public schools. The social background of the pupils reflected this. Two were the sons of a banker who kept 12 servants. Others came from clergy households or went on to be clergymen themselves. Parents also included a solicitor, a West End surgeon and gentlemen of private means who kept significant numbers of servants. The school closed in about 1857 when Hall Place was purchased by Magdalen College, Oxford.

Opposite Hall Place was a house later to be known as Leigh House, which belonged to the Beaconsfield solicitor John Parton. In 1856 he sold the property to James Russell, the former master of the Free School. Russell took in paying pupils, of which there were six in 1861.

Another large boarding school was established at The Yews, 27 London End, which until 1857 had been the home of Beaconsfield's leading surgeon, John Crook Rumsey. In 1861, the house was occupied by Mary Campbell Rumsey and her two sisters, who were running a small boarding school for girls, but by 1871 it was the home of Humphrey Sandwich, physician. By 1881 the house was rented by the Rev. William Chambers, a 'clergyman without cure of souls', who was also running a small school there with four pupils, probably training for the priesthood. Two of these were the sons of clergyman, who kept several servants, and one was the son of a Sheffield ironmaster who kept nine servants.

82   *Hall Place as occupied by the Rev. Bradford's School, c.1820. The top storey was removed when the house became the Rectory in 1869.*

The income that could be obtained from such clerical tuition can be seen from an advert in 1855 when a clergyman, using a Beaconsfield postal box, advertised for pupils at £100 per year below 16 and £120 above, to be housed in his parsonage in the south of Buckinghamshire.[6] In 1891 these premises were temporarily occupied by Arthur Baker, headmaster of the National School, before he moved into a new school house called Edith Lodge in Windsor End. The school at 27 London End was later called Norfolk House by Cecil Marcon, who relocated to a large house in Penn Road in 1907. This building is now part of Alfriston Special School, but still has the date and Marcon's initials over the door.

At least three Beaconsfield houses were used as schools for girls. The first was Wendover House, 24 London End. This was run by Etienne Jean Millet, professor of music, who had two assistant teachers and 13 pupils in 1841. Millet had come to Beaconsfield in 1835 when he married Cecilia Boddy, daughter of William and Elizabeth Boddy. By 1851, Etienne and Cecilia Millet had moved to larger premises at Wycombe End House, where they had four assistant teachers, 29 girl boarders and two servants. When Cecilia Millet died in

83   *The garden of The Yews, 27 London End, used as a boys' school from 1860-80.*

1874 the school was taken over by her niece, Cecilia Boddy, who had 17 pupils in 1881. The last proprietor of the school was Louisa Mallet, who renamed the house as Beechcroft around 1890. The third girls' school was at Leigh House, on the opposite side of Wycombe End, which had previously been the home of James Russell. In 1883, Bertha Mary Harrison advertised her ladies' school at Leigh House, Beaconsfield, in *Kelly's Directory*. She was followed at Leigh House by Selina Bolton and then by the Misses Clarke.

84   *Norfolk House School, Penn Road, 1914.*

85 *Wendover House, London End, used as a girls' school in the 1840s.*

86 *Two girls' schools in Wycombe End: Wycombe End House (the house in the centre with bay windows) and Leigh House (extreme right).*

After 1906, several girls' schools opened in the New Town. The best-known of these was Oakdene, begun in a house of that name in Reynolds Road by Louise Watts. The school moved to purpose-built premises, designed by Burgess, Myers & Holden in 1914. High March School was begun by Edith Warr in a house of that name in Station Road. By 1928, the school had moved to Ledborough Lane. Enid Blyton's daughters attended this school. Lillie le Pla, daughter of the Congregational minister, opened a boarding school in Baring Road in the 1920s. A boys' and girls' school was opened at St John's, Gregories Road, in about 1912, by Lawrence Solomon. In 1916, the school moved into purpose-built premises called New Gregories School in Gregories Farm Lane.[7] The school closed in the 1980s but the building is still there.

Between 1841 and 1891, pupils at boarding schools accounted for five or six per cent of Beaconsfield's population. In 1851, amongst towns in the county, only Winslow approached this figure, although at Stoke Poges three substantial schools accounted for eight per cent of that parish's population. At Beaconsfield, taking the

period as a whole, there were about twice the number of boys than girls. Only by 1901 did it seem that the absence of a railway, coupled with greater competition, led to these small schools declining. For the most part the schools educated the children of the solid middle class, rather than those of the professional classes, a fact best codified in the name of one of the establishments, which was the 'Middle Class School'.

In 1881, pupils at Beaconsfield's boarding schools came from a variety of backgrounds. Several pupils came from farming families with 300 or more acres, employing 10 or more men and keeping domestic servants. Others were children of significant retailers, employing assistants and domestic servants. Some were children of publicans. Notable by their absence were pupils whose fathers were professional men. Of the 17 girls at Miss Boddy's school, 11 have been traced. Their parents included two substantial farmers, a Hammersmith teacher of music and some substantial London retailers, including two from Stamford Street. Two sisters came from Slough, where their father was a wine merchant, keeping four domestic servants. Two had widowed

87   *Oakdene School, designed by Burgess, Myers & Holden, 1913.*

mothers, one possibly a clergyman's wife. By 1891, most of these girls would have been married. A few were living with their parents, who, in most cases, had few domestic servants. One was a book-keeper in her father's grocery shop in High Street, Slough. One was a governess and another possibly a cook to a London West End clergyman. One of the daughters of the music professor, by then retired, was living with him at Ifield in Sussex with a single servant.

The boys at Denman's school had a similar background to these girls. One parent was a surgeon dentist in 1871 and was therefore nearest to the professional classes. His son had become his assistant by 1891. It is not clear whether he had any training other than that of the school at Beaconsfield. The most numerous group amongst the fathers was that of the publicans, but there were several clerks, farmers and retailers. Local fathers included Lord Chesham's farm steward and Lord Boston's head gardener. By 1891 the boys had started work. Some went back to the family businesses being, it is hoped, better equipped to deal with the growing needs of commerce. Some went into new forms of activity. John Hedges, the son of an Aylesbury licensed cake merchant, was recorded as a civil engineer living with his parents. John C. Gurney, son of a Saunderton farmer, was in Gateshead as an analytical chemist's assistant. London was the dominant birthplace of both girls and boys at the schools, with 40 per cent coming from the capital. Only 18 per cent were born in Buckinghamshire, 20 per cent from other Home Counties and six per cent from overseas.

The total number of teachers recorded in the censuses shows that about half were resident in the boarding schools and half lived elsewhere in the town. Most teachers were in Beaconsfield only for a short time. Some were recorded in directories but had disappeared by the time of the next census. Thus, not including the boarding schools, the two sources reveal 50 different individuals while only 43 are recorded in the census. Of

	1851	1861	1871	1881	1891	1901
Boarding Schools	12	8	8	13	11	2
Others	10	8	4	10	10	11
TOTAL	22	16	12	23	21	13

Table 6 *Teachers in Beaconsfield, 1851-1901.*

these 43, only eight were found in more than one census. Only 13 had been born in Beaconsfield and of these, four were pupil teachers and one a music teacher.

National Schools

The first public day school in Beaconsfield was started in about 1840, funded entirely by the Misses Du Pre of Wilton Park. The school was conducted in part of a former ribbon factory in Wycombe End, belonging to William Child, builder.[8] The first schoolmaster appears to have been James Russell, who was living near the former *Bull Inn* in 1841. Anne Hinton was the schoolmistress in 1847. James Russell was living near the school in Wycombe End in 1851 and was still the master in 1854 when a committee was formed to establish a National School for boys, which, if conducted correctly, might attract grants from the Diocese, the National Society and from the Committee of Council of Education.

A Church School Committee was formed, comprising the rector, the Rev. John Gould; his curate, the Rev. Seymour E. Major, who was appointed secretary; John Charsley, solicitor, London End; Edmund Sheppard of Little Hall Barn, who was the treasurer; Etienne Millet, who ran a school for girls in Wycombe End House; William Dawkins of Whites Farm; and John Smith, surgeon, of London End. They arranged to rent the ground floor of the former ribbon factory for £18 per year from William Child, whilst the upper room was rented at £9 per

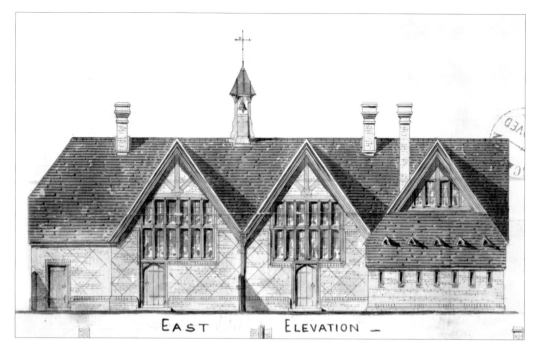

88   *The National School, Windsor End, designed by Henry Woodyer, 1872.*

year to the Misses Du Pre, who continued to run their school for girls only. The committee did not appoint James Russell as master; he set up his own boarding school at what was later known as Leigh House. Instead, the committee appointed John Rudland as the master, but he left in September 1854 to be replaced temporarily by John Slatter, the parish clerk.[9]

The school continued in the old ribbon factory for nearly 20 years. For much of this period the master was Richard Hedges, who lived near the *Saracens Head.* His salary and other costs were met by payments from the parents. In 1861, it was resolved to charge the better off, including farmers and tradesmen, 6d. per week for the first son and 3d. a week for other boys of the same family. In 1863, the school was closed temporarily when smallpox broke out in Factory Yard. In 1864, William Child refloored and painted the schoolroom and repaired the privies. In the same year, the Misses Du Pre transferred responsibility for the girls' school, then conducted by Miss Pearl, to the Church Schools

Committee. No government grant was available, however, whilst the schools remained in these unsuitable premises.[10]

Following the Education Act of 1870, many towns elected school boards, which levied local rates to build new schools. The Act did provide, however, for voluntary schools to receive Government grants if they met the basic standards. The Church of England responded quickly to the threat of independent schools and put forward plans to improve National Schools around the country. At Beaconsfield, the energetic new rector, the Rev. Samuel James Bowles, employed his brother-in-law, Henry Woodyer, to design new National Schools.[11] Woodyer had recently restored the parish church and designed new buildings at Eton College. In December 1870 a site for the school was agreed at the south-west corner of the churchyard, on land given by Magdalen College, Oxford, the owner of the Rectory, and John Hargreaves of Hall Barn. The building was erected in 1872 by William Child at a cost of £1,623, of which £355 came from a Government grant. The school was officially opened on 12 May 1873. The old school in Factory Yard still belonged to James Peet of Derby. He sold it in 1888 to Hubert John Rolfe, whose executors sold it to Lord Burnham in 1909.[12]

The headmaster of the new National School was Feargus Owen Warner, who had charge of about 240 pupils: 70 boys, 70 girls and 100 infants. Warner had left by 1883 and was replaced by Arthur Baker, who stayed at the school until his retirement in 1920. Two of his colleagues also spent their entire careers at Beaconsfield. The mistress of the girls' school, Esther Heath, came before 1877, as did Sarah Fry, the mistress of the infants' school. Miss Heath and Miss Fry lived together, first as lodgers at Miss Stevens' house in London End and later as tenants at Wiggenton Farm. Miss Heath retired in 1920.

After the 1903 Education Act, the former National School became a Church of England primary school. A well-loved teacher from this period was Mary Cordelia Wright. She was born in Chalfont St Peter in 1881, the daughter of George Wright, an organist and music teacher. When George Wright moved to Beaconsfield in about 1886, Cordelia entered the infants' school in Windsor End. At this time, children were put into standards and moved up with age and ability. Most left at the age of 10 or 11 when they finished Standard 4. Clever and better-off children could stay until the end of Standard 7, when they were fourteen. Cordelia Wright is first mentioned in Miss Heath's log book in 1895 when, as a 14 year old, she helped in the infants' school whilst a teacher was off sick. She passed the examination for Standard 7 in October 1895, but did not leave the school until February 1897, just after her 16th birthday, as she was still acting as an unofficial teacher's assistant. In September 1897, when she was 18, a vacancy arose for a monitor and Cordelia Wright took the post.

At that time there was, in addition to the girls' headteacher Miss Heath, one qualified assistant teacher and two monitors. Monitors were paid very little and spent part of their time teaching and part being taught and had to take exams every year. The school inspector gave recognition to Cordelia Wright as an unqualified assistant teacher under Article 68 on his annual visit to the school in 1899. She was given a salary of £35 per year in 1900. Cordelia Wright took her scholarship examination at the end of 1900 and heard that she had passed the following March. At this time she was living with her parents at Bank House, 25 London End.

As a part-qualified teacher, Cordelia Wright had to move schools and, in the summer of 1901, she left for a school in Reading. She completed her qualifications in 1903. Cordelia Wright continued to live in Beaconsfield. Her sister, Bessie, has described how, when the railway line was built in 1904, Cordelia Wright played the harmonium at church services for the railway navvies at Davenies Farm. In April 1910, after 17 years as monitress, pupil and qualified teacher, Cordelia Wright returned to teach at Beaconsfield. Although she taught all subjects, she was particularly interested in music, singing and what Miss Heath described as 'observation walks'.

When both Arthur Baker and Miss Heath retired in October 1920, the school managers took the opportunity to join the boys' and girls' schools together, but Cordelia Wright was acting head of the girls' school until the following June. She wrote the final words in the girls' school log book:

> This completes the history of the Girls' Dept: – Tomorrow June 1st, the Girls' and Boys' Departments are to be amalgamated, and the mixed department will be in the charge of Mr Dyer the Headmaster. Signed Cordelia Wright. Teacher-in charge.[13]

Cordelia Wright became teacher of the Standard 3 children in the mixed school and soon became unofficial deputy to the new headmaster, Samuel Dyer. Her job included directing school productions and the school orchestra. When the school was divided into primary and secondary schools in 1932, Cordelia Wright went with Mr Dyer to the new secondary school in Aylesbury End. Miss Wright had a lengthy absence in 1933 when she nursed her mother through her last illness and contracted pneumonia herself. She took time off before her own retirement to nurse and sort out the affairs of Miss Heath, who, according to the log book, 'had been looked after by Miss Wright for many years'.

The Secondary School

By 1932, the Church of England School in Windsor End had outgrown its 1872 building and a new 'secondary' school was built on the west side of Aylesbury End. Samuel Dyer and Cordelia Wright moved to the new school, taking the 9-14 year olds with them. This was the basis of the secondary modern school which survives today as the Beaconsfield school. Samuel Dyer was a forceful character and used to hire a train each summer to take the children and their parents on a trip to the seaside. When the war broke out in 1939, five London schools were evacuated to Beaconsfield to share the school site. In order for this to happen, local children attended school in the morning and the evacuees attended in the afternoon. So that everyone had enough education, all school holidays were cancelled. Both Samuel Dyer and Cordelia Wright retired in 1940.

The secondary school was extended in 1946 in advance of raising the school leaving age to fifteen. When the new hall and domestic science kitchens were opened in 1965, Cordelia Wright, then aged 84, attended a special prize-giving. The bulk of the school was rebuilt in 1998. Little now remains of the 1930s building, except the bell turret and the plaques which stood over the two entrances, with the words 'boys' and 'girls'. These have been preserved in the modern school to mark the respective toilets. Today the school has about eight hundred pupils.

The original school in Windsor End closed in 1957, although some classrooms were used subsequently by the secondary school. The building is now used as a Masonic Hall. A new Beaconsfield Church of England Primary School was built in Maxwell Road and opened by Princess Alexandra, on 8 January 1958. It is now called St Mary and All Saints Church of England School and has 182 pupils aged four to eleven. A county primary school, Butler's Court School, was opened in Wattleton Road in 1966. It now has 425 pupils aged four to eleven. Prior to 1958, those pupils who passed the 11+ examination went to grammar schools in High Wycombe. In that year, Beaconsfield High School, a grammar school for girls, was opened in Wattleton Road. It now has 1,000 pupils.

Eleven

Local Government

Until the 1830s, Beaconsfield was run by a vestry, a regular parish meeting, which appointed several unpaid officials, such as churchwardens, surveyors of highways and overseers of the poor. There is an unbroken run of rate books and overseers accounts starting in 1678 and running through until 1835. These not only show how the overseers of Beaconsfield raised money to relieve the poor of the town, but they also list a variety of payments to travellers and vagrants moving through Beaconsfield to and from London. By the late 18th century, the numbers requiring poor relief were so great that the overseers established their own workhouse. Here the governor employed claimants in manufacturing commodities like lace and gave shelter to the deserving poor who could no longer live independently. The building used was the former *Chequers Inn*, London End.

The following are some of the rules to be observed in the workhouse:

Rules and Orders for the Poor House of the Parish of Beaconsfield Bucks to be strictly observed by the Governor and Paupers therein.

1. That every person be employed by the Governor in such work as is suited to his or her strength and capacity.

2. That the Governor take proper Care to keep the House and all Persons therein, thoroughly clean and wholesome. For which purposes, he shall employ such of the Poor, inhabiting the said House, as he shall think best qualified to assist him: as also in providing and dressing Victuals for the use of the House. Any poor person, refusing such office, to be punished by confinement, loss of meals, or in such manner as the Churchwardens Overseers and Governor or either of them shall judge right. A second offence of the same sort, to be laid before a Justice of the Peace, who will punish with imprisonment or otherwise at his discretion according to Law.

3. That the Governor shall give the best apartments and show a reasonable indulgence to such persons, as have been creditable Housekeepers and have been brought to poverty by misfortune.

4. That those who are able to work be called and set to work by six o'clock in the morning from Lady Day to Michaelmas, and by eight from Michaelmas to Lady Day, and that they continue to work the accustomed hours having the usual time allowed for meals and rest.

A 1785 inventory of the household furniture in the workhouse shows that the building included a hall or living room, kitchen, pantry, brewhouse and a governor's room. There were 10 bedrooms with 24 beds, 10 of which were in the long chamber or dormitory. There was also a bedroom for the governor and, nearby, a silk room, probably for the storage of silk thread for lacemaking.

This generous provision for the poor was sustained until 1834, when, under the new Poor Law Act, Beaconsfield entered into a poor law union with the towns of Amersham and Chesham and all the surrounding villages. A new Union Workhouse was built at Amersham and all the poor of all these parishes were transferred in 1838.

The new Union Workhouse was a potent symbol of change and also a sign that Beaconsfield was falling behind neighbouring towns in providing modern facilities. A chance to catch up was provided by the Public Health Act of 1848, which enabled English towns to elect Local Boards of Health and levy rates to improve housing, water supplies and sewage disposal. Both

John Hargreaves of Hall Barn and James Du Pre of Wilton Park supported an application to the new General Board of Health for an inquiry into setting up a Local Board of Health for Beaconsfield. This approach also had the support of the non-conformists in the town, who were anxious to limit the powers of the vestry, which was largely controlled by the churchwardens.

The inspector's report was published in 1850.[1] Figures placed before the inspector suggested that the health of the town had deteriorated. The crude measure of the health of a town was the annual number of deaths per thousand of population. Over the period 1838-44, there had been an average of 19 deaths per 1,000 in Beaconsfield, but this had risen to 24 per 1,000 in 1842-8. The average annual totals of 33 for 1838-44 and 36 for 1845-6, compared with 46 in 1847 and 53 in

89 *The former Chequers Inn, used as a parish workhouse from 1767-1838.*

1848. Two local doctors, John Crook Rumsey and John Hutchinson, gave evidence. Rumsey suggested that during the time of Dr Ferris, a magistrate and physician, the health of the town had improved by attention to its drainage and ending the practice of keeping pigs in the town, but that these improvements seem to have lapsed. Hutchinson observed 'wherever there is the most filth, there I find the most fever'. The solicitor, John Charsley, stated that 'the present state (of the town) has a serious effect in preventing the occupation of some of the best houses in the town and some very desirable inhabitants have threatened to leave if there is no alteration in the future'.

The inspector noted that there were surface drains on either side of London End draining to the Stone pond, the liquid in which regularly

overflowed and at points the drains were almost stagnant. In Wycombe End there was a surface drain on one side and a barrel drain on the other leading to Hicks Meadow. In Aylesbury End, open surface drains on either side merged into one to finish in Wattleton pond. In Shepherds Lane, open ditches on either side became stagnant in large pools until the water evaporated. In Windsor End, a barrel drain was used for the churchyard. The matter passing down all these drains 'consists of house slops and in some cases of the solid matter from the privies. The liquid refuse frequently overflowing and their state particularly in hot weather is represented as being most offensive'. Privies and cesspools of many of the cottages were in an even worse

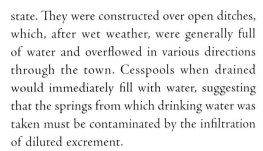

state. They were constructed over open ditches, which, after wet weather, were generally full of water and overflowed in various directions through the town. Cesspools when drained would immediately fill with water, suggesting that the springs from which drinking water was taken must be contaminated by the infiltration of diluted excrement.

The inspector found the worst conditions in Everett's Yard, Hedgelerly Lane, Barrack Yard and Blake's Rent in Aylesbury End. The cottages in Everett's Yard consisted of two rooms, one up and one down, each 11ft by 6ft, with the ground floor 7ft 3in in height and the upper, 8ft. There was only one pump and one double privy for the nine houses and the pump was frequently affected by overflows of the privy. In 1848, of the 70 cases of typhus, 12 were found in this yard. It progressively spread from one cottage to another, including five out of seven members of the More family, who all slept in the same bedroom. The state of Barrack Yard was 'extremely bad' and several cases of fever occurred there. He also noted that the town was 'not free of that hot-bed of disease and immorality, the common lodging house'. There were three such houses, one of which was also a beerhouse. Each of them had only two bedrooms, and 12 persons had been seen sleeping in one room measuring 10 feet square. The inspector found in favour of the petition and made recommendations on the supply of water and drainage.

Beaconsfield Local Board of Health

Set up in 1850, the new Local Board of Health quickly became involved in wider matters than health, including the repair of highways. In 1855, the Local Board, seeing the 'destination of many of the agricultural labourers … from want of work and the high cost of provisions … resolved that as immediate relief alone can meet the case, the surveyor be and is hereby ordered to employ all that may be willing to work on the parish highways until further ordered'. A public meeting was held at the *Saracens Head* on 22 October 1855 to take steps to find work through the winter. Another responsibility taken on by the Local Board was the control of the fire engine. Apparently a committee had been formed in 1847 but had failed to act, so in 1855 the Local Board took control, albeit reappointing the existing engineer in charge. He was Charles Smith, a 39-year-old harness maker, born in Yorkshire, who was not challenged in the job and served until 1866.

The Local Board was initially dominated by local farmers. The chairman was Thomas Hearn, a tenant of James Du Pre at Davenies Farm. He was sponsored by William Rolfe of Wattleton Farm and William Dawkins of Whites Farm, both owner-occupiers. These three dominated the poll for a new Local Board in 1851, with far more votes than any of the other six candidates. They were joined by Edmund Grove, a farmer and coal merchant who lived in the western part of the former *Kings Head*; two builders, William Child of Wycombe End and John Spring of Windsor End; John Hare, a market gardener and corn merchant living near the windmill in London End; John Wassell Hitchcock, a plumber living on the south side of London End; and Simeon James Blake, a butcher on the corner of London End and Shepherds Lane.

The second retailer to serve on the Local Board was James Turketine, a baker, born in Suffolk, who had moved into a shop on the south side of London End in the 1840s. He was replaced in 1855 by a grocer, William Fowler of Aylesbury End, and later by two other grocers, Uriah Day of Market Place and Joseph Marshall of London End. At first, the professional men of the town failed to get elected to the Local Board, but the doctor Harding Ress served on the Local Board in the 1860s and the solicitor George Allington Charsley in the 1870s. The schoolmaster Arthur Denman also joined the Local Board in the 1870s

as did the estate agent John Rolfe. The first clerk and surveyor to the Local Board was Edward William Mackie, a saddler, living on the north side of London End. He was later replaced by the former National School teacher Richard Hedges. When the two roles were split, Hedges continued as surveyor, with G.A. Charsley as clerk.

Chairmen of Beaconsfield Local Board of Health

1850-1	Thomas Hearne
1851-2	John Wassell Hitchcock
1852-3	William Dawkins
1853-4	Simeon James Blake
1854-5	Edmund Grove
1855-6	John Spring
1856-7	John Lever
1857-8	Simeon James Blake
1858-60	Joseph Rance
1860-1	Thomas Hearne
1861-2	David Batchelor
1862-3	Simeon James Blake
1863-4	John Wassell Hitchcock
1864-6	Simeon James Blake
1866-71	George Rance
1871-5	John Wassell Hitchcock
1875-84	William Rolfe
1884-5	Edward Lawson
1885-6	William Rolfe
1886-91	Arthur Denham
1891-2	Walter Hearne
1892-4	Hubert John Rolfe

The problems that led to the setting-up of the Board were not quickly solved. In 1855, Henry Blinko, a butcher living near to Dr Rumsey in London Road, was ordered to fill up a hole in his yard, then used as a dung hole. William Taylor was to open, clean out and repair the drain from his washhouse and empty an overflowing privy. William Chapman, a gardener in Lakes Lane, was instructed to discontinue using a certain shed in his occupation as a pigsty, but disobeyed the order. Nearly 20 years later, William Barlow of the High Street (a brewer in 1871 and carpenter in 1881) was not alone in being ordered 'to remove their pigs to a place not injurious to health and that they discontinue the keeping of pigs in their present sties'.

In 1862, the Local Board of Health gave permission for the U.K. Telegraph Company to erect posts and wires in return for 'an annual rental of 1d. for each post so erected. And they place on every post (not being less than six in number) one good sized Street Lamp, provided with Hollidays Patented Burner, to be lighted with Hollidays Mineral Gas, at the expense of the said Company during the usual hours of lighting Lamps for the next two winters.'

The problem of sewage was tackled very gradually. By 1860, sewage pipes had been laid on the south side of London End and most householders had carried their drains into them. James Du Pre, Mrs Elizabeth Rance and Messrs John and Nathaniel Charsley had, however, declined to do so, presumably preferring to use their existing cesspits. The last two of these complied within 14 days, but the fact that they had to be told to do so after everyone else suggests that the enthusiasm that John Charsley had had for the formation of the Local Board had worn thin. Even in 1883, Dr Brickwell, Medical Officer of Health, called attention to the continuance of foul closet accommodation in Shepherds Lane and Lakes Lane. He also stated that the drainage of the town passing into the meadow occupied by Mr Honour was in a state dangerous to the inhabitants. In 1893 G.A. Charsley, acting for Arthur Riversdale Grenfell of Butler's Court, wrote to the Local Board, drawing attention to an open drain or ditch which ran from Aylesbury End, through the garden of Benjamin Bagley and the ground of Mr Harding, and discharged itself onto Mr Grenfell's property. He stated that:

This drain … is full of the matter of the foulest and most detestable description and causes a most horrible nuisance to the part of the Town and Houses near which it passes. Mr Grenfell informs me that there have already been sore throats and Scarlet Fever in his Lodges where the stench caused by the inflow on to his property from this ditch is positively unbearable. I am therefore instructed to give notice that unless this crying nuisance is abated on or before the 1st of October, my client will take such steps as he shall be advised by the proper authority to prevent the discharge from this foul and fetid drain or ditch, going on his property.

Another recurring problem was the lack of an isolation hospital. In 1881, during an outbreak of smallpox, it was proposed that an advertisement be inserted at once in *The Times* and the *Telegraph* for a second-hand corrugated-iron building, suitable for a hospital. In November of that year, the Local Board was asked by the Local Government Board whether it intended to apply for any loan permissions in the next year. The Local Board replied that they might wish to raise a loan of £500 for a hospital, but nothing more was done. In 1899, during an outbreak of typhoid fever, Sir Edward Lawson placed the New Hall, later to be called the Burnham Hall, at the disposal of the Council as a temporary hospital.

The Local Board was not anxious to extend its activities or to incur extra expense. When G.A. Charsley, the last clerk to the Turnpike Trust, enquired if the Local Board wished to have the turnpike running through the district under their control, the Board considered that 'from the very efficient state of repair in which the Turnpike Roads have been kept, it is inexpedient that any alteration be made in the management thereof, and as there is little local traffic thereon, it be continued as heretofore'. The Local Board did exercise some control over the annual fair. In 1866, the clerk was directed to charge all shows or stalls standing or erected within the town 2s. 6d. per day and night, large shows and dancing booths with three caravans or carriages 5s. per day and night and wild beast shows with more than three caravans or carriages

90 *The police station, built by Buckinghamshire County Council, 1870.*

10s. per day and night. It was also ordered that the shows should not be erected on the wasteland next to the churchyard, or allowed to remain more than one night on the highway.

The Urban District Council

Following the Local Government Act of 1894, the functions of the Local Board were taken over by the new U.D.C. Meetings continued to be held at the Reading Room in the Broadway until new Council Chamber were built in the New Town in 1915. There was some continuity between the two bodies. The officers of the Local Board continued to be employed by the new Council and the several members of the Local Board in 1893 and 1894 were elected to the Council in 1895. The main difference was the disappearance of John Thomson of Wilton Park Farm, and the election of Sir Edward Lawson of Hall Barn and Thomas Lane, proprietor of the *White Hart*. Lane was to become a key figure on the U.D.C. and a county councillor.

In its earliest years the Council had to deal with much the same problems as the Local Board. In July 1895, Arthur Riversdale Grenfell threatened the Council with an injunction unless the open drain leading to his property was remedied. Obviously nothing was done, as in June 1896, his brother, Sir Francis Grenfell, made a specific proposal to the Council:

> That the filtering bed should be made at the top of my field and that by this means the water flowing into my pond should be purified and made clean and stand analysis. Though I cannot consider this a solution of the drainage question, it may suffice until some better is adopted, and I agree to your proposal if concurred in by the Council under the following conditions: that it be emptied at least once a fortnight by the U.D.C.; that the men who empty it should enter and leave my ground at a place I shall select; that the work be begun at once and finished within three weeks; that if this proves ineffectual, other steps be eventually taken; these proposals to be embodied in a memorandum to be signed by myself and the Clerk to the Council; and the U.D.C. being tenants of the ground subject to six months' notice.

This was not the end of the story, for a full sewerage system was not begun until 1898, when Sir Edward Lawson made land available from the Hall Barn Estate. The scheme cost £3,000 and it was not until 1902 that it seems to have been completed.

The Amersham, Beaconsfield and District Waterworks Company

In July 1896, a letter was received from the Local Government Board enquiring as to what was being done by the Council about the water supply. A reply was sent indicating that a water supply was about to be provided by the formation of a private company. This was the Amersham, Beaconsfield and District Waterworks Company, registered in 1895. The plan was to sink a well 260ft below the surface of the Misbourne Valley at Amersham and pump the water up to a reservoir 500ft above sea level on the ridge at Coleshill, midway between Amersham and Beaconsfield. The promoters intended to supply water to the parishes of Amersham, Beaconsfield, Chalfont St Giles, Chenies, Chesham Bois, Coleshill, Gerrards Cross, Penn, Seer Green, and part of High Wycombe. The rapid development of all these districts, particularly of Amersham on the Hill, Beaconsfield and Gerrards Cross, could not have taken place without the vital water supply provided by this company. On completion of the works in October 1897, the engineer, Edmund Alderson Sandford Fawcett, wrote to the directors, including Sir Edward Lawson of Hall Barn, describing the route of the water pipes:

> An aqueduct or line of pipes commencing at the aforesaid reservoir passing through Coleshill aforesaid, and terminating about the centre of the town of Beaconsfield, with distributing branches carried along the various roads and streets in the town and parish of Beaconsfield aforesaid.[2]

The area covered by the Amersham, Beaconsfield and District Waterworks Company experienced dramatic growth during the period before the First World War. The Amersham, Beaconsfield and District Water Order of 1914 gave the company power to build a water tower next to the Coleshill reservoir, by which means the water level was raised a further 100ft above the surrounding countryside. The Amersham, Beaconsfield and District Water Company was taken over in 1951 by the Rickmansworth and Uxbridge Valley Water Company, and is now known as Three Valleys Water plc.

Despite the introduction of mains water to the town in 1897, the Medical Officer of Health reported in 1899 that there were still 25 wells in different parts of the town which produced water unfit for drinking and domestic use. Cottagers were still in the habit of emptying slops into the street gullies. A major outbreak of typhoid led a lady in South Wales to send a cheque for £50 in relief of the expenses of the epidemic. The Medical Officer of Health's report in 1901 caused further embarrassment to the Council. A deputation lead by A.E.W. Charsley, including several former Local Board members, protested against many of the statements in the report, which had been repeated in the London and other papers, and asked that the Council should take steps to contradict the injurious statements which had been made.

Building Regulations

In 1903, the Railway Company proposed to erect some accommodation for staff at the new station then being built at Beaconsfield. When they enquired as to what building regulations the Council had in place, they were told that there were at present no building bye-laws. As the New Town began to develop, the Council was repeatedly asked for copies of its bye-laws and had to tell purchasers of houses that any problems were a matter for them and their builder. Some plans submitted to the Council were simply returned without comment. When the architect Julian Burgess wrote to the Council in May 1907 with respect to removal of house refuse and the condition of drains at his premises, he was told that, in the absence of bye-laws, the responsibility for drainage rested on him. Even as late as 1910, when Arthur Vernon & Son enquired about laying out new streets, they were told that the Council would not intervene in the case of new roads commenced before its bye-laws were passed. Although the Council began drafting bye-laws controlling building and other matters in 1908, these were not finally approved until October 1910.

In 1906, Beaconsfield U.D.C. was chaired by John Rolfe of Wiggenton House, agent to Lord Burnham. The vice-chairman was his brother, Robert Rolfe. There were seven other elected members. The clerk was G.A. Charsley, solicitor; the treasurer was Arthur Kiddall, manager of the Capital and Counties Bank; the Medical Officer of Health was A.H. Turner, a local G.P.; the surveyor and rate collector was Herbert Watson, a surveyor from London End; and the sanitary inspector was Percy Coleman, a plumber from London End. From 1906, Council officers had to cope with a large increase in work and there were petitions to the Council for increases in salary. The Council, which met at the Reading Room in the Broadway, had no separate offices until the Council Chamber was built in 1914. The architect Julian Burgess offered space in his offices. When James Honour was appointed surveyor in 1907, he was required to provide his own office space. James Honour had been a member of the Council from 1899 and combined the role of Surveyor with that of assistant overseer and rate collector. These roles were split in 1908 when a new surveyor was appointed.

The New Sewage Works

After 1906, the disposal of sewage again became a serious problem for the Council and its surveyor. In 1908, there was an outbreak of scarlet fever in

Wycombe End where the pail system of disposing excrement was still in use. The first time a new house was discussed at the Council was in April 1907, when Mr R. Seller wrote with a plan for a new house. He was told that the Council had no objection, but because there was as yet no extension to the sewer he had better make temporary arrangements. In September 1907, the owners of property and land in the New Town were invited to meet the Council to discuss the question of a sewerage scheme for that part of the district, but no scheme was built until about 1912. In the absence of adequate controls, builders often provided cesspools which were too small. An owner of a house in Ledborough Lane wrote to the Local Government Board in 1908 with a complaint about a cesspool, which was then examined by the Inspector of Nuisances. Perhaps following another complaint, a special report on the cesspool at Omea, Reynolds Road, was addressed to the Local Government Board, by the surveyor and the Medical Officer of Health. Solicitors acting for General Schomberg of Boyne House, Grove Road, wrote asking on what authority the General had been called upon to construct a larger cesspool, and why he had been charged 7s. 6d. for emptying the existing one. The General's neighbour in Grove Road wrote a similar letter and this argument went on for sometime. In 1910, the High Court found against the Council in a case brought by Robinson and another, described as owners of a building estate, who sued following the failure of the Council's contractor to satisfactorily dispose of sewage from cesspools. These problems were solved in 1915 when the Holtspur sewage works was built at a cost of £13,000.

Another major problem was the condition of the roads. Beaconsfield U.D.C. did not adopt the Private Street Works Act of 1892 until 1910. In January 1908 proposals were brought forward to fund the reconstruction of the road from the Old Town to the railway and to the parish boundary at a cost of £3,000 but, after a vote, only the section to the station was supported. By July 1908, however, proposals for Windsor Road, Burnham Road, Amersham Road, Candlemas Lane, Ledborough Lane and Penn Road were made, with priority being given to the last two. Nothing came of these proposals and, despite complaints from the County Council, the Local Government Board advised in 1909 that the road schemes should be delayed, as it would soon be necessary to lay gas mains, sewers and surface water drains. Ledborough Lane was so bad that one resident in 1909 submitted photographic evidence of its poor state. The Council made a proposal to adopt Baring and Reynolds Roads in 1910, but this did not happen until during the First World War.

Although the railway opened in April 1906, the desirability of lighting the road from the Old Town to the new station was not considered until August that year. Eventually 12 gaslights (initially oil) were authorised. The Council also objected to the Uxbridge and District Electric Lighting Extension Order, possibly because they feared it would lead to the introduction of Electric Tramways through the district along the main London to Oxford road. Their objections were ignored, but no trams arrived and nor did electricity until about 1912. In November 1906, the question of a noticeboard indicating the road to the station was raised. Signs outside the station to Knotty Green and Penn, as well as Beaconsfield, were not considered until four months later, and even then it was suggested that they were the responsibility of the railway company. The Council also fought a battle with the National Telephone Company to ensure that

91 *The opening of the new sewage works, 29 July 1915. Front centre, Thomas Frederick Lane, Chairman of Beaconsfield U.D.C. Extreme right, William Gurney, Chairman Amersham R.D.C.*

lines were put underground every time a new one was proposed.

Partly because of such problems and partly perhaps because they considered themselves neglected, a North Beaconsfield Residents Association was formed and, for a time, each meeting of the Council was subjected to several letters from this body. In 1909 the North Beaconsfield Association complained about the bad condition of the roads and footpaths, after companies and builders had opened them for ditches. The association was quite separate from the Rate Payers' Association, which may have been more orientated to the Old Town, and whose main concern was to keep down expenditure.

The first sign of tension between New and Old Towns appeared on 30 October 1906 when 'residents near the new Railway Station' requested the removal of house rubbish. In November, Mrs Elliott had asked that the houses there should have a Sunday delivery of letters. The service of the New Town was still not satisfactory in 1908 when a further approach was made to the Postmaster General.

It was not until 1913 that residents of the New Town joined the Council. These were Thomas Galloway Cowan of The Firs, Burke's Road, a London solicitor; Roland Townsend of Cicester, Baring Crescent, a schoolmaster; Edward Norcross of Cestria, Ledborough Lane, a land agent, and

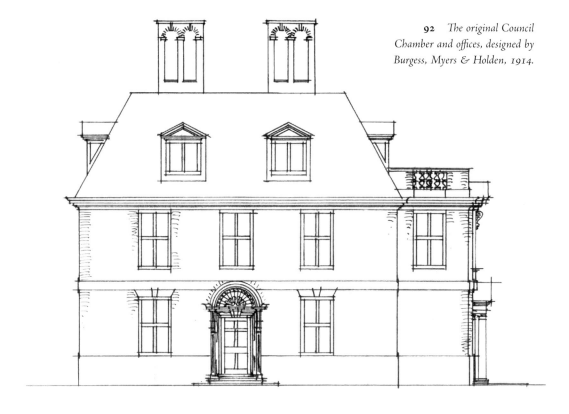

92   The original Council Chamber and offices, designed by Burgess, Myers & Holden, 1914.

93   *The new Council Hall, designed by Burgess, Holden & Watson, opened in 1936.*

William Edmund Vare of Burke's Cottage, Burke's Road, a sanitary engineer. In 1914, W.E. Vare himself commissioned the architects Burgess, Myers & Holden to design a Renaissance-style block of offices on the corner of Burke's Road and Station Road. The building was completed in 1915 and included a new Council Chamber. In 1915, Vare applied for permission to convert part of the building into flats. The offices of Beaconsfield U.D.C. remained there until 1936, when the new Council Hall was built to the north of the railway bridge.

In 1921, the number of members of the U.D.C. was increased from nine to fifteen. In 1934, the boundaries of the urban district were extended to take in parts of the parishes of Burnham, Taplow and Wooburn, including Holtspur. This increased the area of the urban district from 4,395 to 5,314 acres By 1935, only two of the members of the U.D.C. were from pre-railway families and one of these, Edward William Tilbury, a retired builder, had greatly profited from the construction of the New Town.

Council Housing

In 1912, Lord Burnham offered an acre of land in Aylesbury End for working-class housing, but the Council considered the site too small. It eventually obtained rights over three acres and, after a competition won by Burgess and Myers, a plan was drawn up for 34 cottages, each with 10 poles of land. They were to be constructed with hollow walls and have an 11ft square parlour, a 12ft by 18ft combined living room and kitchen with a dresser, larder and range, a scullery containing a copper sink and tip-up bath, a W.C. and a coal cellar. Upstairs there was to be a landing measuring 6ft by 3ft, three bedrooms 11ft square, 12ft by 11ft, and 7ft by 9ft. The rooms were to be 8ft in height except the scullery (7ft 6in) and concrete and cement floors with 1¼ inch boards. Gas was to be laid on. It was calculated that £16 18s. would be needed per annum to cover repayments on water, loans and that with 6s. 6d. a week rent the scheme would be self-supporting. It is worth noting that with about seven hundred square feet of floor-space, these cottages would have fallen short of the 1912 Local Government Board's standard of 820 square feet to 1,230 square feet. However, by the time the proposals had been worked up in 1914, the First World War intervened and the scheme was abandoned because of a considerable increase in costs.

At the same time as this scheme was being discussed, a private development of small houses north of the Old Town was built called the Cottage Homes Estate. Plots were laid out around a new road called Horseshoe Crescent and several small houses were built there before the First World War. This development was on land belonging to Williams Brewery, whose tenant, Thomas F. Lane, a member of the U.D.C., was heavily involved in the project. The architect Stanley Hamp prepared plans of a block of three cottages to be built in

Beaconsfield in 1909.[3] By 1925 there were 40 houses in Horseshoe Crescent and a further three under construction.

It was only in 1919 that the council estate at Lakes Lane and Malthouse Square was commenced. The first of the 52 three-bedroom houses in Malthouse Square were ready for occupation by 1922.[4] The first 26 tenants were approved by the Housing Committee in May of that year. In the 1930s, further council houses were built on the Amersham road, including 22 houses at Ronald Road. The Amersham Road Estate was also built in the 1930s, on 13¾ acres of land nearer the railway. There were 124 houses fronting Maxwell Road, Hyde Green and Waller Road. Some of these houses, such as 34-40 and 35-41 Maxwell Road, were built in blocks of four, with a central entry to the rear gardens. The cast-iron drain-water heads

94 *Council houses in Ronald Road, designed by Burgess, Holden & Watson, 1928.*

95 *Members of Beaconsfield U.D.C., 1974.*

BACK

| H.E. Hibbert Ass. Finance Officer | L.R. Peacock Deputy Clerk | Cllr R.L.J. Baile Medical Officer | Cllr D.E. Simpson Public Health Inspector | Dr B.H.Burne | Mr P.J. Bunce |

CENTRE

| Cllr A.M. Dyer | Cllr T.D. Easton | Cllr E.E. Biestro | Cllr G.H.D. Roundell Green | Cllr I.St.L. Kynoch | Cllr F.H. Laramon |

FRONT

| Cllr B.M. Yorke Hill | Cllr J.K. Kirkconel | Cllr R.M. Scarles | F.I. Knowles | F.V. Harris | Cllr J.V. Shapland |

above these entries carry the date 1933. A further 26 houses at Fernhurst Close, adjoining Ronald Road, were completed in 1939.

The building of council houses continued after the Second World War, in part to house the workers at the Rotax (later Perkin Elmer) electrical engineering works on Maxwell Road, which employed 500 people. By 1947, 80 houses were under construction in Candlemas Mead and many more were to be built in Maxwell Road, Garvin Avenue and Chesterton Green. In 1958, a new Church of England School was built on Maxwell Road, at the heart of this estate.

Reorganisation of Local Government

With the reorganisation of local government in 1974, Beaconsfield U.D.C. joined most of Eton Rural District in a new unit called Beaconsfield District Council. The council chose to centralise its operations at the former R.D.C. offices in Slough. New offices were planned for Beaconsfield New Town, but the scheme was dropped. The name of the Council changed to South Bucks District Council, and the offices eventually moved to Denham in 2005.

Chairmen of Beaconsfield Urban District Council, 1895-1974

1895-1907	Hurbert John Rolfe, Wiggenton House		1945-7	George Alfred Angus, Highbury, 29 Lakes Lane
1907-8	John Stay, The Manse, Lakes Lane		1947-9	Stanley Nicholson Whitehead, Walkwood, 65 Burke's Road
1908-17	Thomas Frederick Lane, 1 Windsor Lane		1949-50	Patrick Hugh Gold, The Spinney, Bearswood End
1917-19	Joseph Edward Harding, Wilton Park Farm		1950-2	Thomas James Thompsett, Wolmer, 70 Lakes Lane
1919-20	Thomas Galloway Cowan, The Firs, 37 Burke's Road		1952-5	Clare Alix Whitworth Holloway, Staceys, 26 Ledborough Lane
1920-2	John Eyre, Three Gables, Station Road		1955-7	Brian Ernest Wisker, Minsmere, Brownswood Road
1922-7	Edward William Tilbury, Marlborough House, 45 Wycombe End		1957-9	Alice Mary Bakewell, Methuen, Burnham Avenue
1927-9	Hugh Charles King, Byeways, Ledborough Lane		1959-61	Owen Standidge Puckle, Pigeon House Cottage, 26 Grove Road
1929-31	Robert Upton Morgan, Woodside, Baring Road		1961-3	Eleanor Margaret Diamond, Alderley Cottage, Wilton Road
1931-3	Reginald Thomas Smith, Hedgereley End, Hedgerley Lane		1963-5	Herbert Arthur Harding Gray, Orchard Cottage, 23 Candlemas Lane
1933-5	Percy Cyriac Skinner, Farm End, Burke's Road		1965-7	Derek Rivers Mullins, Woodstock, 79 Burke's Road
1935-7	William Arthur Whitworth, Dilkusha, Gregories Road		1967-9	James Dill Smith, Flat 22, Block A, Bulstrode Court, Gerrards Cross
1937-8	Norman William Gurney, Woodlands, Burke's Road		1969-71	John Langrigg Kirkonel, Benalata, 14 Beechwood Road
1938-41	Robert Hamilton Trench, 30 Windsor End		1971-2	Noel Kenneth Scott Bramer, 2 Woodside Close
1941-3	William Edmund Vare, Burke's Cottage, Burke's Road		1972-4	Ronald Michael Scarles, 5 Butler's Court Road
1943-5	Francis Graham, St Andrews, 72 Ledborough Lane			

Twelve

Beaconsfield's Population in the Nineteenth Century

Beaconsfield's dual character as an agricultural village and a small town is revealed in the decennial censuses of population. The population of many Buckinghamshire villages peaked in about the middle of the 19th century, after which there was a drift of population into the towns and to larger towns and cities outside the county. Beaconsfield had a modest increase of population until mid-century and then declined, suggesting an over-dependence on agricultural employment. Buckinghamshire towns with vigorous economies increased in size dramatically during the 19th century, with Chesham more than doubling its population and High Wycombe enjoying a fourfold increase. Beaconsfield, however, had no staple industry like brush or chairmaking which could expand to provide employment.

With a substantial increase in the birth rate, Beaconsfield's population grew strongly from 1,149 in 1801 to 1,763 in 1831. The population then fell to 1,524 in 1871, whilst modest rises in 1881 and 1891 were followed by a fall in 1901. The number of houses in the parish however remained remarkably steady at between 333 and 360.

Prior to 1851, church records show a considerable excess in the number of baptisms compared with the number of burials, but in a town with a strong non-conformist tradition need to viewed with care.

From 1837 birth and deaths were recorded by the government. Beaconsfield was included with Seer Green and Penn in a sub-registration district. Figures for this area suggest, after allowing for the natural increase in the population from an excess of births over deaths, an 11 per cent net migration from the area in both 1841-51 and 1851-61 increasing to 19 per cent in 1861-71. Thereafter the percentage net outflow of population was not so high. The high migration can be put into perspective if a calculation is made of what the population might have been without it; from 1841 to 1901 it would have grown from 1,732 to 2,843 (i.e. a size that it was not to reach despite the development of the New Town until about 1914).

Although generally births exceeded deaths, the parish was far from healthy. The decline in the death rate occurred despite poor housing conditions and an urban environment in such a small town that was not conducive to good health. Epidemics were common and in the spring quarter of 1861, the Registrar General reported that deaths in the sub-district were considerably more numerous than births, with several fatal cases of scarlatina. The reason for

	1801	1811	1821	1831	1841	1851	1861	1871	1881	1891	1901
Population	1149	1461	1736	1763	1732	1684	1662	1524	1635	1773	1570
% change		27.2	18.8	1.6	-1.8	-2.8	-1.3	-8.3	7.3	8.4	-11.4
Absolute Change		312	275	27	-31	-48	-22	-138	111	138	-203
Deaths in 10-year period ending						462	487	500	485	400	355
Births in 10-year period ending						309	295	277	242	233	220
Natural Increase in 10-year period ending						153	192	223	243	166	134
% net migration						-10.6	-11.4	-19.2	-7.5	-1.6	-10.6
% population Male	50.7	46.3	49.1	49.5	48.2	47.5	48.9	49.6	49.1	48.7	48.3
Houses occupied					339	345	342	333	336	349	360
Empty houses					16	18	16	36	34	25	25
Being built					3		6		3		
TOTAL					358	363	364	369	373	373	385

Table 7   *Beaconsfield's population, migration and housing numbers, 1801-1901.*

this was that 'the poor people are not accustomed to sufficiently ventilate and purify their homes'.[1] From 1841 to 1901 there were considerable variations in both birth and death rates, with deaths increasing during epidemics to twice the rate in good years.

Some variation in the total population revealed on one night by the decennial censuses can be traced to the presence or absence of the owners of the great houses. Hall Barn and Wilton Park might be expected to house a large family and an even larger number of servants, but for most of the

census nights, their owners were not at home. Only in 1891 was one of these houses occupied, when Pascoe Du Pre Grenfell was in residence at Wilton Park, with a total of 41 guests and servants.

The town's location on the London to Oxford road might have revealed some overnight stays by travellers at the inns, but the censuses were taken on a Sunday night when there were few travellers. What few lodgers are recorded at inns and public houses may have been medium-term residents. The majority of boarders in the town were pupils at the boarding schools. Variations in

	1800-9	1810-19	1820-9	1830-9	1840-49	1841-50
BIRTHS	355	491	483	422	332	462
BURIALS	374	300	337	374	354	309

Table 8   *Beaconsfield baptisms and burials, 1800-50.*

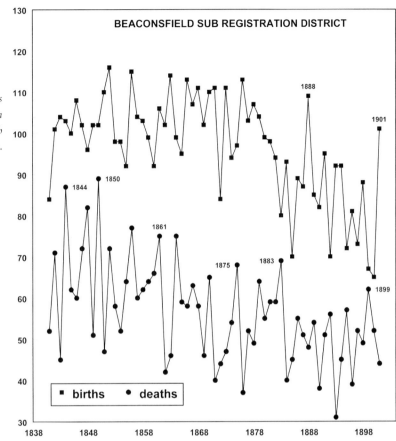

Table 9 *Births and deaths in Beaconsfield's sub registration district.*

the number of such temporary residents, although contributing in part to the substantial fall in the population between 1861 and 1871, were not the prime reason for the fluctuations in the town's population. The substantial fall of 203 between 1891 and 1901 was largely attributable to the 41 people missing from Wilton Park and the 98 pupils absent from the boarding schools. It was only slightly offset in 1901 by the presence of some railway construction workers.

The detailed census figures show about ninety per cent of the population was housed within the town until 1891, compared with 85 per cent in 1901. These figures conceal the importance of agriculture to the town as well as the parish, which underlies most of the decline in its population in the mid-Victorian period.

Genteel Households

With two great mansions, two redundant coaching inns and several substantial houses built by professionals or tradesmen, Beaconsfield had plenty of attractive residential property in the early 19th century. This was often let out for short terms. In 1802, Wycombe End House, which had been built by the solicitor Robert Charsley but always let to wealthy tenants, was advertised in *The Times*:

> To let for the summer, a commodious family house, completely furnished at Beaconsfield, Bucks, 23 miles from London, on the great road to Oxford, containing 11 rooms, and also a wash house, coach house, 3 stall stable, excellent cellars, a garden well-stocked with fruit and every useful vegetable, situated at the West End of Beaconsfield, within

gates, and looking into Waller's beautiful Park. Enquirie of Mr A Mitchell, No 51, Gracechurch Street or at Beaconsfield, where the servants will show the house.[2]

In 1811 the house on the north side of London End, later called The Elms, was advertised for sale in *The Times*. This was described as 'a most desirable and substantial brick-built residence with offices of every description, brewhouse, wash house, double coach-houses, four-stall stable etc., handsome pleasure and kitchen-garden'.[3] The house remained empty for some time before it was purchased by the solicitor John Charsley. Short lets were perhaps easier to obtain than sales of the larger houses. Thus, when Robert Crook of Hall Place died in 1812, the house was repeatedly advertised whilst occupied as a boarding school.[4] It was only sold in 1818 when the schoolmaster managed to raise the finance to buy the freehold.

Beaconsfield's proximity to London made it an excellent location for the occasional man of independent means who did not want to live in the capital itself. Rentals were probably lower than closer to town. Little Hall Barn in Windsor End was let to a succession of wealthy tenants, including the writer William Hickey. He described it as 'a pretty little cottage' when he arrived in 1806, but he found Beaconsfield 'a trifling' place with 'a very limited society'. He spent his time going in rotation to the houses of different friends, and going up to London every six weeks. Living with him was Munro, his favourite Indian servant. Munro expressed a desire to become a Christian and was taught by the Rev. Bradford. He was baptised as 'William Munnew' in 1809.[5] In 1827, Little Hall Barn was let to John and James Cundee for 21 years at a rent of £50 7s. per year.[6] John Cundee outlived his brother and died at Beaconsfield in 1842. There was a sale of his furniture in October of that year.[7]

Many of the temporary residents were widows or spinsters and most were found only in a single

edition of the *Kelly's Directory* or in one census year. This fleeting association with the parish arose in part because most were not native to Beaconsfield and can be expected to have moved to and from London. As spinsters or widows who had left the parental or marital home, most were elderly and many could be expected to die between censuses. The healthy gravel soil was advertised as a special attraction to those fearful of their health. These conditions combined to make the small town an attractive destination. Some residents, like Lady Kirkwall, took a house in Beaconsfield so as to be near to their sons whilst at local boarding schools. Her sons were taught by the Rev. Bradford at Hall Place, Bradford having earlier been tutor to their father. Lady Kirkwall's mother-in-law, the Countess of Orkney, lived at Burke House, 20 London End, from 1823 until her death in 1831. Lady Willoughby, the mother-in-law of Lord Carrington, lived at the same address in 1841. All these wealthy tenants could be expected to have two or more domestic servants.

After 1841, Beaconsfield's residential role seemed to decline. In the census of that year, only five 'independent' households are found with two or more servants. It is impossible to say to what degree this reflected the absence of a railway and to what extent it arose from the greater attractions of seaside resorts for the retired. Other than the owners of Hall Barn and Wilton Park, almost all those who kept three or more domestic servants were local professional men or the proprietors of boarding schools. This compares unfavourably with other parts of southern Buckinghamshire. There were a number of reasons for this. The two major estates dominated land ownership so that it was difficult for incomers to establish 'hunting lodges'. The absence of significant local businesses meant that there were few second-generation business families or widows living a genteel lifestyle. The boarding schools occupied many of the larger houses, thus excluding some of the gentry who might

	1851	1861	1871	1881	1891	1901
TOTAL POPULATION	1,684	1,662	1,524	1,635	1,773	1,570
Boarding Schools	81	79	75	102	87	0
Lodgers in PHs	17	20	13	14	23	1
Other Lodgers	79	62	53	45	56	60
Rough Sleepers	5	20	0	0	0	0
TOTAL ABOVE	200	212	156	185	186	86

Table 10 *Temporary accomodation in Beaconsfield, 1851-1901.*

otherwise have found the town attractive. Those seeking the picturesque were now moving to areas overlooking the Thames or one of the Chiltern valleys. The fear of disease spreading from the poorer areas of the town was suggested to the new Local Board of Health as a reason why some were discouraged from living there.[8] The genteel households would normally be expected to provide some leadership in the community. With short lets being so common, however, and the small number of genteel households headed by men, this was rarely the case in Beaconsfield. When a committee was formed in 1854 to establish a National School, only one such household was involved along with the rector, the curate, a private school master, a doctor, a farmer and the solicitor John Charsley.

Servants

According to Mrs Beeton, the number of servants was directly related to income. Those with an income of at least £150 per annum would be expected to keep one servant; those with £300, two servants; those with £500, three servants; those with £750, four servants; and those with £1,000 five servants. With this in mind, it is illuminating to count those households with domestic servants listed in the various censuses. Even though this approach risks missing those genteel households who were absent on census night, it is preferable to relying on directory listings of 'private residents'. From 1841 to 1901, excluding the two mansions, the private schools and those who had pupils, there was only one household with four or more servants, that of the solicitor G. A. Charsley. Even he reduced his establishment to two servants in 1891 and 1901.

There were 18 private households with two or more servants found in the period 1841-1901. Seven were found in two or more censuses. In three cases, the owner was absent and the house was in the care of domestic servants. Only six were headed by men. These included one clergyman resident in 1881 at The Yews, who with five servants had four pupils, a second clergyman also in 1881, and a 70-year-old fundholder resident at Little Hall Barn in 1861. Two were residents at The Grange in the north of the parish, which had been owned by wealthy Londoners from the middle of the 18th century. The last of the six was Henry Johnston who lived at Parkside, London End, from about 1888. He was one of the few 19th-century upper middle-class arrivals, who immersed themselves in the life of the town. He was a member of the U.D.C., manager of the Amersham, Beaconsfield and District Water Company, secretary of the Beaconsfield Chair Manufacturing Company and also ran a gymnasium for boys.

No. of Servants	Private Households				Professional Households *				Retail and Craft Households etc.			
	1	2	3	all	1	2	3	all	1	2	3	all
1841	9	3	2	14	1	0	3	4	15	3	0	18
1851	6	2	0	8	2	3	1	6	18	2	0	20
1861	4	2	1	7	3	2	2	7	7	1	0	8
1871	9	2	1	12	0	2	3	5	4	1	0	5
1881	6	3	2#	11	1	2	1	4	6	3	0	9
1891	4	4	1	9	2	2	1	5	7	2	0	9
1901	3	3		6	2	3	1	6	12	1	0	13

*Professional = clergy, doctors, vets, dentists, solicitors
#These were Little Hall Barn where there was a housekeeper and two servants and The Yews where a clergyman without cure of souls had four private pupils aged 16-19

Table 11 *Servants in private, professional, retail and craft households, 1841-1901.*

Agricultural Employment

In Beaconsfield the terms 'agricultural labourer' and 'labourer' seem to have been interchangeable. Individuals who in one census were recorded as the former were in the next shown as the latter and vice versa. There is no reason to expect that the considerable difference in numbers between 1851 and 1861 was due to anything except this. Two other occupations, those of sawyer and woodman, may well be described as agricultural labour in the censuses. Indeed, it can be expected that over the year, individuals might have been involved in all these occupations, something that no census captured. In 1851, more than half of adult males were working on the land. This proportion fell to 36 per cent by 1901, despite the increase in the number of gardeners by that date.

In many ways the town was simply an extra large village. One indication of this is perhaps the compliment that Disraeli paid the cottagers of Beaconsfield when speaking to the dinner of the Royal South Buckinghamshire Agricultural Association's award giving in 1862:

I was not surprised that (the first prize for cottage garden produce) was obtained by an inhabitant of Beaconsfield because I have observed for a long time that the allotment gardens there are managed on principles which are sounder and regulated by discipline which was more accurate than those which prevailed in any other part of the county … It showed that the people of Beaconsfield have recognised the important truth that a cottage garden should not be bad potato field.[9]

The servicing of the two main estates was perhaps not as important up to 1881 as it was to become in the long Edwardian summer up to 1914. The value of timber to the estates was considerable, but was probably a diminishing one. Certainly the number working in forestry fell from 1851 onwards. They were largely replaced by gardeners and gamekeepers, whose numbers increased from five to seven. The importance of shooting meant that most of those employed cultivating the land on the estates would also have played some role in servicing the sporting activity. Hall Barn under Lord Burnham was run with modern accounting principles and it is possible to create a detailed picture of the estate before 1914 from the surviving ledger accounts.

The substantial increase in the number of grooms in 1891 and 1901 must have been related to the two estates. Eight grooms were recorded in the Wilton Park stables and six at Hall Barn in 1891. Most of the grooms were spread across the town, many heading their own households.

	1851	1861	1871	1881	1891	1901	1911
Chelsea House 13 London End	Unoccupied	Rev. S.E. Major (1)	Hannah Rees (1)	Sarah Roadnight (1)	Sarah Roadnight (3)	Fred White (0)	
Essex House 15 London End	Edmund Grove (1)	Maria Green (0)	Jane G. Grove (2)	Owner absent (1)	Elizabeth Myers (2)	Elizabeth Myers (1)	Elizabeth Myers (1)
17 London End	Mary Jackson (2)	Catherine Charsley (1)	Barnard Beckam (1)	Barnard Beckam (1)	Eliza Hemsted (2)	Eliza Hemsted (2)	
The Elms 21 London End	Unoccupied	George A. Charsley (4)	George A. Charsley (4)	George A. Charsley (4)	George A. Charsley (2)	George A. Charsley (2)	George A. Charsley (3)
The Yews 27 London End	Dr John C Rumsey (3)	Mary C. Rumsey (1)	Dr H. Sandwich (5)	Rev. Wm Chambers (5)	Arthur Baker (0)	Cecil Marcon (2)	Owner absent (2)
18 London End	Elizabeth Boddy (1)	Elizabeth Boddy (2)	Elizabeth Boddy (2)	Alfred W. Hitchcock (0)	Rev. B.S. Kirby (1)	Mary E. Whitfield (1)	
Burke Lodge 20 London End	John Smith (1)	Unoccupied	William H. Bacon (1)	Rev. E.B. Finlay (2)	Arthur R. Grenfell (1)	Unoccupied	Bailey Gibson (4)
Burke House 22 London End	John Parton (2)	Unoccupied	Catherine Charsley (3)	Catherine Charsley (2)	Dr Francis Johnson (1)	Dr Wm W. Kennedy (2)	Julia Inglefield (5)
Wendover House 24 London End	Unoccupied	Dr Harding Rees (4)	Dr F.J. Wadd (2)	Dr Thomas Parrott (2)	Unoccupied	Tom Mundy (0)	James R.N. Stopford (5)
Hall Cottage Windsor End	Rebecca Hall (2)	Unoccupied	Unoccupied	George Withall (2)	George Withall (2)	Unoccupied	John M. Figgis (2)
Little Hall Barn Windsor End	Julia Crick (2)	Edmund Sheppard (3)	Unoccupied	Emily Parker (3)	Emily Parker (2)	Emily Parker (1)	Esther Young (4)
The Grange Amersham Road	William Dawkins (2)	William Dawkins (3)	Charles N. Biggs (1)	George H. Wood (2)	Charles F. Sage (2)	James Gurney (1)	Owner absent

Table 12 *Servants in Beaconsfield households, 1851-1901,*

	1851	1861	1871	1881	1891	1901
Males aged 15-69	474	467	415	429	503	481
Farmers	14 (+2 >70 +1 widows)	13	13	14	15	8
Farmers Son	5	4	2	2	7	8
Ag Labourers	82	133	99	89	103	69
Ag Lab living in	12	9	7	2	4	0
Ag Other	2	1	2	5	2	4
Labourers	83	13	41	50	33	35
Woodmen	7	9	5	3	7	6
Sawyers	33	24	8	11	5	2
Gamekeepers	5	5	6	7	7	7
Gardeners	15	17	16	13	14	33
Total above	258	228	199	198	198	173
% working on the land	54	49	48	46	39	36
Grooms	7	7	11	7	28	20

Table 13   *Men aged 15-69 working on the land, 1851-1901.*

Craftsmen

The craftsmen associated with the agricultural activities of the parish and the passing trade enjoyed by the town were an important element of the male population. The growing affluence of southern Buckinghamshire will have assisted in supporting these men. What is remarkable is how constant the numbers were in the various trades until 1901, when a large number of bricklayers were recorded. Eight had been born outside the parish. Five of the brickmakers' labourers aged under 20 were born locally, so theirs may have been 'new jobs'. They are more likely to have been employed in Lord Burnham's improvements and some of the new houses appearing on the edges of the Old Town rather than in railway construction. There were 23 navvies working on the railway, of whom eight were born in the parish and only five outside Buckinghamshire. There was no railway camp and the navvies were spread around the town, with one in the police cells on census night.

Women's Employment

The censuses provide only a glimpse of the employment of women. In 1851, about forty per cent of women in Beaconsfield were employed outside the home, although by 1901 the figure had fallen to 32 per cent. Such work was mainly done by unmarried women.

	1851	1861	1871	1881	1891	1901
Bricklayer	11	16	11	10	12	26
Building	3	3	5	7	7	5
Carpenter	9	14	14	13	12	18
Painter	3	1	3	3	8	12
Plumber	1	3	7	4	3	9
Blacksmith	7	8	5	4	7	5
Wheelwright	3	2	3	4	2	1
Hurdle maker	2			3	1	4
Well Sinker	3			1		
Saddler	5	4	3	4	3	4
Chalk Drawer	1					
Charcoal Burner	1	1	3			
Sweep	1	1	2	1	2	3
	50	53	56	54	57	87

Table 14   *Tradesmen and craftsmen, 1851-1901.*

	1851	1861	1871	1881	1891	1901
Total 15+	565	540	485	505	571	528
Boarding Scholars	6	6	5	11	7	0
	559	534	480	494	564	528
Occupied	202	239	160	198	212	167
% Occupied	36.1	44.8	33.3	40.1	37.6	31.6
Lacemakers	62	77	36	37	25	22
Dressmakers etc	24	34	28	42	29	13
Domestic Servants	64	69	52	60	90	64
Retail Workers	3	13	10	16	17	18
Public House Workers	9	5	0	1	7	5
Laundress & Charwomen	17	13	17	16	16	19
Teachers	11	10	8	15	15	9
Other	12	18	9	11	13	17

Table 15   *Womens' employment, 1851-1901.*

Children's Employment

Employment opportunities for girls were limited although it should be expected that the census will have under-recorded their occupations. Only two of those aged under 10 were shown as lace-makers. The percentage of those aged 10-14 who were in employment reached its height in 1871, helped by the chair factory, but then fell with under 12-year-olds in employment reducing to only six per cent in 1901.

GIRLS 10-14	1851	1861	1871	1881	1891	1901	
Boarding Scholars	18	16	18	11	10		73
Chairmakers		6	7	2			15
Domestic Servants	3	6	6	9	8	6	37
Labourers			1	1			2
Lacemaking	3		1	2	1	1	8
PH staff		1					1
Pupil Teachers				1			1
Total Employed	6	13	15	15	9	7	64
Total	102	107	91	102	121	110	633
Total Excl Boarding Scholars	84	91	73	91	111	110	560
% Occupied	7	14	21	16	8	6	11

Table 16 *Children's employment – girls, 1851-1901.*

The percentage of boys aged 10-14 in employment fell from a peak of 50 per cent in 1861 to 22 per cent in 1891 and 1901. Agriculture or labouring accounted for more than half of the employment of these boys in all years except 1901.

Migration and London

The schoolmaster of an Oxfordshire parish told Rider Haggard that 'three quarters of the young men and all the young women left the parish at 19 or 20 years of age, only the dullest remaining.' Whilst this was no doubt an exaggeration, and Beaconsfield had far more opportunities for its youngsters than a small rural parish, the census figures do show significant emigration from the town. The birthplaces given in the 1851 and 1901 censuses provide a glimpse into the way in which people moved about the country. Beaconsfield's stagnation in this period can be seen from the fact that in 1851, the proportion

of those born in the town but living elsewhere was 45 per cent. By 1901, 62 per cent of those born in Beaconsfield had moved away. This loss of talent was not made up by outsiders coming into the town. In 1851, 40 per cent of the residents had been born outside the town, whilst by 1901, that proportion had only risen to 44 per cent.

The inter-relationships between the town and London in the 19th century were very important. London must have been an outlet for the parish's poor. In 1839, James Fisher, a 12 year old from Beaconsfield, was charged at Queen Square Magistrates' court for sleeping in the open air. He said he was without friends at Beaconsfield as his mother had died and his father had been transported for machine-breaking. He lay in haystacks in the summer and came to London in the winter.[10] The table compares the places where those born in Beaconsfield were living in 1851 and 1901 with the birthplaces of those

Boys, 10-14	1851	1861	1871	1881	1891	1901	Total
Agriculture	18	20	9	20	10	5	82
Building	1	3	1	1	1	2	9
Chair making		6	3				9
Crafts	6	6	2	2	0	1	17
Servants						1	1
Gamekeeper						2	2
Gardener	1	2	2	1		3	9
Errand boy	3		1	1	4	1	10
Labourer	3	1	7	4	1		16
Teacher	1						1
PH staff				1	1		2
Post						1	1
Retail	5	2	1	5	2	4	19
	38	40	26	35	19	20	178
Boarding scholar	21	27	32	40	30	6	156
Grand Total	115	107	112	142	117	96	689
	94	80	80	102	87	90	533
	40.4	50	32.5	34.3	21.8	22.2	33.396
% in agriculture	47.4	50	34.6	57.1	52.6	25.0	47.4
% Labourers	13.6	2.44	23.5	12.5	20.8	4.76	13.6

Table 17 *Childrens' employment – boys, 1851-1901.*

resident in Beaconsfield in the same years. In 1851, 12 per cent of those born in Beaconsfield were living in London and a further six per cent in Middlesex, while by 1901 these figures had both become 11 per cent. It is sometimes forgotten that for every migrational flow there is a counter flow. In 1851, four per cent of Beaconsfield's residents had been born in London, whilst by 1901 that figure had risen to five per cent. In 1851, 1.4 per cent of those born in Beaconsfield were in Wycombe and a similar percentage were in Uxbridge. By 1901, 3.3 per cent of those born in Beaconsfield were found in Wycombe, whilst only 0.4 per cent were in Uxbridge. The increase in migration from Beaconsfield to Wycombe was proportionate to the increase in Wycombe's population. Wycombe, however, was a much greater lure to the populations of local villages than it was to natives of Beaconsfield. In 1851, no fewer than 12 per cent of those born in Penn lived in Wycombe, whilst this figure had risen to 17 per cent in 1891.

| | Those Born in Beaconsfield | | | | | Those Resident in Beaconsfield | | | | |
| | 1851 | | 1901 | | % change | 1851 | | 1901 | | % change |
	No.	%	No.	%	%	No.	%	No.	%	%
Beaconsfield	996	55.4	864	39.2	-13	996	60.8	864	54.7	-13
Bucks South	257	14.3	265	12.0	3	252	15.4	261	16.1	4
Wycombe	25	1.4	72	3.3	188	34	2.1	34	2.1	0
Bucks North	8	0.4	17	0.8	113	28	1.7	27	1.7	-4
Berkshire	53	2.9	99	4.5	87	42	2.6	41	2.4	-2
Herts South	34	1.9	28	1.3	-18	13	0.8	15	1.0	15
Uxbridge	26	1.4	8	0.4	-69	8	0.5	2	0.0	-75
Hillingdon	24	1.3	26	1.2	8	1	0.1	1	0.0	0
Middlesex	53	2.9	189	8.6	257	13	0.8	21	1.5	62
London	217	12.1	250	11.3	15	62	3.8	79	5.0	27
Surrey	14	0.8	72	3.3	414	6	0.4	19	1.2	217
Essex	0	0	49	2.2		10	0.6	19	1.2	90
Other South-East	24	1.3	102	4.6	325	17	1	35	2.2	106
Oxfordshire	14	0.8	19	0.9	36	32	2	34	2.2	6
All Others	53	3.1	144	6.4	172	123	7.4	117	8.7	-4.8
Total excl. boarding school pupils		100		100			100		100	

Table 18 *Migration to and from Beaconsfield in 1851 and 1891.*

Thirteen

The Railway and the New Town

With the opening of Brunel's Great Western Railway through Slough in May 1838, the people of Beaconsfield were only seven miles away from a mainline railway station. In 1854, the G.W.R. branch from Maidenhead to High Wycombe brought the railway even closer, with a station at Wooburn Green. In 1895, a Harrow, Uxbridge and High Wycombe Railway was promoted, which was to pass through Gerrards Cross and Beaconsfield. This had the backing of the Metropolitan Railway. The Great Western Railway responded by proposing to build a new mainline through High Wycombe to Paddington, also passing through Beaconsfield. The U.D.C. discussed the rival schemes in 1897 and supported the Great Western line, but only after a rare split vote. The railway came a step nearer in 1899 when the G.W.R. formed a committee with the Great Central Railway to build the new

96   *Beaconsfield Station, 1910, with Station Parade on the right.*

mainline to London as a joint venture. Their line was to use the existing section of the G.W.R. Aylesbury branch, from Princes Risborough to High Wycome, from where a new line to London would be constructed, passing just to the north of Beaconsfield. Although the line took several years to build and did not open until April 1906, there was an immediate impact on the local economy. Speculative building began on Shepherds Lane, Park Lane and Candlemas Lane and the agents of William Baring Du Pre of Wilton Park and Earl Howe of Penn House began to mark out building sites in their fields near the proposed station.

Development near the Old Town

Development on the edges of the Old Town was something familiar to local builders. Indeed, two terrace blocks of houses in Shepherds Lane had been built in about 1900. In one block of five terraced cottages, accommodation varied from five to six rooms. In 1910, these cottages were valued between £128-160 and were rented for £7-9 per year.[1] It is not clear whether the developers of these houses anticipated the building of the railway. The

terraced houses in Candlemas Lane were built at much the same time and aimed at a similar market. Built in eight blocks, they were typical of 19th-century developments in which a small builder built several houses, sometimes keeping one for himself, and selling the rest on to an investor. Here the builders were Sidney Grice of Knotty Green, and William Child and Edward Tilbury, both long-established Beaconsfield builders. At the time of the 1910 valuation, rents ranged from £15 per year for a '3 up 3 down' cottage to £19 per year for a '4 up 4 down' cottage and £24 for Wilton Park View, a '3 up 3 down' cottage with a bathroom. The values of the houses ranged from £245-320.[2]

The terraced houses in Candlemas Lane were built quickly. By the time of the 1910 valuation, only six of the 31 plots had not been built upon and by 1925 only two pieces of land were left for later infilling. Larger houses in Candlemas Lane were slow to appear, with only one (Fernhurst) being listed in 1925, but between then and 1939, plots on either side of the road were developed northwards to Station Road, with 19 houses on the east side and 12 on the west side. The land on which Fernhurst was built was bought by Arthur Charsley in 1903 for £600. A house with seven bedrooms, reception rooms and a housekeeper's room was built, valued at £2,000. In 1909, the house was leased for 10 years by Joseph Peal, a wholesale stationer from Ealing, at a rent of £120 per

97 *Bull Farm Cottage, Park Road, designed by P. Morley Horder, 1910.*

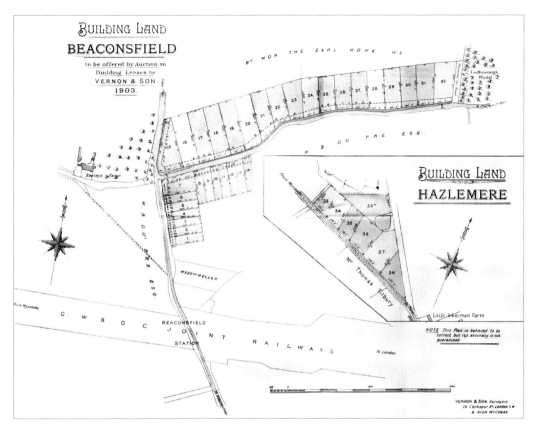

98   *Building plots at Penn Road and Ledborough Lane, 1903.*

year. In 1911 he had three live-in servants. In 1934 the house was acquired for a convalescent home by Roman Catholic sisters, who had a rather brutalist building added in the grounds.

By 1903, when building plots in Park Lane were sold, the railway was eagerly awaited. Although the houses had views over Wilton Park, there remained uncertainty as to the best market to aim for. Two semi-detached houses, built by the local builder Jesse Reeves and valued at £500 each, were built next to a house designed by the well-known architect P. Morley Horder, valued at £1,150. One house owned by Richard Perryman, a local corn dealer, was valued at £960 and let at £55 per year to Admiral Cragie. Another, owned by the builder Benjamin Bagley, was let to Captain, later Rear Admiral, Tudor and after him to surgeon Rear Admiral Dennis. These men were in the forefront

of a new tradition for this inland town of housing naval officers. However, next door was The Meade, owned and occupied by A.R. Morford whose family grocery business was in London End. It seems unlikely therefore that the first residents of these houses were commuters to London.

Ledborough Lane

Some of Earl Howe's land on Ledborough Lane and Penn Road was divided into 32 building plots by the High Wycombe estate agent Arthur Vernon in 1903.[3] The sale plan shows 18 fairly evenly sized lots on the north side and seven on the south side of the road, plus another seven plots on the east side of Penn Road, south of its junction with Ledborough Lane. Most of the plots were purchased by local builders, G. & F. Bagley, who built old-fashioned villas like Cestria,

99   *Ledborough Lane, 1912.*

100   *Meldon, Ledborough Lane,
the home of Mrs Smythe, 1910.*

5 Ledborough Lane, mostly to the designs of the local architects Burgess & Myers. One of their better houses was Meldon, 19 Ledborough Lane, built by G. & F. Bagley and occupied by Mrs Smythe. By the time of the 1910 valuation map, there were houses on 17 of the 25 plots, which was rapid progress by Beaconsfield standards. By 1924 development was continuous as far as Ledborough Wood.

Curzon Avenue

In May 1906, a further 105 acres of Earl Howe's land was released, including land either side of

Penn Road over the U.D.C. boundary in the parish of Penn. The plots ranged in size from one-quarter of an acre to seven acres. There were 76 small plots north of Ledborough Lane within the parish of Beaconsfield earmarked for 'country cottages', with a minimum value of £200. There were 11 more plots here for 'superior country cottages' with a minimum value of £250. All these were to be accessed from a network of new roads called Curzon Avenue, Richard Road, Francis Road and George Road. There were five plots on the east side of Penn Road, between Ledborough Lane and Curzon Avenue, intended for 'moderate sized houses' valued at £300, and a further five plots, north of Curzon Avenue, for houses valued at more than £400. Another seven plots north of the U.D.C. boundary were for houses valued at more than £500. The 15 plots for 'superior country residences', with a minimum value of £750, were mostly on the west side of Penn Road, north of the hamlet of Knotty Green. The plots were to be conveyed leasehold to the individual or firm which offered the highest annual ground rent. The deposit was the first year's rent in advance. This may reflect some nervousness on the part of Earl Howe's agents that there was not sufficient capital available for developers to buy the freeholds outright.

Only very gradually did houses appear in Curzon Avenue, Richard Road, Francis Road and George Road, as they were known in the 1920s. Curzon was one of the surnames in Earl Howe's family and his Christian names were Richard George. Francis was the name of his son and heir. The modern names of Sandelswood Lane, Assheton Road, Bearswood and Brownswood Road did not appear until about 1930, although their alignments were all set out by at least 1910. The new names were local woodlands, with the exception of Assheton, another surname in Earl Howe's family.

Penn Road

The earliest houses built on Penn Road were modest houses on small plots south of Seeleys Farm and Ledborough Lane. Calumet, however, situated on the corner of Seeleys Lane, was valued at £3,000, probably the highest-rated house built in the New Town. In 1910 it was rented by George Hart from Mrs M.E. Thurlow, of The Towers, Salisbury. With three reception rooms and seven bedrooms, it was described by the valuers as 'well built and fitted throughout' and 'too good for the neighbourhood'. Earl Howe began to release land from Seeleys Farm on the west side of Penn Road in about 1910. The builders G. & F. Bagley bought Seeley's Orchard and built 12 large houses there to the designs of Burgess & Myers. Most of these houses were completed by 1915, suggesting that there was a strong demand for houses with a frontage onto an existing road. Ennerdale, 41 Penn Road, belonged to James Bruce Ronaldson, who held an appointment at a London hospital but was also Hon. Medical Officer for the Children's Convalescent Home in Beaconsfield. Cherry Trees, 49 Penn Road, was occupied by Stephen Bird, a member of the Bird brewery family of High Wycombe.

On the opposite side of the road, the large building plots released in 1906 were gradually developed. Milton Mount, 42 Penn Road, was built in 1912 on a two and a half-acre plot with

101 *Enid Blyton in the garden of Green Hedges, c.1950.*

102   *Upton Leigh, 46 Penn Road, designed by Burgess, Myers & Holden, 1914.*

a gardener's cottage in the grounds. It had eight bedrooms and belonged to the London bookseller Charles Maggs. This house was later owned by the children's writer Enid Blyton, who renamed it Green Hedges. In 1946, the Blyton household included a cook, a house-parlour maid and a gardener.[4] Green Hedges was demolished in the 1970s and replaced by several houses in a new road called Blyton Close. Next door was Upton Leigh, designed by Burgess, Myers & Holden in

1914. In the 1920s, this was the home of Kenneth Oswald Peppiatt, chief cashier of the Bank of England. Further to the north was Chiltern Place, 58 Penn Road, another eight-bedroom house with a gardener's cottage. This was briefly the home of Evelyn Alice Eyre, sister of Earl Howe, who had married John Eyre in 1896. She died in 1913 of injuries sustained in a pony trap accident near the house. By 1918, John Eyre had moved to Three Gables, Station Road. The most northerly

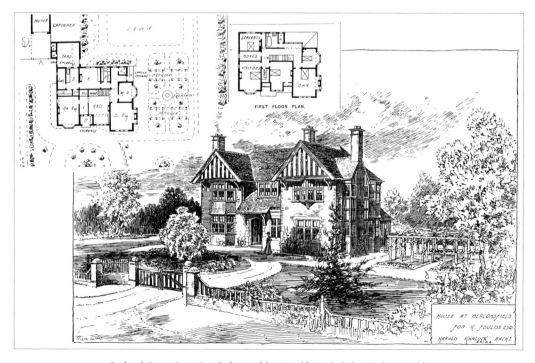

103   *Orchard Dene, Penn Road, designed by Harold Harlock for Herbert Foulds, 1906.*

104 *The Farm Cottage, Knotty Green, extended by Burgess & Myers, for J. Bailey Gibson, 1910.*

105 *Netherlands, Knotty Green, built for architect Julian Burgess in 1907.*

of these houses, White Cottage, 64 Penn Road, was valued at £1,500 and was occupied by H.E. Burgess, an accountant who later became the Senior Official Receiver.

Development continued along Penn Road over the U.D.C. boundary into Penn. The area was attractive to new residents and developers as it was within a mile of the railway station and there was no need to wait for the laying out of new roads. The rising ground afforded good views over the surrounding countryside and the large plots gave ample room for gardeners' cottages, lodges and chauffeurs' flats. Some very substantial houses were built on the east side of the road on land purchased by the local estate

agent John Rolfe. Orchard Dene, 70 Penn Road, was designed by Harold Harlock A.I.R.B.A., for Herbert Foulds in 1906. There were large stone-mullioned windows to the hall and an inglenook fireplace in the drawing room.[5]

The architect Julian Burgess built his own house called Netherlands just off Penn Road in 1907. The land, formerly part of Knotty Green Farm, was purchased from Robert Henry Rolfe for £250. The house featured Dutch gables, casement windows under brick relieving arches, and an inglenook fireplace inside. The prominent architect Charles Henry Biddulph-Pinchard, who was to play a key role in the Penn branch of the Council for the Protection of Rural England,

106   (Left) Hollymount,
Penn Road, designed by
C.F.A. Voysey, 1907.

107   (Below) Plan of building
plots at Baring Road and
Reynolds Road, 1905.

lived at nearby at Eghams Close, Knotty Green
Road. His house was designed in the style of
a Tudor manor house. Hollymount, designed
by the leading Arts and Crafts architect C.F.A.
Voysey, was built for company secretary Charles
Thomas Burke in 1907.

Some very large houses were built on the
west side of the road on land formerly part of
Baylins Farm, released by Earl Howe in 1906.
West Witheridge was built in 1906 for Henry
Dixon Davies, a London solicitor. When West
Witheridge was advertised for sale by Savill's
in 1927, the land extended to 11½ acres; there
were 15 bedrooms, a garage for three cars and a
chauffeur's flat. In 1919, Baylins Farm itself was
altered and extended by the architects Forbes &
Tate for the London furnisher Ambrose Heal.

Baring Road and
Reynolds Road

William Baring Du Pré's land north-west of the
railway was laid out in 63 small building plots
by Arthur Vernon in October 1905.[6] The plan
shows Baring Road and Reynolds Road, as yet
un-named, running parallel west of Penn Road but
not linking up. The lots were sold off piecemeal to
local builders like Frank Froude, E. & C. Goodyer

and T.W. Hanson. Development was quite rapid, with a variety of small houses being built, some detached, some semi-detached and some even in blocks of three. The row of three cottages, 48-52 Baring Road, was designed by Francis Duck and built by Claude Baldwin, both of Gerrards Cross. Most of the houses were built to let, with, initially at least, the builders continuing to own the property. Some were sold on as investments, as was common elsewhere, to local tradesman and others. The valuation records suggest that many were vacant in 1910, perhaps because too many small houses were being built for the available rental market.

By the time of the 1910 valuation map, 65 houses had been built and a further 14 are shown in outline. By 1924, 97 properties had appeared, but there were many empty plots, particularly on the north side of Baring Road. The 1910 process of valuation was largely via the length of frontage with £1 10s. being a typical figure. When converted into values per acre, the smaller lots were then worth more than those with long gardens. It was these smaller plots, particularly

109   *Reynolds Road, 1914.*

those on the western curve of the road (sometimes called Baring Crescent), that were first built on, largely with houses worth less than £500.

In Reynolds Road there were three substantial houses. The first house on the south side belonged to Mrs Thurlow, who also owned Calumet. It had eight bedrooms, three sitting rooms and a garage and was valued at £1,500. One of the early tenants was the Rev. Edward Domett Shaw, then Archdeacon and, from 1914, Bishop of Buckingham, who lived there until about 1920. After 1920, the 'Bishop's House' was occupied by Dr Sheffield Airey Neave, an entomologist and secretary of the Zoological Society. The other two substantial houses were on the north side of the road. Little Seeleys, 8 Reynolds Road, was valued at £1,100 and leased in 1907 for 21 years by Dr Jones from J. Wooster at £55 per year. It

had four bedrooms, a sitting hall, two reception rooms and verandas back and front. There were two doctors Jones resident here. Denmill, 12 Reynolds Road, was owned by Mary A. Rowntree and valued at £1,250. It was designed by Fred Rowntree, the Quaker architect, who was building the model village at Jordans.[7] Fred Rowntree had moved to Burke's Road by 1911 and was succeeded at Denmill by a long-term resident, Ernest A. James, head of a firm of auditors.

The poet Robert Frost was an early resident of Reynolds Road. From 1912-14 he lived with his wife and four children, in a three-bedroomed bungalow, rented from the estate agent A.C. Frost.

110   *Denmill, 12 Reynolds Road, 1910.*

It stood next to open countryside and the cherry orchards of Seeleys Farm and was described as a 'low stucco cottage, with a large grassy lawn in front, set behind hedges of laurel and red osier dogwood'.[8] It was valued at £400 and sold in 1917 for £430.

The Woodside Estate

The Woodside Estate was laid out for development at the same time as Baring Road and Reynolds Road, but very little had happened by 1910. The five houses on the valuation map are all shown in white, indicating development considerably after that date. A large area of building land had been sold to Robinson and Roods and their development company, the Circle Land Company, and another large plot had been purchased by the builder H.J. Flint. The Old Town grocer Edward Morford also owned building plots

here. The architect Herbert Green was living in Woodside Avenue in 1914.

The One Tree Meadow Estate

This was the final area lying north of the railway to be developed before 1939. The absence of earlier development was strange, given the close proximity to the station. However, William Baring Du Pre may have thought that the sale of the land elsewhere was sufficient in the New Town's early years. The road pattern was laid out later than the areas described above and in a grand manner. A short initial part of Warwick Road was shown in the valuation map as being developed and two semi-detached houses were built in about 1910, but otherwise the area was still agricultural. Oakdene School was opened in 1915 and St Michael's Church and its parsonage was built in 1917 to the designs of G.H. Fellowes Prynne. By

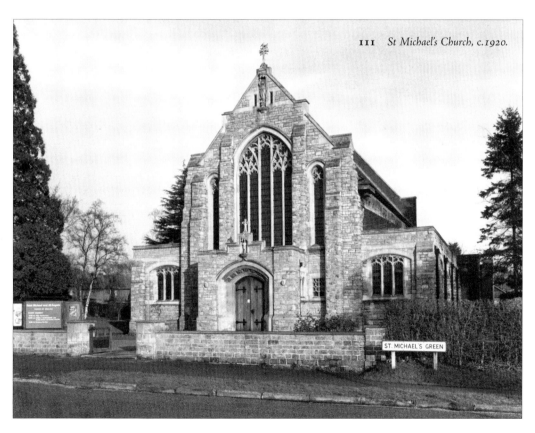

111 *St Michael's Church, c.1920.*

1924, only two further buildings had appeared: Meadow House, later called Broadfield, on the north-east corner of Wilton and Grenfell Roads, and St Michael's Corner, in what was then called Church Square.

By 1925, there were three new, two empty and three occupied houses in Caledon Road. One house called Little Gable was occupied by a Harold Belbin, a stockbroker who was an early resident of Reynolds Road. Colonel G. Wardle moved from Baring Road to occupy One Tree Cottage. Miss Homan of St Michael's Corner moved there from Station Road. This pattern of relocations suggests that, unlike those in the Baring Road area, the houses were built for owner occupation and rented accommodation was becoming less attractive to private residents.

It is perhaps a reflection of the slow development of the One Tree Estate that Roland Callingham could afford to buy several acres of land for his Bekonscot model village, which opened in 1929. By the end of 1936, Bekonscot had attracted 188,356 visitors and problems with car parking were already apparent. By April 1939, Princess Elizabeth had visited three times and Princess Margaret twice. By 1948, the number of visitors had grown to 730,000.

The Burke's Estate

Having divided his land north of the railway into building plots, William Baring Du Pre chose to sell Gregories Farm, south-west of the railway, to a single developer. He sold the farmhouse and 293 acres of land in 1907 to the local estate agents James and William Gurney for £58,690. The Gurneys borrowed £39,000 of the purchase price from Francis Baring Du Pre and the remainder was provided by Howard Montague Mackusick, who had already given the Gurneys a mortgage on their land at Gerrards Cross. A plan of roads and building plots was drawn up by the local surveyor Legender Myers,

who had recently formed a partnership with architect Julian Burgess.

Sales of building plots, planned for 10 July and 24 July 1907, were cancelled when several of the lots were sold by private contract. Lots 1-3, 21-38 and 60-3, mostly fronting Station Road, were bought by Frank Nash, a grocer from Chalfont St Giles, for £4,665. Gregories farmhouse and 27 acres of land were purchased by A.E.W. Charsley for £11,258. Another sale was advertised for 8 August 1907, when nearly 50 lots were to be sold at between £350 and £500 per acre. The advertisement claimed that 'the estate offers perhaps the healthiest situation on the new line, lying at 400ft, with soil made up from gravel and sand'. It was also stated that 60 extra lots were in preparation. Some very large plots, especially those on the western side of the estate, were marked with the maximum number of houses that could be erected there. Thus, a 13¼-acre plot was shown with a maximum of 30 houses (i.e. an average of 0.44 acres per plot). Another indicated an average size of 0.38 acres per plot, while 21 acres split into four lots was to average 0.275 acres per plot. Other large areas seem to have been excluded from the sale. Chiltern Hills Road was sketched in, but the land around it was not included in the sale. In all, the plan showed 160 lots.

The August 1907 auction was held in a marquee on the estate. The auctioneer, T.A. Bamford, said that earlier auctions had not taken place as, although plans had been drawn up, the plots had been sold in blocks to gentlemen 'who knew a good thing when they saw it'. 'His clients had bought the estate at such a price that they could afford to sell at such prices that purchasers would be sure of making a profit.' The auction was meagrely attended, although the *Bucks Free Press* correspondent noticed that several 'speculators' who usually deal in land were present, including Messrs W. Weston, Raffety, Gee, Wooster, Bagley, Reeves, Payne, Hearne, Nash etc. Whilst the reporter could not have been expected to identify any potential

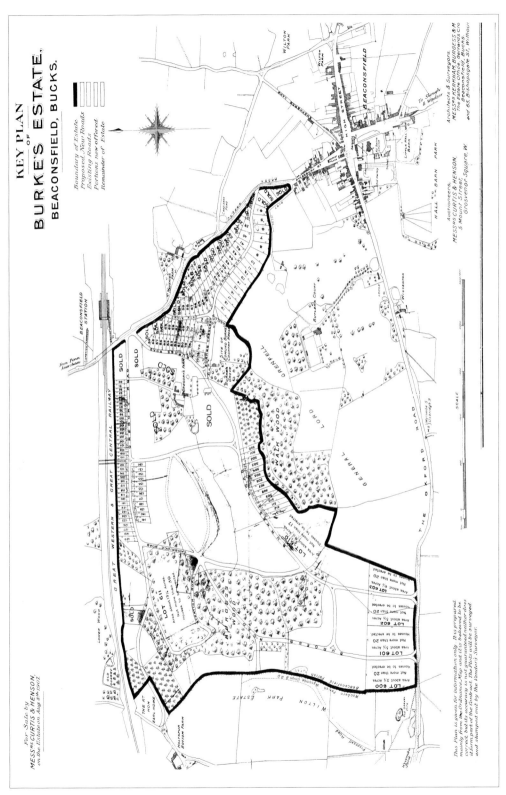

112 *Plan of Burke's Estate, 1907.*

113   *Overroads, Grove Road, the home of G.K. Chesterton.*

London purchasers, other evidence suggests that they would have been scarce. No plots were actually sold at the auction, even though land was offered at £350 per acre. A few were subsequently sold singly. Bamford himself must have bought some lots as he was still listed as an owner in 1909-10. By the time of the 1910 valuation, the main owners of land on the estate were James and William Gurney, A.E.W. Charsley, Frank Nash, A.C. Frost, and Burgess and Myers.

Station Road

The west side of the Burke's Estate had a long frontage to the old road to Penn, which was just then acquiring the name of Station Road. The 1907 sale plan shows 18 building plots here, but most had been purchased by a developer, Frank Nash of Chalfont St Giles, before the sale. Nash sold on to a variety of investors before development was complete. Such speculation was probably a result of the frontage to an established road, making development easy. One of the first houses was Overroads, on the corner of Grove Road, designed by architects Burgess & Myers

for Frederick William Lane, a newsagent from Chalfont St Giles. In 1909, Lane rented the new house to the author and journalist G.K. Chesterton. Some of the houses were substantial. Steyning, with five bedrooms and three reception rooms, was let at £85 but was sold before 1910 to the dentist Frederick Bailey Penfold. Northgate, 64 Station Road, had three receptions rooms and six bedrooms and was let at £100 per year. It was occupied by Hugh Edward Clerk, former Chief Engineer in Madras, from 1920 until his death in 1942.

Station Road attracted some very high-status residents. John Eyre J.P., who had married Evelyn Curzon, sister of Earl Howe, lived at Three Gables, 26 Station Road, from 1918-28. He was Chairman of the U.D.C., 1920-2. This house was demolished and flats built on the site as early as 1968. Lady Edith Curzon, another sister of Earl Howe, married Harry Walter Franklin and was left a widow in 1915. She lived at Willington, 62 Station Road, from 1924 until her death in 1936. The house was then occupied by her daughter, Violet, who had married Edmond de Ayala of the champagne family in 1924. This, too, has now been replaced by flats. At Oak House, 46 Station Road, was James Edge Partington, who moved from Wyngates, Burke's Road. He served on the U.D.C. in the 1920s and died at Beaconsfield in 1930. A large house called Penn Croft, 18 Station Road, was demolished in the 1960s to build the shops south of the cinema.

The east side of Station Road was dominated by Davenies Farm, which was bought by the architect Stanley Hamp for £2,100 in 1909. Hamp converted the farmhouse and barn into a large country house and was living there with his mother in 1911.[9] Davenies became a school in 1940. Hamp also designed White Barn,[10] which was bought in 1922 with two acres of land for £4,500 in order to relocate the childrens' convalescent home from London End. This site is now occupied by a car showroom.

Gregories Road

The north side of the Burke's Estate was laid out as Gregories Road, running parallel to the railway. The corner plot of over an acre, next to Station Road, had already been sold to Legender Myers and others by the time of the auction. This was valued in 1910 at a high rate for the town of £875 per acre. The elegant shops called Burke's Parade were built here, including the offices of estate agent A.C. Frost and architects Burgess & Myers. Part of this site remained undeveloped in 1924 and eventually housed the telephone exchange and some more shops. Between this site and the railway footbridge, there were 21 plots on the 1907 sale plan. These were bought

by five different developers. Beyond the bridge were 18 more building plots.

Development was slow, with only seven houses built on this side of the road by 1910. The first houses were modest in size, and generally rented out by builders, such as Frank Froude and T.W. Hanson. Dalehurst, 60 Gregories Road, was owned by Burgess & Myers and occupied by Myers himself in 1915. North Dene, 74 Gregories Road, next to the footbridge, was built by F. & O. Nash and sold in 1910 to the High Wycombe estate agent Percy Charles Raffety for £550. Raffety lived at North Dene until the 1950s. Numbers 112 and 114 Gregories Road were built in 1919 by Henry Brown, a builder from Stoke Newington, who developed the North Park Estate in Gerrards Cross. Salter's Acre, 116 Gregories Road, was built in 1920 by the architect Walter Holden, by then a partner in Burgess, Holden & Watson. There were 22 houses on the north side of the road by 1925.

Gregories Farm, bounded by Gregories Road, Furrzefield Road and Burke's Road, was purchased in November 1907 by the sitting tenant,

114 *Gregories Road, c.1912.*

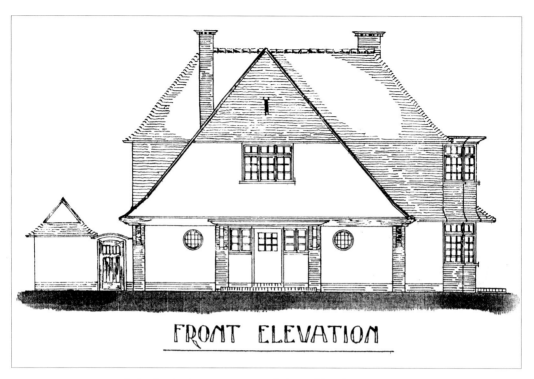

115   *Orchard Dale, Gregories Farm Road, designed by Johnson & Boddy, 1912.*

116   *Salter's Acre, 116 Gregories Road, designed by Walter Holden, 1920.*

A.E.W. Charsley, for £11,258. Charsley was still living at the farmhouse in 1911. With the help of the estate agent A.C. Frost, he sold off a few building plots, including St Johns, 31 Gregories Road (now demolished), which was used as a private school by Lawrence Solomon until 1916, when he moved to New Gregories School, near to the old farmhouse. In 1911, The Gables, 45 Gregories Road, was let to Reginald Ratcliffe Whistler, a bank clerk. The house was owned by the builder Frank Froude until 1919, when it was sold to the sitting tenant, Sidney Bryant, for £1,025. Orchard Dale, on the road to Gregories Farm, was built for A.C. Frost in 1912 and designed by Johnson & Boddy. It was bought by William Birch, the son of a leading High Wycombe chair manufacturer. Some plots remained vacant and were often taken on as extra gardens. Lyttelton, 39 Gregories Road, was not built until 1920 when the land was purchased for a modest £225.

Beyond Furzefield Road, the 1907 sale plan had 12 building plots before Cambridge Road. Ravenswood, 81 Gregories Road was built in 1914. This house was designed by Stanley Hamp and owned by Charles Howard Bowser. A cine-film made by Bowser's grandson features the house and the chauffeur driving the family's Rolls Royce, which was later owned by Peter Ustinov.[11] By 1925 there were 19 houses on the south side of Gregories Road, with two vacant plots added to existing gardens. These were not touched until the 1960s. There were 70 houses in Gregories Road by 1958. In the 1930s, Stanley Hamp developed several flat-roofed houses on the corner of Gregories Road and Cambridge Road. Some of these have now had pitched roofs added, but Whitelands, 75 Gregories Road, remains in its original state.

At the far end of Gregories Road, 13 acres of land with a new road called Stratton Road were earmarked for 30 large houses. One of the first of these was Bekken Cottage, 41 Stratton Road, designed by the London architects Ashley & Newman. Stratton Wood, 28 Stratton Road, was designed by Cornelius Wheeler in 1912 for William S. Fowler. Stratton End, 24 Stratton Road, was designed in 1913 by Ashley & Newman for Manfred Jefferson.[12] The Corner Cottage was designed by Walter Holden in 1921 for the society photographer Richard Neville Speight.

117 *The Corner Cottage, Stratton Road, c.1925.*

118   *Stratton End, 24 Stratton Road, 1924.*

Burke's Road

Burke's Road joined Gregories Road and Station Road at a junction which became known as Five Ways when Maxwell Road was developed on the south-east side of the railway. The east side of Burke's Road, as far as Burke's Crescent, was developed quickly. Rowardennan, 5 Burke's Road, later called Maryton, was built in 1910 for the estate agent Norman William Gurney. It was designed by Stanley Hamp and featured in Gurney's advertising of the Burke's Estate.[13] It is very similar to Thornton (later The Lantern House), 9 Burke's Road, which was occupied in 1911 by a widow, Sophie Skinner. Mrs Skinner's son, Cyriac, became

119   *An advertisement for the Burke's Estate, featuring 5 Burke's Road, designed by Stanley Hamp, 1910.*

a major-general and lived opposite at Farm End, 10 Burke's Road. He was Chairman of the U.D.C 1933-5 and served on the County Council. Also in the same cottage style is Oriel Lodge, 19 Burke's Road, which was occupied in 1911 by George William Borradaile, a retired Indian Army colonel. N.W. Gurney himself was living in this part of Burke's Road in 1911, at a house called Hasfield, named after the Gloucestershire village where his wife was born.

On the west side of Burke's Road, three houses were built near to the junction with Gregories Road. Altons, 2 Burke's Road, was owned by the architect Fred Rowntree. He designed a gardener's cottage for the site in 1914. The house was demolished in the 1960s and a car park made on the site. Next was Elmslie, 4 Burke's Road, also designed by Rowntree, which is now

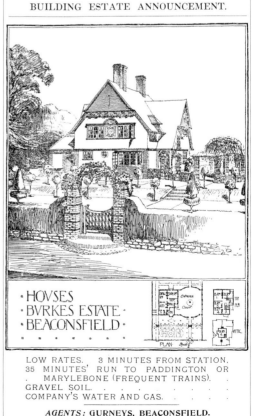

BUILDING ESTATE ANNOUNCEMENT.

· HOVSES ·
· BVRKES ESTATE ·
· BEACONSFIELD ·

PLAN

LOW RATES.   3 MINUTES FROM STATION.
35 MINUTES' RUN TO PADDINGTON OR
.   MARYLEBONE (FREQUENT TRAINS).   .
GRAVEL SOIL.   .   .   .   .   .   .
COMPANY'S WATER AND GAS.   .   .   .   .

AGENTS: GURNEYS, BEACONSFIELD.

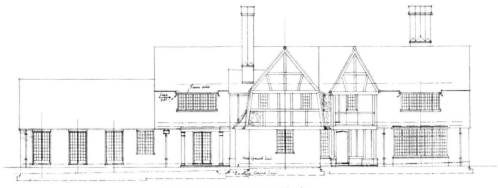

SOUTH-WEST ELEVATION

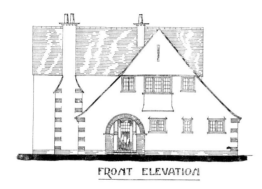

FRONT ELEVATION

120 *(Above) Manawatu, 12 Burke's Road, designed by Burgess, Holden & Watson for A.C. Frost, 1935.*

121 *(Left) Fairlawn, 34 Burke's Road, designed by Johnson & Boddy, 1910.*

Brinchley House Child Care Centre. Yewlands, 6 Burke's Road, was designed by Johnson & Boddy. It was occupied from 1911-39 by Arthur Treacher Stephens, a prominent solicitor with chambers at Lincoln's Inn. Further development along this side of the road was limited by a large pond and the driveway to Gregories Farm, which belonged to the solicitor A.E.W. Charsley. Charsley soon released some building plots south-west of the farm. Uplands, 28 Burke's Road, was built in 1910 and occupied in 1911 by William Gordon Edwards, of 'private means'. The house was later called Timbers and has recently been replaced by Coningsby House. Both Uplands and Heatherdene, 30 Burke's Road, were designed by Johnson and Boddy. The same firm also designed Fairlawn, 34 Burke's Road in 1910 and Wyngates,

42 Burke's Road in 1912. Wyngates was occupied by the anthropologist James Edge Partington, whose collection was given to the Pitts-Rivers Museum. The gap near the lane to Gregories Farm was filled in 1935 by the building of Manawatu, in which the estate agent A.C. Frost and his family lived until the 1980s. Some plots on Burke's Road remained undeveloped whilst others, situated a long way from the railway station, were built upon. Woodlands, on the corner of Ellwood Road and Burke's Road, was probably built before the First World War. Alterations were made to the house in 1918 for the estate agent N.W. Gurney. He lived there from 1928 and served on both the Urban District and County Councils. He died at Beaconsfield in 1973.

It was the southern side of Burke's Road, with gardens backing onto Walk Wood, where some of the most elegant houses were built. Burke's Grove, 27 Burke's Road, with its mansard roofs, was the

SOUTH ELEVATION :

SOUTH ELEVATION.

122 (*Above*) *Wyngates, 42 Burke's Road, designed by Johnson & Boddy, 1912.*

123 (*Left*) *Woodlands, Burke's Road, extended for N.W. Gurney, 1918.*

home of James Ransome F.R.I.B.A. He bought a large plot of land and developed Cherry Tree Cottage (now By The Wood), 31 Burke's Road, and The Barn, 49 Burke's Road, all of which have mansard roofs. Ransome designed an extension to Cherry Tree Cottage for Margaret Millar, in 1913. Miss Millar was a member of the U.D.C. in the 1920s. Homewood, 35 Burke's Road, was occupied in 1911 by Richard Neville Speight, a court photographer, patronised by many of the European royalty. Speight moved to Stratton Road in about 1920. Rookwood, 43 Burke's Road, was designed by Davis, Boddy & Green in 1912. Coniston, 51 Burke's Road, was designed by Herbert Green in 1913 and has recently been

refurbished. Unfortunately, Walkwood, 65 Burke's Road, designed by Walter Holden for Stanley Whitehead, Chairman of the U.D.C. in 1947, has been demolished.

Grove Road

A third road turning out of Station Road was called Grove Road. One of the first houses to be built on the east side was Martindale, 38 Grove Road, which was sold for £1,191 in 1908. In 1911 it was occupied by John Martin Danavall, a retired colonel, who died at Beaconsfield in 1912. This house is now called Little Briars. Next door at the Brown House, 34 Grove Road, was Frances Wace,

124 *Burke's Road, c.1910.*

125 *Burke's Grove, 27 Burke's Road, 1962.*

126 *Coniston, 51 Burke's Road, designed by Herbert Green, 1913.*

NORTH ELEVATION :

a widow, and her daughter, with four servants. The name of this house has changed to Kerry Croy. On the opposite side of the road, Grove Cottage, 33 Road was built in 1910 for the estate agent N.W. Gurney. It is the reverse image of Meryton, 5 Burke's Road. Grove Ash, 31 Grove Road, was one of several houses developed by W.E. Vare of Burke's Cottage.

At its junction with Burke's Crescent, Grove Road turns east back towards Station Road. By 1925, only Marchington, 24 Grove Road, and Hillside, 4 Grove Road, had been built on the north side. The land in between was owned in 1910 by the London builder, Alfred Beach Faulkner, and went undeveloped until nine new houses were built there in the 1930s.

The plots on the south side of Grove Road and Burke's Crescent were bigger and land here was valued at £600 an acre. Boyne House, 9 Grove Road, was first occupied by Lieutenant General Schomberg of the Royal Marines, who was living there in 1911. The house was later occupied later by Sir Arnold White, retired Chief Justice of Madras, and later by Canon William Lee Harnett, formerly Vicar of Wolverton, who died at Beaconsfield in 1937. Boyne House has been redeveloped. Another early house, Highfield, 15 Grove Road, was built in 1915 and occupied by Harry Tempest Vane, a leading figure in the motor industry, having been Managing Director of Dunlop up to 1904 and then of Napier's of Acton. He died in Beaconsfield in 1942. Middle Meadow, 19a Grove Road, was owned by Sir Charles Alan Bennett, a High Court Judge, who lived there from 1915 until his death in 1943. This house has also been redeveloped. Pigeon House Meadow, built in 1915 by W.E. Vare, was first occupied by Maurice Beresford Wright, a leading psychologist.

Burke's Crescent

Linking Grove Road to Burke's Road was Burke's Crescent, on which three large houses were built. Kingswear House, 10 Burke's Crescent, was designed in 1910 by James Ransome F.R.I.B.A. for the engineer, Basil H. Joy. It is very similar to Northgate, Station Road. Burke's Wood House, 8 Burke's Crescent, was designed in 1911 by Albert Cockerell, who also designed Morven, 23 Grove Road and Hambledon, 25 Burke's Road. These houses were built for W.E. Vare, who lived nearby at Burke's Cottage, 2 Burke's Crescent. This was a converted cottage and had a huge garden, part of which is occupied by two modern houses. Vare also built the Council Chamber on the corner of Burke's Road in 1915 and was later to become Chairman of the U.D.C. In 1958, Burke's Cottage

127 *Kingswear, Burke's Crescent, 1911.*

was owned by David Gomme, joint-Managing Director of the Wycombe furniture makers.

Beaconsfield in 1911

The early release of the 1911 census enables us to examine the 164 households in the New Town, and a further 20 or so new houses just over the border in Knotty Green. The geographical origins and social character of the residents have been analysed in seven areas: the Burke's Estate including Station Road; Baring and Reynolds Roads; Ledborough Lane and the Curzon Estate; Station Parade and Penn Road south of Ledborough Lane; individual houses like The Grange which predate the railway; new houses in Knotty Green; and older houses in Knotty Green.

The prime distinction between these areas was the small size of the households in the Baring Road area, the large number of those households with no living-in servant and the very small number with two servants. Elsewhere there were only 16 households with three or more servants, although additionally there were a number of gardeners living in cottages adjoining the larger houses in Knotty Green. Only one of the houses with five servants was occupied by a private resident, Charles James Blomfield, who had been an assistant to one of the great Victorian church architects, Sir Arthur Blomfield. He lived for a short time on the east side of Penn Road, somewhere north of Ledborough Lane. Norfolk House School and the *Railway Hotel* also had five servants. Two of the four houses with four servants were in Knotty Green, one housing a solicitor and the other a stockjobber. One was a farm. The other two were the Brown House in Grove Road (owned by Mrs Wace, the widowed wife of a Norfolk clergyman) and Redlands, the largest house in Curzon Avenue (owned by Professor Arthur Whitfield of Kings College, a consulting dermatologist physician).

There were only six households on the Burke's Estate with no living-in servants. One of these belonged to A.E.W. Charsley, living at Gregories. Perhaps as a local man he relied on daily help. Only two of the 13 houses in Ledborough Lane had no servants. In the Curzon Avenue area, five out of 15 households had no servants. They included a builder involved in the estate's development, a dispatch manager, a commercial agent, a clerk on the stock exchange and an assistant keeper at the Wallace Collection.

Overall there were 56 household heads in what might broadly be termed professional occupations, 35 in commerce, 28 retired or living on private means, nine widows, nine wives (some of whom

Area	Number in Household											No. of Houses	Population
	1	2	3	4	5	6	7	8	9	10	22		
Burke's Estate	2	2	11	5	7	6	2	1	1	0	0	37	161
Baring Road	8	15	14	17	5	2	2	0	1	0	0	64	208
Curzon Avenue	1	2	10	8	6	0	5	1	0	1	0	34	150
Station Area	3	6	7	6	3	2	1	0	0	1	0	29	104
Pre-railway	2	2	0	1	1	3	1	0	0	0	0	10	40
Total New Town	16	27	42	37	22	13	11	2	2	2	0	174	663
Knotty Green New	1	2	1	5	2	6	1	1	0	0	1	20	111
Knotty Green Old	20	1	0	1	1	0	1	0	0	0	0	24	38
Grand Total	37	30	43	43	25	19	13	3	2	2	1	218	812

Table 19 *Size of households in Beaconsfield, 1911.*

AREA	NO. OF SERVANTS						HOUSES WITH SERVANTS	TOTAL NO. OF SERVANTS	% HOUSES WITH SERVANTS	SERVANTS AS % OF POP.
	0	1	2	3	4	5				
Burke's Estate	6	15	11	4	1	0	31	53	84%	33%
Baring Road	40	20	4	0	0	0	24	28	38%	13%
Curzon Avenue	9	9	14	0	1	1	25	46	74%	31%
Station area	20	7	0	0	0	1	8	12	29%	12%
Pre-railway	9	0	0	1	0	0	1	3	10%	8%
Total New Town	84	51	29	5	2	2	89	142		
Knotty Green New	2	5	7	3	2	1	18	41	90%	37%
Knotty Green Old	24	0	0	0	0	0	0	0	0%	0%
GRAND TOTAL	110	56	36	8	4	3	107	183		

Table 20 *Numbers of domestic servants in Beaconsfield, 1911.*

may have been widows), 16 domestic gardeners and other servants living outside their employer's house (12 of these were in Knotty Green), and 11 were in the building trades with a further 10 surveyors and six architects – most of these were involved with the development of the New Town. Probably more than half the heads of households living within Beaconsfield were commuters. There would have been sons and some lodgers doing this as well. Significantly more than half of the major new houses in Knotty Green were headed by commuters.

The motivations of a move to Beaconsfield can only be guessed at from census data. It has already been noted that many were setting up their first home. An initial attempt to trace the place of residence before the move indicates that this was very rarely anywhere except London and the Home Counties, although a few were probably returning from various outposts of the Empire. Within the Greater London area there was a tendency to move out along the axis formed by the new railway line, or two or three miles on either side of it. Willesden, Wembley and Ealing in particular contributed a number of the new residents. Others moved from the western extremities of Middlesex, including Staines and Uxbridge. One stockbroker moved from Windsor Road, Slough.

So far, only five have been traced who moved from Wycombe: the Archdeacon Shaw, Albert Edward Barnes, a furniture designer, from his parent's home in the aspiring area of Priory Avenue to Baring Road; and also moving from Priory Avenue to Baring Road was a commercial traveller and his wife. Two moved from Wycombe to Station Parade: a newly widowed chair manufacturer's wife who took in boarders in her new home and a newly married draper who in 1901 had lodged at a public house in Wycombe.

No. of Servants	Road	House Name	Occupier's Surname	Christian Name	Age	Profession
5	Penn Road		Blomfield	Charles James	49	Architect
5	Knotty Green	Norfolk House School	Marcon	Cecil Thomas	44	Schoolmaster
5	Penn Road	Railway Hotel	Borlase	Thomas	47	Publican retired
4	Grove Road	Brown House	Wace	Frances Anne	51	Widow
4	Curzon Avenue	Redlands	Whitfield	Arthur	42	Consulting Physician
4	Knotty Green	Whichert House	Prestone	Charles Sansone	45	Solicitor
4	Knotty Green	Farm Cottage	Pawle	Levis Shepherd	51	Stock jobber
3	Grove Road	Boyne House	Schomberg	Herbert St George	66	Lieut. Gen. Army Retired
3	Burke's Road	Burke's Cottage	Vare	William Edmund	35	Sanitary Engineer Contractor
3	Burke's Road	Cherry Tree Cottage	Joy	Basil Hambert	40	Consulting Engineer Printing Motor Works
3	Burke's Road	Hollywood	Morris	William George Wingate	33	Solicitor
3	Penn Road	Davenies	Hamp	Anne Mary	71	Mother of architect
3	Amersham Road	Barnhurst	Chaplin	Percy Frank	28	Gentleman
3	Knotty Green	Drews	Cuthbert	Gordon	34	Produce broker
3	Knotty Green	Witheridge	Davies	Henry Dixon	52	Solicitor
3	Knotty Green	Orchard Dene	Foulds	Herbert	65	Independent

Table 21 *Beaconsfield houses with three or more servants, 1911.*

Occupation	Burke's Estate	Baring Road	Curzon Avenue	Pre-Railway	Station Area	Knotty Green New	Knotty Green Old	Total
Solicitor	4	2	1			4		11
Architect	1	2	1			2		6
Stockjobber		2	5		1	2		10
Doctor	2		2		1			5
Arts, Publishing, Religion	2	3	2			1		8
Civil Servant	2	2	6					10
Accountant	1	3	2					6
Commerce	5	13	6		5	6		35
Law		1					1	2
Surveyor	3	4			2	1		10
Private Means	4	3	1	1		3		12
Retired	3	4	3		2	1	3	16
Widow	4		2	2			1	9
Wife	1	6	1		1			9
Retail	1	6			11		1	19
Boarding House Keeper		2			1			3
Builders etc.	1	6	1		3			11
Railway		3			1			4
Inside Servant	2							2
Outside Servant	1	1	1	1			12	16
Farmer				3			4	7
Labourer		1		3	1		2	7
Grand Total	37	64	34	10	29	20	24	218

Table 22 *Occupations of heads of households in Beaconsfield, 1911.*

Endnotes

Chapter One – Lords of the Manor

1. Dugdale, *Monasticon Anglicanum*, vol. 4, p.574.
2. Pipe Rolls Soc., vol. 9, p.26.
3. Cartulary of Missenden Abbey, vol. 2, item 416.
4. Inquisition Post Mortem 17, Edward IV, no.25.
5. British Library Harleian Rolls, S.1.
6. Nottingham University Library, Mi 6/170/89.
7. TNA SC, 11/76.
8. Lipscomb, G., *History and Antiquities of the County of Buckingham*, vol. 3 (1847), p.209.
9. L & P, Hen VIII, xx (2), g. 1068 (50).
10. CBS, D 247.
11. TNA, SP 11/8/52.
12. TNA, C 142/126/150.
13. TNA, C 142/217/116.
14. TNA, CP 25/2/274 6 JAS I TRIN.
15. TNA, Feet of Fines Bucks., Easter 22 Jas I.

Chapter Two – Great Houses

1. Feet of Fines Bucks., case 19, file 78.
2. TNA, CP 25/1/20/94.
3. *Ibid.*
4. British Library (B.L.), Egerton Rolls, 8325.
5. CBS, Hall Barn Deeds, AR 93/2006/16.
6. TNA, C 137/76/6.
7. B.L., Harleian Roll, S.1.
8. CBS, Hall Barn Deeds, AR 93/2006/25.
9. TNA, C 140/61/25.
10. Certificate of Musters for Bucks., 1522, Bucks. Record Soc., vol. 17 (1973).
11. TNA, 142/44/97.
12. Steele Mss, Bod. Lib. Mss. Top. Gen. E. 79.
13. TNA, Feet of Fines, Div. Co., Mich 37, Henry VIII.
14. CBS, D 247.
15. Lipscomb, G., *History and Antiquities of the County of Buckingham*, vol. 3, p.157.
16. TNA, *Catalogue of Ancient Deeds*, vol. 1, A 679.
17. *Valor Ecclesiasticus* (Record Commission), iv, 221.
18. CBS, Hall Barn Deeds, AR 93/2006/72.
19. Northants. Record Office, O, xxii, 3.
20. Glouc. Rec. Off. D 6148/3/2.
21. Feet of Fines Bucks., Easter 22 Jas I.
22. CBS, Report by N.W. Alcock on Beaconsfield Manor and Beaconsfield deeds at the Library of Congress (1985).
23. Will of Walter Waller, proved PCC 22 January 1629.
24. Cal. S.P. Dom. (1637), p.398.
25. CBS, D 16/1/18.
26. CBS, BAS 927/38.
27. British Library, Add. Mss. 47030.
28. CBS, BAS 98/21.
29. Spencer, A. (ed.), *Memoirs of William Hickey*, vol. 4 (1790-1809), 5th edn (1925), pp.473-5.
30. *The Times*, 4 June 1831.
31. CBS, AR 40/76, Box 2, Bundle 23.
32. CBS, Hall Barn, AR 40/76, Box 2, Bundle 23.
33. CBS, AR 40/76, Box 3, Bundle 28.
34. *The Times*, 20 May 1873.
35. *The Times*, 9 April 1874.
36. CBS, Rev. Cooke's Diary, 24 Feb 1897.
37. Lawson, L., *Of Old I Hold: My Life in a Newspaper Family* (2008).
38. Cartulary of Missenden Abbey, vol. 2, item 407-8, 410-11.
39. Cartulary of Missenden Abbey, vol. 2, item 416.
40. Pope Nich. Tax. (Record Commission), 45.
41. Bodleian Library, Mss Ch. Bucks., 1061.
42. Calendar of Close Rolls (1364-8), p.86.
43. Bodleian Library, Mss Ch. Bucks., 1040.
44. CBS, Hall Barn Deeds, AR 93/2006/16.
45. British Library Harleian Roll, S.1.
46. TNA, C 140/61/25.
47. CBS, D 247.
48. CBS, D 247.
49. TNA, C 142/73/12.
50. CBS, DX 179/1.
51. TNA, C 142/647/37.
52. TNA, C 126/18.
53. CBS, DX 179/9.
54. CBS, D 69/5/4/2.
55. Broad, J., *Buckinghamshire Dissent and Parish Life*

1669-1712, Buckinghamshire Record Society, vol. 28 (1993), p.100.
56. CBS, D 69/1/5.
57. *Beauties of England* (1801), p.392.
58. CBS, Q/H/20.
59. CBS, DX 805/5/2.
60. CBS, D 69/1/26.
61. *The Times*, 29 July 1882.
62. *South Bucks Free Press*.
63. *The Times*, 5 December 1898.
64. *The Times*, 16 November 1937.
65. Bodleian Library, Mss. Ch. Bucks., 887.
66. *Ibid*. Mss. Ch. Bucks., 903.
67. *Ibid*. Mss. Ch. Bucks., 904.
68. *Ibid*. Mss. Ch. Bucks., 1159.
69. Nottingham University Library, Mi 6/170/89. Transcrption by A.H. Packe, CBS, D/11/3/7a.
70. TNA, Feet of Fines, Div. Co. Mich 37, Henry VIII.
71. TNA, C 2/Eliz/T 1/41.
72. *Ibid*.
73. TNA, C 3/272/31.
74. TNA, C 142/435/113.
75. Bodleian Library, Mss. Ch. Bucks., 122.
76. Steele, Mss. Bodleian Library, Mss. Top. Bucks., e. 8-9.
77. Cal. S.P. Dom. (1637), p.398.
78. Campbell, C., *Vitruvius Britannicus*, vol. 2 (1717), p.47.
79. Will of Frances Fuller proved PCC, 7 Feb 1735.
80. CBS, D 69/4/2.
81. *Gentleman's Magazine*, xviii (1748), p.284.
82. CBS, Rate Book, PR 14/5/3.
83. CBS, Land Tax, Q/RPL/4/1.
84. *Gentleman's Magazine*, xxix (1754), p.578.
85. Dixon, W., *Edmund Burke and his Kinsmen*, Univ. of Colorado Studies, Ser. B. (1939), 1, no. 1, p.35.
86. TNA, C 12/2132/21.
87. Garvin, V.G. Gregories, 'Bucks., the House of J.L. Garvin', *Architectural Review*, April 1930.
88. Beaconsfield Historical Society, 1950 Sale Catalogue.
89. Arjowiggins, *Butler's Court: The History* (2007).

Chapter Three – Farms and Farmers

1. CBS, PR 14/5/2.
2. CBS, AR 40/76, Box 3.
3. *Studio Yearbook of Decorative Art* (1921).
4. Lipscombe, G., op. cit., vol. 3, p.197.
5. DX 1122/21.
6. CBS, DC 18/22/6/103.
7. *The Times*, 21 June 1955.
8. CBS, D/X 805/5/2.
9. Missenden Cartulary, Bucks. Record Society, vol. 10 (1955), p.90.
10. CBS, Wakefield Collection, D 247.
11. *Ibid*.
12. TNA, Chancery Inquisitions Post Mortem (Ser. 2), ccclix, 136.
13. CBS, Wakefield Collection, D 247, Box 2.
14. CBS, AR 40/76, Edward Lawson, Box 3.
15. *Ibid*.
16. CBS, AR 40/76, various, Box 4.
17. CBS, Hall Barn Deeds, AR 93/2006/25.
18. TNA, Feet of Fine, Bucks. Mich. 6 Eliz.
19. British Library, Additional Charters, 5163.
20. CBS, Hall Barn, AR 40/76, Edward Lawson, Box 3.
21. *Ibid*.
22. TNA, Feet of Fines, Bucks., Easter, 22 Jas I.
23. CBS Hall Barn Deeds AR 93/2006/126.
24. CBS, Hall Barn, AR 40/76, Edward Lawson, Box 3.
25. Cartulary of Missenden Abbey, item 410.
26. CBS, D 69/4/2.
27. Guildhall Library, Sun Insurance, Mss. 11936/337/519241.
28. Hertfordshire Record Office, DE/HL/12097.
29. CBS, Hall Barn, AR 40/76, Edward Lawson, Box 3.
30. TNA, PROB, 20/442.
31. TNA, PROB, 3/23/18.
32. CBS, Land Tax, 1783.
33. CBS, Hall Barn, AR 40/76, Edward Lawson, Box 3.
34. CBS, 1831 Survey, 40/76.
35. TNA, CP, 25/1/91/114, no. 117.
36. Lipscomb, G., *History and Antiquities of the County of Buckingham*, vol. 3, p.199.
37. Hertfordshire Hearth Tax returns, TNA, E 179/375/30.
38. Transcript supplied by Family Chest (2008).
39. Worcestershire Record Office, 705:349 12946/502734.
40. Recited in 1828 deed of covenant for production of deeds, CBS, Hall Barn (1976), Deposit Box 2.
41. CBS, Hall Barn, AR 40/76, Box 2.
42. Magdalen College Archives.
43. CBS, Hall Barn, AR 40/76, Box 2.
44. CBS, Hall Barn, map (1763).
45. CBS, Hall Barn, AR 40/76, Edward Lawson, Box 3.
46. CBS, Hall Barn Estate Map (1763).
47. CBS, DX 1122/21.

Chapter Four – The Oxford Road

1. TNA, WO 30/48.
2. Calendar of the Sessions Records, vol. 1, 1678-94, p.311.
3. *Ibid*. vol. 2, 1694-1705, p.46.
4. Lipscomb, G., *History and Antiquities of the County of Buckingham*, vol. 3 (1847), p.181.
5. Kingston, H., *History of Wycombe* (1848).
6. *Bucks Free Press*, 26 October 1867.
7. CBS, Q/RX/9.
8. *Middlesex Advertiser*, 25 January 1929, 13 February 1931.
9. CBS, DX 1122/21.
10. Bates, A., *Directory of Stage Coach Services 1836* (1969).
11. *London Gazette*, 10 March 1672.
12. Calendar of the Sessions Records, vol. 1, 1678-94, p.422.
13. Gibbs, R., *Buckinghamshire: A Record of Local Occurences*, vol. 3 (1880), p.120.

Chapter Five – Inns and Innkeepers

1. CBS, D/X 423.
2. TNA, PROB 5/931.
3. Taylor, A.W., *History of Beaconsfield* (1983), p.13.
4. Guildhall Library, Sun Fire Insurance, Mss. 11936/11/17497.
5. Guildhall Library, Sun Fire Insurance, Mss. 11936/55/83295.
6. CBS Q. *See also* notes in the Wulcko Papers, CBS, D 119.
7. CBS, DX 776/11.

8. Guildhall Library, Sun Fire Insurance, Mss. 11936/32/54238.
9. CBS, DC 18/39/1.
10. Guildhall Library, Sun Fire Insurance, 89298.
11. CBS, D 69/7/3.
12. *Ibid.*
13. Guildhall Library, Sun Fire Insurance, Mss. 11936/17/31197.
14. CBS, Hall Barn, AR, 40/76, Box 11.
15. *Ibid.*
16. Guildhall Library, Sun Fire Insurance, Mss. 11936/250/374122.
17. *Ibid.* 374123.
18. CBS, Hall Barn, AR, 47/76, Box 35.
19. CBS, Hall Barn, AR, 40/76, Box 11.
20. *Country Life*, 13 April 1929.
21. TNA, PROB, 3/24/98.
22. CBS, D 69/4/4.
23. CBS, D 69/1/5.
24. Guildhall Library, Sun Fire Insurance, Mss. 11936/296/452210.
25. Day, K., *Recollections of Old Beaconsfield* (1969) p.7.
26. *The Times*, 8 December 1874.
27. Rouse, E.C., 'Domestic Wall Paintings at No. 1 London End, Beaconsfield', *Records of Buckinghamshire*, vol.18 (1966), p.78.
28. CBS, Hall Barn Deeds, AR/2006/92, 95.
29. CBS, Hall Barn, AR, 40/76, Box 7-8.
30. CBS, D 247.
31. CBS, Hall Barn (1976), Deposit Box 7.
32. Guildhall Library, Sun Fire Insurance, Mss. 11936/22/37929.
33. CBS, Hall Barn, AR 40/76, Box 7.
34. Guildhall Library, Sun Fire Insurance, Mss. 11936/132/176128.
35. CBS, DX 1122/21.

Chapter Six – Professional Men

1. Bodleian Library Steele Mss.
2. Lee, F.G., *History of Thame Church* (1883), p.220.
3. *Ibid.*
4. CBS, D 69/7/3.
5. CBS, Wakefield Collection, D 247.
6. TNA, C 202/125/2.
7. Guildhall Library, Sun Fire Insurance, Mss. 11936/336/519035.
8. Hall Barn, AR 40/76, Edward Lawson, Box 3.
9. *Bucks Gazette*, 15 January 1831.
10. TNA, TI 4193.
11. *London Gazette*, 29 July 1853.
12. Godley, A.D., *Aspects of Modern Oxford* (1894).
13. *Bucks. Free Press*, 5 December 1913.
14. *Ibid.* 22 July 1913.
15. CBS, DC 18/39/1.
16. Quarter Sessions Records. vol. 1, 1678-94, p.483.
17. CBS, PR 14.
18. Guildhall Library, Sun Insurance, Mss. 11936/293/445744.
19. *The Times*, 9 August 1815.
20. *The Times*, 11 November 1836.
21. *London Gazette*, 16 May 1845.
22. *London Gazette*, 11 April 1854.

23. CBS, AR 47/76, Box 35, Bundle 7.
24. Spencer, A. (ed.), *Memoirs of William Hickey*, vol. 4 (1790-1809), 5th edn (1925), p.472.
25. *The Times*, 6 April 1821.
26. Lipscomb, G., *History and Antiquities of the County of Buckingham*, vol. 3 (1847), p.193.

Chapter Seven – Trade and Industry

1. Calendar of Charter Rolls, I, 441.
2. Calendar of Charter Rolls, II, 122.
3. CBS, Hall Barn, AR 47/76, Unnumbered Box, Item 115.
4. Beaconsfield Urban District Official Handbook (1947), p.15.
5. Guildhall Library, Sun Fire Insurance, Mss. 11936/290/442286.
6. CBS, DX 805/5/2.
7. CBS, MacKinnon, F., Mss., *Notes on the History of Beaconsfield and District*, p.60-1.
8. CBS, D 69/1/2.
9. Guildhall Library, Sun Fire Insurance, Mss. 11936/267/400770.
10. CBS, D 69/1/26.
11. Calendar of the Quarter Sessions, vol. 4, 1712-8, p.8.
12. CBS, D 69/7/3.
13. Guildhall Library, Sun Fire Insurance, Mss. 11936/257/382804.
14. CBS, PR 14/5/2.
15. Guildhall Library, Sun Fire Insurance, Mss. 11936/132/176128.
16. *London Gazette*, 4 March 1864.
17. TNA, PROB 3/23/18.
18. CBS, Hall Barn, AR 40/76, Box 5, Bundle 57.
19. Guildhall Library, Sun Fire Insurance, Mss. 11936/339/521163.
20. *Ibid.* 261/391790.
21. CBS, PR 14/5/2.
22. Beckett, I.F.W., *Buckinghamshire Posse Comitatus 1798*, Buckinghamshire Record Scociety, vol. 22 (1985).
23. *Ibid.*
24. CBS, Q/H/20.
25. *London Gazette*, 20 December 1878.
26. CBS, PR 14/12/9.
27. Guidhall Library, Sun Insurance, Mss. 11936/274/414749.
28. Day, K., *Further Recollections of Old Beaconsfield* (1990), p.16.
29. CBS, Hall Barn, AR 40/76, Box 3.
30. CBS, Hall Barn, AR 40/76, Box 3.
31. *London Gazette*, 18 January 1880.
32. *London Gazette*, 21 November 1905.
33. Guildhall Library, Sun Insurance, 11936/313/478924.
34. *The Times*, 25 January 1956.
35. *Bucks Life*, April 1967.

Chapter Eight – Shops and Shopkeepers

1. Guildhall Library, Sun Fire Insurance, 22/37929.
2. CBS, AR 40/76, Box 7.
3. CBS, AR 40/76, Box 8.
4. Guildhall Library, Sun Insurance, Mss. 11936/30/50608.

5. *Ibid.* 257/382380.
6. *Ibid.* 261/389436.
7. *London Gazette*, 6 February 1838.
8. *The Times*, 6 September 1824.
9. CBS, AR 40/76, Box 8.
10. CBS, AR 40/76, Box 8.
11. CBS, DC 18/22/6/15, 17.
12. Magdalen College Archives.
13. Guildhall Library, Sun Fire Insurance, Mss. 11936/276/416943.
14. CBS, AR 40/76, Box 7.
15. Guildhall Library, Sun Fire Insurance, 22/37929.
16. Guildhall Library, Sun Fire Insurance, 257/382804.
17. Day, K., *Recollections of Old Beaconsfield* (1969), p.6.
18. Guildhall Library, Sun Fire Insurance, 339/522095.
19. CBS, AR 40/76, Box 8.
20. *The Times*, 15 August 1861.
21. CBS, D GR/19/18.
22. CBS, DC 18/22/6/191.
23. CBS, DC 18/22/6/57.
24. CBS, DC 18/22/6/203.

Chapter Nine – Churches and Chapels

1. Glynne, S., *Ecclesiastical and Architectural Topography of England* (1849).
2. *Building News*, 3 January 1890, p.5.
3. Certificate of Musters for Buckinghamshire, 1522, Buckinghamshire Record Society, vol. 17 (1973).
4. Records of Buckinghamshire, vol. 9 (1907), p.311.
5. Calendar of State Papers, Domestic (1637), p.398.
6. Records of Buckinghamshire, vol. 7 (1892), p.99.
7. *Ibid.*, p.103.
8. *Ibid.*, p.113.
9. Magdalen College Archives, D – Y 46.
10. *Ibid.* D – Y 55.
11. *Ibid.* D – Y 57.
12. *Buckinghamshire Returns of the Census of Religious Worship, 1851*, Buckinghamshire Record Society, vol. 27 (1991).
13. Magdalen College Archives. (This deed is listed in the catalogue but is missing from the parcel).
14. Magdalen College Archives, EX 224/15.
15. Quiney, A., 'Altogether a capital fellow and a serious one too. A brief account of the life and work of Henry Woodyer', *Architectural Review*, vol. 38 (1995), pp.192-219.
16. Diary of Rev. G.A. Cooke.
17. Broad, J. (ed.), *Buckinghamshire Dissent and Parish Life 1669-1712*, Buckinghamshire Record Society, vol. 28 (1993), p.100.
18. Brown, C.E. and Parry, L.L., *A Short History of Beaconsfield and Holtspur United Reformed Church, 1704-1974* (1974).
19. *Buckinghamshire Returns of the Census of Religious Worship, 1851*, Buckinghamshire Record Society, vol. 27 (1991).
20. CBS, DVD 1/97.
21. Summers, W.H., *History of the Congregational Churches in Berks, South Oxon and South Bucks* (1905).

22. CBS, Hall Barn, AR 40/76, Box 3.
23. *Ibid.*
24. CBS, Hall Barn, AR 40/76, Box 4.

Chapter Ten – Schools

1. Guildhall Library, Sun Insurance, Mss. 11936/327/502130.
2. *Bucks Herald*, 31 August 1878.
3. Magdalen College Archives.
4. Fitzmaurice, E., *Life of Granville George Leveson Gower, 2nd Earl Granville 1815-1891*, p.12.
5. *The Times*, 11 February 1836.
6. *The Times*, 19 January 1855.
7. *Buckinghamshire Countryside*, May 1999, p.14.
8. CBS, Tithe Award (1846).
9. Warr, E.B., *Early Schooldays in Beaconsfield: History of the Church of England Schools 1854-1914* (1968).
10. *Ibid.*
11. CBS, AR39/65, No. 4.
12. CBS, Hall Barn, AR 40/76, Box 3.
13. CBS, Log Books, 1873-1920, AR 80/2007.

Chapter Eleven – Local Government

1. Report to the General Board of Health on a Preliminary Inquiry into the Sewerage, Drainage and Supply of Water, and the Sanitary Condition of the Inhabitants of the Parish of Beaconsfield (1850).
2. CBS, AR 47/1976, Unnumbered Box, Item D.
3. The Studio, 15 September 1909, p.296.
4. CBS, DC 18/1/32.

Chapter Twelve – Beaconsfield's Population in the Nineteenth Century

1. 25th Annual Report of the Registrar General (1861), 1863, p.xxi.
2. *The Times*, 5 May 1802.
3. *The Times*, 26 October 1811.
4. *The Times*, 9 August 1815.
5. Spencer, A. (ed.), *Memoirs of William Hickey*, vol.4 (1925), pp.472-5.
6. CBS, AR 40/76, Edward Lawson, Box 3.
7. *The Times*, 25 October 1842.
8. CBS, DC 18/39/6.
9. *The Times*, 9 October 1862.
10. *The Times*, 7 January 1839.

Chapter Thirteen – The Railway and the New Town

1. CBS, DVD 1/97.
2. TNA, Valuation Office Field Books, IR 58.
3. Bucks. Arch. Soc. AYBM: 1937.577.
4. Cox, D., *Memories of Green Hedges*.
5. CBS, DX 795/1 (k).
6. CBS, D GR/ 19/18.
7. *Studio Yearbook of Decorative Art* (1910), p.71.
8. Bober, Natalie S., *Robert Frost a Restless Spirit* (1998), p.91.
9. *Studio Yearbook of Decorative Art in 1921*, p.62.
10. *Studio Yearbook of Decorative Art in 1921*, pp.55, 60-1.
11. Scottish Screen Archive, 3116.
12. *Studio Yearbook of Decorative Art* (1924).
13. *Where to Live Round London* (1910), p.5.

Index